Statistics for the Terrified

Second Edition

Gerald Kranzler
University of Oregon

Janet Moursund
University of Oregon

Prentice Hall, Upper Saddle River, New Jersey 07458

Library of Congress Cataloging–in–Publication Data

Kranzler, Gerald.
   Statistics for the terrified / Gerald Kranzler, Janet Moursund. —
2nd ed.
    p. cm.
   Includes index.
   ISBN 0–13–955410–6
   1. Statistics. I. Moursund, Janet. II. Title.
QA276.12.K73 1998
519.5—dc21   98–9811
                                        CIP

Editorial Director: Charlyce Jones-Owen
Editor-in-Chief: Nancy Roberts
Executive Editor: Bill Webber
Acquisitions Editor: Jennifer Gilliland
Assistant Editor: Anita Castro
Director of Production and Manufacturing: Barbara Kittle
Senior Managing Editor: Bonnie Biller
Production Editor: Randy Pettit
Manufacturing Manager: Nick Sklitsis
Prepress and Manufacturing Buyer: Lynn Pearlman
Marketing Director: Gina Sluss
Marketing Manager: Mike Alread
Cover Design Director: Jayne Conte
Cover Design: Karen Salzbach
Cover Art: Edvard Munch; "The Scream"

This book was set in 10/12 Century Old Style by Pine Tree, Inc.
and printed and bound by Courier-Westford.
The cover was printed by Lehigh.

 © 1999 by Prentice-Hall Inc.
Simon & Schuster/A Viacom Company
Upper Saddle River, New Jersey 07458

Printed in the United States of America
10 9 8 7 6 5 4 3 2 1

ISBN 0-13-955410-6

Prentice-Hall International (UK) Limited, *London*
Prentice-Hall of Australia Pty. Limited, *Sydney*
Prentice-Hall Canada Inc., *Toronto*
Prentice-Hall Hispanoamerica, S.A., *Mexico*
Prentice-Hall of India Private Limited, *New Delhi*
Prentice-Hall of Japan, Inc., *Tokyo*
Simon & Schuster Asia Pte. Ltd., *Singapore*
Editora Prentice-Hall do Brasil, Ltda., *Rio de Janeiro*

Dedication

Jerry Kranzler, friend and colleague, is the primary author of this
book. He developed the ideas in it, through working with genera-
tions of students. Nearly all of them began Jerry's statistics class
wishing they were anywhere but in a stats class; nearly all of
them ended their work feeling glad about the course, proud of
their progress, and amazed at how Jerry had done it. As Jerry's
co-author, and in his absence, I take the liberty of dedicating this
second edition to him. Jerry, thank you for your friendship, your
wisdom, your humor, and your love of learning. We miss you.

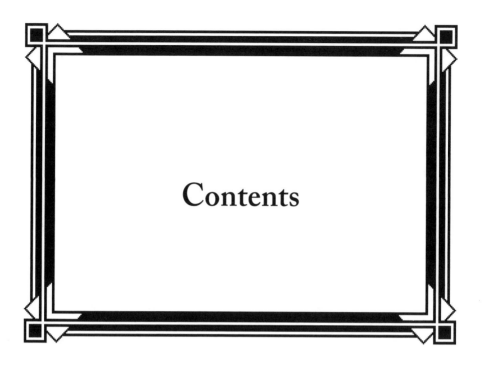

Contents

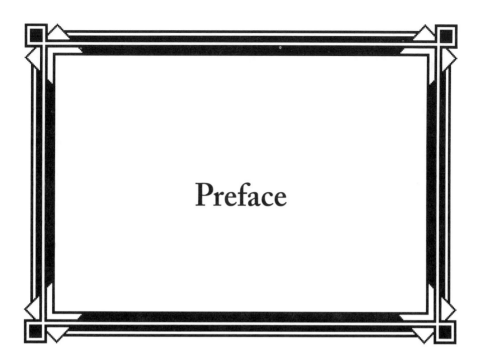

Preface

A book like this, one that has grown over so many years, has made friends with a lot of people. And I want to acknowledge those people, to say "thank you" for their nudges and pats-on-the-back and occasional less friendly, but equally useful bits of information.

When I've read other books, especially textbooks, I've tended to skip over all that "front stuff." I expect most readers will do the same thing here. But if you've gotten this far, maybe you're different; if so, please accept my thanks in advance for reading this. The people whom I shall be acknowledging really do deserve your notice and appreciation.

First on the list of folks to thank, of course, must be all the students. I can't list names and won't even try to pick out a representative few; they know who they are. They made this book, it's about them and for them, and if it weren't for them, you wouldn't be reading any of this.

Jerry Kranzler, though a coauthor, needs to be recognized here. Jerry died shortly after the first edition of *Terrified* was published, but his sense and spirit live on in every page of the new edition. Jerry did the greater part of the work for this book; his vision began it and his experience gave it form and structure.

Fellow faculty in the DABCS (I won't spell it out, but isn't "Department of ABCs" a great acronym within a College of Education?) at the University of Oregon have been enormously encouraging. Suzie Prichard, secretary and good friend, made even bad days bearable by her encouragement and sense of humor. And friends and colleagues in that other world, outside of academia, have been patient and understanding when I've grumped and whined over a difficult passage. Thank you, thank you all.

Then there are the good folks at Prentice Hall: editorial staff, reviewers, and probably others that I don't even know about. Anita Castro, who has steered me through the revision process with unfailing good humor, and Randy Pettit, Production Editor, whose email comments cheered my days. And the reviewers: Sandra A. McIntire, Rollins College; and Eugene R. Gilden, Linfield College, who will never know how useful they have been. And, finally, Sarah Streett of Colorado State University, who patiently sorted through the entire manuscript and corrected errors that I never even knew were possible!

Words are poor things for expressing sincere feelings, and these paragraphs are woefully inadequate to express my gratitude. I hope that all of the people I've mentioned, especially those who couldn't be named specifically, will understand how much their support has really meant.

—Janet Moursund

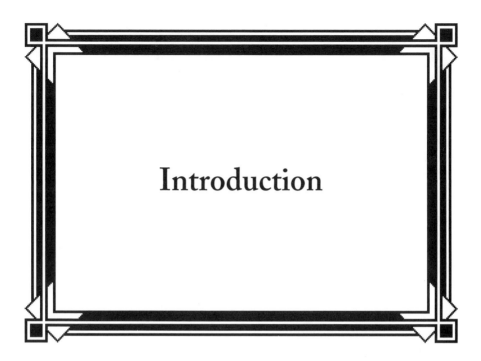

Introduction

"You haven't told me yet," said Lady Nuttal, "what it is your fiancé does for a living."

"He's a statistician," replied Lamia, with an annoying sense of being on the defensive.

Lady Nuttal was obviously taken aback. It had not occurred to her that statisticians entered into normal social relationships. The species, she would have surmised, was perpetuated in some collateral manner, like mules.

"But Aunt Sara, it's a very interesting profession," said Lamia warmly. "I don't doubt it," said her aunt, who obviously doubted it very much. "To express anything important in mere figures is so plainly impossible that there must be endless scope for well-paid advice on how to do it. But don't you think that life with a statistician would be rather, shall we say, humdrum?"

Lamia was silent. She felt reluctant to discuss the surprising depth of emotional possibility which she had discovered below Edward's numerical veneer.

"It's not the figures themselves," she said finally, "it's what you do with them that matters."

—K. A. C. Manderville, *The Undoing of Lamia Gurdleneck*[1]

---

[1]In the first edition, we confessed that we did not know the origin of this quotation, and asked for help in finding it. Thanks to Dr. Keith Baggerly of the Rice University Statistics Department, we can now share with you the following information: The quote first appeared as an introductory blurb for volume II of "The Advance Theory of Statistics" by Maurice Kendall and Alan Stuart. Many statisticians really liked the quote, and tried to track down the book to find out more about the mysterious statistician fiancé, but to no avail. The mystery was solved in 1992, with the

Another statistics book! There are so many statistics books on the market now that it seems strange even to me that there be another one. However, as a teacher of statistics, I have been dissatisfied with available books because they seem aimed at students who whizzed right through college algebra and considered taking math as a major just for the sheer joy of it. Most of my students in counseling and education programs are not like that. Many of them would respond with a hearty "true" to many of the following self-test statements. I invite you to test yourself, to see if you too fit the pattern.

1. I have never been very good at math.
2. When my teacher tried to teach me long division in the fourth grade, I seriously considered dropping out of school.
3. When we got to extracting square roots, thoughts of suicide flashed through my mind.
4. Word problems! My head felt like a solid block of wood when I was asked to solve problems like, "If it takes Mr. Jones 3 hours to mow a lawn and Mr. Smith 2 hours to mow the same lawn, how long will it take if they mow it together?"
5. Although I never dropped out of school, I became a quantitative dropout soon after my first algebra course.
6. I avoided courses like chemistry and physics because they required math.
7. I decided early that there were some careers I could not pursue because I was poor in math.
8. When I take a test that includes math problems, I get so upset that my mind goes blank and I forget all the material I studied.
9. Sometimes I wonder if I am a little stupid.
10. I feel nervous just thinking about taking a statistics course.

Did you answer "true" to many of these items? If so, this book may be helpful to you. When writing it, I made some negative and some positive assumptions about you:

1. You are studying statistics only because it is a requirement in your major area of study.
2. You are terrified (or at least somewhat anxious) about math and are sure you cannot pass a course in statistics.
3. It has been a long time since you last studied math, and what little you knew then has long since been forgotten.

appearance of an article in *Chance* by Fortney, et al. entitled "The Undoing of Maurice Kendall." In short, note that one of the main characters in the quote is the aunt, Lady Sara Nuttal, the author is K. A. C. Manderville, and be aware that Alan Stuart and Maurice Kendall were both very fond of anagrams (Roman lettering, so u's can be written as v's).

4. But with a little instruction and a lot of hard work on your part, you can learn statistics. If you can stay calm while baking a cake or reading your bank statement, there is hope for you.
5. You may never learn to love statistics, but you can change your self-concept. When you finish your statistics course you will be able to say, truthfully, "I am the kind of person who can learn statistics! I'm not stupid."

In this book, I will attempt to help you to achieve two important objectives: (1) to understand and compute some basic statistics, and (2) to deal with math anxiety and avoidance responses that interfere with your learning.

Here is some advice that I think you will find useful as we move along: (1) Because the use of statistics requires you to work with numbers, you should consider buying a calculator. Make sure that the calculator has at least one memory and that it can take square roots (almost all calculators can do this). Before you go out and invest in such a machine, though, check out your personal computer—many desktop and laptop computers come equipped with calculator software that will easily handle the problems in this book. (2) Try to form a support group of fellow statistics students. Exchange telephone numbers and times when you can be reached. Talk about what you are studying and offer to help others (you may learn best by teaching others). When you are stuck with a problem that you can't solve, don't hesitate to ask others for their help. Very likely they have some of the same feelings and difficulties you do. Not everyone gets stuck on the same topics, so even you may be helpful to someone else.

If you are one of the "terrified" for whom this book is intended, there are two appendixes at the end of the book that may be helpful to you. Appendix K, "Overcoming Math Anxiety," will give you some general tools and techniques for dealing with the uncomfortable feelings that many students experience when they find themselves dealing with numbers. And Appendix B provides a review of some of the basic math concepts that you may have once known, but that have gotten rusty through disuse. It also gives some sample problems that will allow you to test your ability to use those concepts. I know that reading an appendix before you even get to the first chapter of a book may seem pretty weird (and probably not politically correct), but I think these may help you to get off to a running start and will be well worth your time and trouble. Of course, if you don't have problems with math, and already know all the basics, you won't learn anything new; but, even so, "Shucks, I know all this" is a great way to begin a statistics class. Especially if you think it may be terrifying!

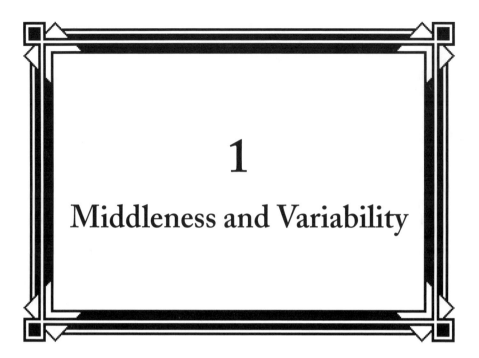

1

Middleness and Variability

The field of statistics is concerned with methods of organizing, summarizing, and interpreting data. "Data" means information: Any collection of information is a collection of data. For statisticians, though, "data" generally means numerical information. Statistics really amounts to a collection of techniques for dealing with sets of numbers: organizing them, summarizing them, figuring out what they mean. This chapter will focus on the "summarizing" part. It will present methods of finding a number that describes a group of numbers.

We often ask questions such as, "What is the average IQ of this class?" or "How much money does the average football player make?" When we ask such questions, we are really asking for a single number that will represent all of the different IQ scores, or player salaries, or whatever. Many people are not aware that there is more than one "average." In this chapter, you will find three methods for computing an average: the mean, the median, and the mode.

Just one number, though, can be misleading. Sets of data not only have a middle, but they have a spread: The numbers in the data set cluster more or less tightly around the middle. The second kind of summarizing technique is finding a number that describes that spread.

Before presenting measures of middleness and spread, however, I need to digress a bit and discuss symbolizing data.

SYMBOLIZING DATA

If you have read, or even looked at, any statistics books, you have probably noticed the use of many symbols unfamiliar to you. These symbols are shorthand ways of referring to numbers, or to manipulations that we use on numbers. A common example is the small "2" that we put high and to the right (that position is called "superscript," by the way, just as the low-and-to-the-right position is a "subscript") of a number to indicate that the number is to be squared—multiplied by itself. It's certainly simpler to write "$5^2 = 25$" than to write "5 times itself is equal to 25." And, as we shall see, other sorts of procedures that can be symbolized quite easily would require lots and lots of words if we had to write them out.

Learning to read statistics material is somewhat analogous to learning to read music or a foreign language: impossible at first, difficult for a while, but relatively easy after some effort. One thing to remember, though: Since symbols are a way of condensing information, a paragraph that is full of mathematical symbols has much more information in it than an ordinary paragraph in a history book or a newspaper article. Don't be surprised if it takes you three or four times longer to get through a page in a statistics book (even this one!) than to get through a page in a nonnumerical book. In fact, one of the challenges for the beginning statistics student is learning to slow down. Force yourself to adjust your reading speed to the density of the information on the page, and you'll find that things get much easier.

Variables

Those of us who are interested in education or the behavioral sciences are concerned mostly with characteristics of people, such as ability, achievement, interests, and personality. When you study people, one of the first things you will notice is that people vary considerably on almost every characteristic. Some people are much brighter than others; some learn more than others in the same amount of time; some are more emotional, or more grumpy, or more talkative than others. In statistics, we call such characteristics *variables.*

It is conventional to designate variables by capital letters near the end of the alphabet. For example, the intelligence test scores earned by a group of five students could be designated with the capital letter X, and achievement test scores earned by the same students could be represented by a Y. The first student's intelligence test score would be X_1; the third student's achievement test score would be Y_3. With X and Y as your two variables, you could ask, "What is the average score on the X variable?" or "Is there any relationship between X and Y?"

The Summation Sign

You will also be introduced to quite a few Greek letters, especially sigma, designated by Σ. The Greek uppercase letter sigma (Σ) directs you to sum (add up) whatever comes after it. If years in school are represented by the letter X, then ΣX directs you to add up all the X scores:

Example

Years in School (X)
5
3
4
6
8
$\Sigma X = 26$

Similarly, if achievement test scores are represented by the letter Y, and the test scores are 82, 71, 69, 50, and 22, then $\Sigma Y = 82 + 71 + 69 + 50 + 22 = 294$. You will find more information about working with the summation sign in Appendix B, "Basic Math Review."

Parentheses

Strange as it may seem, parentheses are an important mathematical symbol. They serve as a kind of recipe, telling us in what order to do things. In a complicated set of cooking directions, it can be important to know whether to add the sugar before you beat the egg whites or afterward; in the same way, it's important to know whether to square a set of numbers before or after you add them together.

The parentheses rule is simple: Work from the inside out. Carry out whatever operations are inside the innermost set of parentheses, and then whatever is inside the next set, and so on. For example, $(((x(x + y)) - 32)/y)^2$ means to (1) add x and y together; (2) multiply the sum by x; (3) subtract 32; (4) divide by y; and finally (5) square your answer. The parentheses are important because doing the operations in a different order will give you a different result. Try it. Let $x = 2$ and $y = 5$, and see what happens when you change the order of operations!

THE MEAN

The *mean* is the most often used measure of central tendency *(central tendency* is a fancy statistical term that means, roughly, "middleness"). The mean is an old acquaintance of yours: the arithmetic average. You obtain the mean by adding up all the scores and dividing by the number of scores. Remember?

Different statistics texts use different symbols to designate the mean. Some use a bar over the letter symbolizing the variable: a group's mean score on variable X would be symbolized $\overline{X}$. Others (this book included) use a capital M, with a subscript indicating the referred-to variable: The mean score on variable X is M_X. If the amount of time needed to thread a needle is designated by Y, then the mean time needed by the people in the Busy Bee Sewing Circle to thread their needles would be M_Y[1].

---

[1]By convention, M_x and M_y are used to designate the mean of a sample, that is, a finite set of something—test scores, people, wallpaper colors, what have you. Sometimes we want to refer to the mean of a less definite, often infinite set: all the fifth-graders in the United States, for example, or the scores that all those fifth-graders would get if they all were given the same achievement test. A large, inclusive group like this is called a *population*, and its mean is symbolized by the Greek letter μ (pronounced "mew," like a kitten). Values having to do with populations are called parameters and are usually symbolized using lowercase Greek letters; for sample values (called *statistics*), we use the normal English-language alphabet.

To be technically correct, we would have to define a *population* as the collection of all the things that fit the population definition and a *sample* as some specified number of things selected out of that population. You'll see why that's important when we talk about inferential statistics in Chapter 6. For now, though, just assume that we are working with samples—relatively small groups of things in which each individual member can be measured or categorized in some way.

The formula for the mean of variable X is

$$M_X = \frac{\Sigma X}{N}$$

This formula says, in words, that the mean of variable X (symbolized as M_X) equals the sum of the X scores (ΣX) divided by the number of scores (N).

Similarly, for the scores on the Y variable, the mean of Y is

$$M_Y = \frac{\Sigma Y}{N}$$

Example

Achievement Test Scores (X)	Reading Comprehension Scores (Y)
14	25
19	37
13	26
9	20
13	19
$\Sigma X = 68$	$\Sigma Y = 127$
$M_X = 68/5 = 13.6$	$M_Y = 127/5 = 25.4$

Have you noticed how complicated it was to describe the mean in words, compared with that short little formula? Formulas, and mathematical relationships in general, often don't translate into words easily. Mathematicians are trained to think in terms of relationships and formulas and often don't have to translate; we do. That's one reason why social science folks can have problems with statistics: We don't realize that we need to translate, and that the translating takes time. We expect to read and understand a page in a stat book as quickly as a page in any other sort of book. Not so! As I said earlier, symbols simply take longer to read, and we need to remember to slow ourselves down. So don't beat yourself up for being slow—you're supposed to be that way!

THE MEDIAN (Md)

When scores are arranged in order, from highest to lowest (or lowest to highest), the *median* is the middle score. Suppose you administered a test to five persons who scored as follows: 113, 133, 95, 112, and 94. To find the median, you would first arrange all scores in numerical order and then find the middle score.

Example

Test Scores
———————
133
113
112   median = Md = 112
95
94
———————

In our example, 112 is the median score because, when scores are arranged in order (highest to lowest), two scores are higher than 112 and two scores are lower than 112.

But suppose you have six scores:

Example

Test Scores
———————
105
102
101
92
91
80
———————

In this example, the number 101 can't be the Md because there are two scores above it and three below. Nor can the number 92 be the Md, for similar reasons. The problem is solved by taking the two middle scores—in our example, 101 and 92—and finding the point halfway between. You do this by adding the two middle scores and dividing by 2: 101 + 92 = 193, divided by 2 = 96.5 = Md. (Did you notice that this is the same as finding the mean of the two middle scores? Good for you!) The Md of our six scores is 96.5. As you can see, now there are three scores that are higher than 96.5 and three that are lower.

Here's another example. Find the median of the following scores: 27, 12, 78, 104, 45, and 34. First, arrange the scores from highest to lowest: 104, 78, 45, 34, 27, and 12. Then, find the point half way between the two middle scores. The two middle scores are 45 and 34. Half way between is 45 + 34 = 79, divided by 2 = 39.5. Thus, Md = 39.5. Easy as pie, right?

THE MODE (Mo)

The *mode* (Mo) is the most frequently occurring score in a set of scores. For example, we are given the following scores:

Example

Test Scores
110
105
100
100
100
100
99
98

Because the number 100 occurs more frequently than any of the other scores, Mo = 100.

But what about the following set of scores?

Example

Test Scores
110
105
105
105
100
95
95
95
90

In this example, both 105 and 95 occur three times. Here we have a distribution with two modes: a *bimodal* distribution. If there were more than two modes, it would be a *multimodal* distribution.

SELECTING A MEASURE OF CENTRAL TENDENCY

It has been said that statistics don't lie, but statisticians do. Paraphrased, we could say that statistics can be employed to enhance communication or to deceive.

Consider Ruritania, a country so small that its entire population consists of five persons, a king and four subjects. Their annual incomes are as follows:

Citizen	Annual Income
King	1,000,000
Subject 1	5,000
Subject 2	4,000
Subject 3	4,000
Subject 4	2,000

The king boasts that Ruritania is a fantastic country with an "average" annual income of $203,000. Before rushing off to become a citizen, you would be wise to find out what measure of central tendency he is using! True, the mean is $203,000, so the king is not lying, but he is not telling a very accurate story either. In this case, either the median or the mode would be a more representative value. The point to be made here is that your selection of a measure of central tendency will be determined by your objectives in communication as well as by mathematical considerations.

VARIABILITY

As we computed measures of central tendency (mean, median, and mode), we were looking for one score that would best represent an entire set of scores. Consider the final exam scores earned by students in each of two classrooms:

Classroom A Exam Scores	Classroom B Exam Scores
160	102
130	101
100	100
70	99
40	98
$\Sigma X = 500$	$\Sigma X = 500$
$M_X = \dfrac{500}{5} = 100$	$M_Y = \dfrac{500}{5} = 100$

Notice that the mean is 100 in both classrooms. But what a difference in variability! (Perhaps you have heard about the man who drowned in a lake with an average depth of 1 foot.) In order to deal with such differences, statisticians have developed several measures of variability that allow us to differentiate between groups of scores like those preceding.

THE RANGE

The simplest measure of variability is the range. The *range* is the highest score (H) minus the lowest score (L). In classroom A,

$$\text{Range} = \text{H} - \text{L} = 160 - 40 = 120$$

In classroom B,

$$\text{Range} = \text{H} - \text{L} = 102 - 98 = 4$$

Because the range is based on only the two most extreme scores, it can be quite misleading as a measure of overall variability. Remember Ruritania, where the king had an annual income of $1,000,000 and the other four people in the sample had incomes of $5000, $4000, $4000, and $2000? The range of this distribution is $998,000, even though all but one of the people in the sample are clustered within $3000 of each other. In this distribution, the range is not as useful a measure as the variance, which is based on all the scores. That's where we go next.

THE VARIANCE (S^2)

The *variance* is the most frequently used measure of variability. The formula for the variance may seem a bit intimidating at first, but you can handle it if you follow the procedures outlined in what follows. Here it is:

$$s^2 = \frac{\Sigma(X - M_x)^2}{N - 1}$$

Before learning how to compute the variance, though, let's discuss the concept of deviations about the mean.

Deviations about the Mean

We can tell how far each score deviates from the mean by subtracting the mean from it, using the formula $(X - M_X)$. Notice that in the following distribution of scores, we have subtracted the mean (5) from each score:

Scores	$X - M_X$
9	9 − 5 = +4
7	7 − 5 = +2
5	5 − 5 = 0
3	3 − 5 = −2
1	1 − 5 = −4
$\Sigma X = 25$	$\Sigma(X - M_X) = 0$

When we add up the column headed "$X - M_X$," the sum of that column equals zero. That is, $\Sigma(X - M_X) = 0$. Another way of expressing this relationship is to say that *the sum of the deviations of scores about their mean is zero.* This generalization is always true, except when you make rounding errors. In fact, another definition of the mean is *that score around which the sum of the deviations equals zero.* The sum of the deviations about the mean would not,

therefore, make a very good measure of variability because it would be the same for every distribution.

   If we square each deviation, however, the minus signs cancel each other out. In the following distribution, look carefully at the column headed $(X - M_X)^2$. Notice that squaring the deviations gets rid of the negative values.

Scores (X)	$X - M_X$	$(X - M_X)^2$
9	$9 - 5 = +4$	16
7	$7 - 5 = +2$	4
5	$5 - 5 = 0$	0
3	$3 - 5 = -2$	4
1	$1 - 5 = -4$	16
$\Sigma X = 25$	$\Sigma(X - M_X) = 0$	$\Sigma(X - M_X)^2 = 40$

   Now we have $\Sigma(X - M_X)^2 = 40$, the numerator of the formula for the variance. To complete the computation, just divide by $N-1$:

$$s^2 = \frac{\Sigma(X - M_X)^2}{N - 1} = \frac{40}{5 - 1} = 10$$

Many students complete the computation of their first variance and then ask, "What does it mean?" Perhaps you have a similar question. Before answering it, let's go back to classrooms A and B (from the beginning of the chapter) and find the variance for each classroom.

Classroom A Exam Scores	Classroom B Exam Scores
160	102
130	101
100	100
70	99
40	98
$\Sigma X = 500$	$\Sigma X = 500$
$M_X = \dfrac{500}{5} = 100$	$M_Y = \dfrac{500}{5} = 100$

The variance for classroom A is

$$s^2 = \frac{\Sigma(X - M_X)^2}{N - 1} = \frac{9000}{4} = 2250$$

And the variance for classroom B is

$$s^2 = \frac{\Sigma(X - M_X)^2}{N - 1} = \frac{10}{4} = 2.5$$

Notice that the values for the variances of classrooms A and B indicate that there is quite a bit of difference between the variabilities of the classrooms. That's what the variance is supposed to do—provide a measure of the variability. The more variability in a group, the higher the value of the variance; the more homogeneous the group, the lower the variance.

Another way to understand the variance is to notice that, in order to find it, you need to add all the squared deviations and divide by $N-1$. Sound familiar? Very similar to the definition of the mean, don't you think? So one way to understand the variance is to think of it as an average[2] deviation squared, or maybe a mean squared deviation.

The preceding formula given for the variance is a definitional formula. It is both accurate and adequate for small sets of numbers in which the mean turns out to be a whole number, but it is inconvenient for general use. For

[2]The difference between this formula and other formulas for "average" values is, of course, that here we divide by $N-1$ rather than simply by the number of scores. The reason? It's fairly complicated, and it has to do with how we will use the variance later on, when we get to *inferential statistics*. I think it would just be confusing to explain it now—okay if we wait for Chapter 6? It is? Thank you . . .

most purposes, it will be better for you to use a mathematically equivalent computational formula. It's not only easier to use, but it minimizes roundoff error.

The computational formula for the variance is

$$s^2 = \frac{N\Sigma X^2 - (\Sigma X)^2}{N(N - 1)}$$

Just take a few deep breaths and try to relax. Calmly analyze what you see. Notice that you know quite a bit already: You know that N is the total number of scores, and ΣX is the sum of all the scores. There are two terms you haven't seen before: $(\Sigma X)^2$ and ΣX^2. Let's look at each one in turn.

$(\Sigma X)^2$: This term directs you to find the sum of the X scores and then square that sum. It's an example of the parentheses rule we talked about earlier: Work from the inside out.

X Scores
10
9
8
7
6
$\Sigma X = 40$

$(\Sigma X)^2 = (40)^2 = 1600$

ΣX^2: This term directs you to square each X score and then sum the squares.

Scores (X)	Scores Squared (X^2)
10	100
9	81
8	64
7	49
6	36
$\Sigma X = 40$	$\Sigma X^2 = 330$

Note that ΣX^2 is not the same as $(\Sigma X)^2$. It is very important that you make this distinction!

Here are two rules that may help you to read statistical formulas:

Rule 1. Whenever you see parentheses around a term, as in $(\Sigma X)^2$, do what's indicated *inside* the parentheses before doing what's indicated *outside* the parentheses. In the last example, you would find ΣX first and then square it: $(\Sigma X)^2 = (40)^2 = 1600$.

Rule 2.   When there are no parentheses, a symbol and its exponent are treated as a unit. When you see ΣX^2, first square and then add the squared numbers. In the preceding example, square each number first and then get the sum of the squares: $\Sigma X^2 = 330$.

Another example:

Scores (X)	Scores Squared (X²)
140	19,600
120	14,400
100	10,000
80	6,400
60	3,600
$\Sigma X = 500$	$\Sigma X^2 = 54{,}000$
	$(\Sigma X)^2 = 250{,}000$

If you have many numbers with which to work, the process of finding the square of each number first, then recording it, and then adding them is tedious. Here's where you can use your calculator's memory. Follow these steps to find ΣX^2 for the scores in the last example:

1. Clear your calculator's memory.
2. Find the square of 140 and enter it into M+. Do the same for each of your X scores without writing any of the squares on paper.
3. After you have entered the squares of all scores into M+, push your memory recall button (usually MR) and you should get the correct answer, which is 54,000 in this example. This is the value of ΣX^2.

Meanwhile, back at the variance formula, we still have

$$s^2 = \frac{N\Sigma X^2 - (\Sigma X)^2}{N(N-1)}$$

Let's apply the formula to the following example:

Math Anxiety Scores (X)
11
9
8
7
6

Just follow these steps:

1. Look at the numerator first (it's as easy as a, b, c).
   (a) Find $N\Sigma X^2$. In our example, $N = 5$. To find ΣX^2, remember to square each score first; then sum the squares: $\Sigma X^2 = 351$. Therefore, $N\Sigma X^2 = (5)(351) = 1755$.
   (b) Find $(\Sigma X)^2$. (Remember, find ΣX first and then square the result.) $(\Sigma X)^2 = (41)^2 = 1681$.
   (c) Find $N\Sigma X^2 - (\Sigma X)^2$. Use what you found in steps (a) and (b): $1755 - 1681 = 74$. Great! You've got the numerator.
2. Now look at the denominator. This part is really easy because all you have to do is multiply N by one less than N. In our example, $N = 5$, so $N(N-1) = 5 \times 4 = 20$.
3. Now divide the numerator by the denominator to find the variance. The numerator was 74 and the denominator was 20, so s^2 equals 74 divided by 20, which equals 3.7. $s^2 = 3.7$.
   To summarize:

$$s^2 = \frac{N\Sigma X^2 - (\Sigma X)^2}{N(N-1)} = \frac{5(351) - 1681}{(4)(5)} = \frac{74}{20} = 3.7$$

Now let's go back and compute the variances for classrooms A and B (from the beginning of the chapter).

Variance of Scores in Classroom A

1. Numerator:
   (a) $N\Sigma X^2 = 5(59,000) = 295,000$
   (b) $(\Sigma X)^2 = (500)^2 = 250,000$
   (c) $N\Sigma X^2 - (\Sigma X)^2 = 295,000 - 250,000 = 45,000$
2. Denominator:

$$N(N-1) = (5)(4) = 20$$

3. Computation of s^2:

$$s^2 = \frac{45,000}{20} = 2250$$

That is, the variance of classroom A is 2250. Notice that this is the same value we got by using the definitional formula. Because the mean was a whole number, there was no roundoff error with the definitional formula.

Variance of Scores in Classroom B

1. Numerator:
   (a) $N\Sigma X^2 = 5\,(50{,}010) = 250{,}050$
   (b) $(\Sigma X)^2 = (500)^2 = 250{,}000$
   (c) $N\Sigma X^2 - (\Sigma X)^2 = 250{,}050 - 250{,}000 = 50$
2. Denominator:

$$N(N - 1) = (5)(4) = 20$$

3. Computation of s^2:

$$s^2 = \frac{50}{20} = 2.5$$

Again, notice that this is the same value you found for the variance of classroom B when you used the definitional formula.

If there is a lesson to be learned here, it is that statistical formulas aren't so much *difficult* as they are *compressed*. There's nothing really hard about following the steps. But we are so used to reading things quickly, that we tend to look once at a long formula and then give up, without taking the time to break it into chunks that we can understand. A good rule of thumb is that any line of formula should take about as long to read as a page of text.

THE STANDARD DEVIATION (s)

When you read educational and psychological research, you will often come across the term *standard deviation,* designated by the letter *s*. Once you have found the variance s^2 of a sample, finding the standard deviation is easy: Just take the square root of the variance. If the variance is 25, the standard deviation will be 5; if the variance is 100, the standard deviation will be 10. To find the standard deviations of the exam scores from classrooms A and B, take the square roots of the variances.

Standard Deviation of Classroom A	Standard Deviation of Classroom B
$s = \sqrt{s^2} = \sqrt{2250} = 47.43$	$s = \sqrt{s^2} = \sqrt{2.5} = 1.58$

Computing the standard deviation is as easy as pressing a button on your calculator, right? But what do the numbers mean? Again, as was true with the variance, the values of computed standard deviations indicate the relative variability within a group. When you know that the standard deviation of classroom A, for example, is considerably higher than that of classroom B, this could alert you to the likelihood that it might be harder to teach students in classroom A because of the much greater degree of heterogeneity in that class.

We'll find more uses for the standard deviation in later chapters, so you'll learn more about its meaning at that time. Meanwhile, take time to practice computing some of the statistics you've learned so far. Find the mean (M_X), range (R), variance (s^2), and standard deviation (s) for each of the following groups of scores. Carry out all calculations to three decimal places and round them correct to two places. Compare your answers with mine.

	Aptitude Test Scores	GPAs	Math Anxiety Scores
	160	4.0	27
	100	3.6	29
	80	3.4	27
	70	3.0	20
	69	2.5	10
$M =$	95.80	3.30	22.60
$R =$	91	1.5	19
$s^2 =$	1443.2	.33	61.30
$s =$	37.99	.57	7.83

PROBLEMS

1. Compute the mean, median, and mode for each of these distributions.

A	B	C	D
3	2	1	2
3	2	3	3
4	2	3	4
6	5	3	4
7	5	5	4
8	7	5	5
10	7	8	7
	8	8	8
	10	8	8
	11	9	
		11	

2. I grew up in a very tiny town in the midwestern United States. The town had seven streets, and the number of buildings on each street was as follows:

Street	Number of Buildings
Main Street	27
Myrtle Street	7
Pine Street	12
Walnut Street	9
1st Avenue	11
2nd Avenue	13
3rd Avenue	3

Use three different methods to find a single number that describes how many buildings there are per street in my home town.

3. Some of the students in Mr. Whimper's math class decided to have a spitball throwing contest, to see who had the best range. Sixteen students participated, and their scores (in feet) were as follows: Andrew, 15; Beth, 12; Colin, 14.8; Derek, 10.3, Elspeth, 15; Fiona, 9.5; Glenn, 3 (he got the giggles, but they wouldn't give him a second try); Harris, 8.9; Iggy, 22 (he was a starting pitcher on the baseball team); Jeanine, 13; Ken, 10.4; Leila, 10.5; Max, 11; Norton, 9.9; Opie, 15; and Penny, 7. What was the median score, and who came closest to it? Which was closer to the mean, the median or the mode?

4. Find the range, variance, and standard deviation for the following sets of values.
   (a) 1, 2, 3, 4, 5, 6, 7, 8, 9
   (b) 10, 20, 30, 40, 50, 60, 70, 80, 90
   (c) −4, −3, −2, −1, 0, 1, 2, 3, 4
   (d) .1, .2, .3, .4, .5, .6, .7, .8, .9
   (e) number of years in school, page 6.
   (f) achievement test scores and comprehension test scores on page 8.
   (g) the test scores on pages 9 and 10.
   (h) the four sets of numbers in Problem 1
   (i) the numbers of buildings in Problem 2
   (j) the spitball distances in Problem 3

2

Frequency Distributions and the Normal Curve

In the previous chapter, you learned some quantitative methods of organizing, summarizing, and interpreting data. You learned how to compute the mean, the median, the mode, the range, the variance, and the standard deviation. You've come a long way! In this chapter, you will learn some graphic methods for describing data, and you will put them all together when you focus on the normal curve.

FREQUENCY DISTRIBUTIONS

Imagine that you have administered a math anxiety test to 100 graduate students and that the scores earned by these persons are as follows (in random order):

Math Anxiety Test Scores Earned by 100 Students

51	50	50	50	51
50	48	49	46	50
45	46	46	47	46
46	46	48	47	46
47	44	49	47	48
49	48	48	49	45
48	46	46	48	48
44	45	44	46	49

Math Anxiety Test Scores Earned by 100 Students

47	49	43	47	46
47	48	43	48	46
48	46	48	46	47
47	47	47	49	49
46	47	47	44	45
45	48	48	48	47
47	49	47	45	48
49	47	45	47	44
48	47	47	46	47
46	47	46	45	47
45	45	47	48	48
46	48	45	46	47

The simplest way to organize and summarize data such as these is to construct a simple frequency distribution. You can do so by following these steps:

1. Figure out how many different score values there are and write them down in order. By looking over all the scores in our example, you can see that the highest score earned was 51 and the lowest score was 43. List the possible scores, from highest to lowest, like this:

Math Anxiety Scores

51
50
49
48
47
46
45
44
43

2. Go through the list of scores, score by score, and make a check each time a score occurs (it's easier to keep track if you group them by 5's). At the end of this process, your data should look like this:

Math Anxiety Scores Tally

51 ||
50 ||||
49 |||| ||||
48 |||| |||| |||| ||||
47 |||| |||| |||| |||| ||||
46 |||| |||| |||| ||||
45 |||| |||| |
44 ||||
43 ||

3. Count up your tallies to find the frequency (*f*) with which each score was earned. Your complete frequency distribution would look like this:

Math Anxiety Scores	Tally	Frequency (*f*)
51	||	2
50	⺍⺍	5
49	⺍⺍ ⺍⺍	10
48	⺍⺍ ⺍⺍ ⺍⺍ ⺍⺍	20
47	⺍⺍ ⺍⺍ ⺍⺍ ⺍⺍ ⺍⺍	25
46	⺍⺍ ⺍⺍ ⺍⺍ ⺍⺍	20
45	⺍⺍ ⺍⺍ |	11
44	⺍⺍	5
43	||	2

You now have a better picture of how the 100 subjects scored on your math anxiety test than you had when scores were just listed in random order. You can see that most of the scores tend to be bunched up around the middle and that relatively fewer people earned scores at or near the extremes of the distribution.

Data such as these are sometimes presented in graphic form. There are many kinds of graphs; one of the most important graphs to understand in the study of statistics is the frequency polygon. That's because the frequency polygon forms the basis for understanding the normal curve.

THE FREQUENCY POLYGON

Graphs have a horizontal axis (known as the *X*-axis) and a vertical axis (known as the *Y*-axis). It is conventional in statistics to place scores along the *X*-axis and frequencies on the *Y*-axis. The frequency distribution of math anxiety scores in graph form would look like that in Figure 2–1.

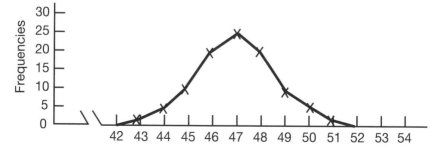

Figure 2–1. A frequency polygon.

Just in case you haven't worked much with graphs, I'll go through this one slowly.

First, look at the X's along the humped line that makes up the shape of the graph. Specifically, look at the X directly above the score of 44. Notice that the X is directly across from the frequency of 5, which indicates that 5 persons earned a score of 44. Similarly, the graph indicates that 20 persons earned a score of 46.[1] Got it? Good!

Second, look at the lines connecting the X's. When constructing a frequency polygon, connect all the X's with a line (you haven't had this much fun since you were a kid). Since the scores 42 and 52 each had zero frequency, we complete the graph by bringing our line down to the base line at these points, indicating that neither of them had anybody scoring there. Now we have constructed a *frequency polygon*—a many-sided figure, describing the shape of a distribution.

Occasionally, a researcher may want to display data in cumulative form. Instead of building a graph that shows the number of scores occurring at each possible score, a cumulative frequency polygon shows the number of scores occurring at *or below* each point. The *cumulative* frequency polygon for the math anxiety score data is shown in Figure 2–2 on page 25.

By finding the point on the line that is exactly above any number on the horizontal axis, and then reading across to the left, we can see how many students scored at or below that point. For example, 38 students had anxiety test scores at or below 46.

A cumulative frequency polygon is particularly useful in illustrating learning curves, when a researcher might be interested in knowing how many trials it took for a subject to reach a certain level of performance. Imagine that the graph here was obtained by counting the number of rounds a beginning dart thrower used during a series of practice sessions. The vertical axis is still "frequencies," but now it represents the number of practice rounds; the horizontal numbers represent the thrower's score on any given round. His worst score was 43, and he had two rounds with that score. He had 7 rounds with scores of either 43 or 44. How many rounds did he throw with scores of 47 or less? Well, find the point on the graph that is right over 47, and trace over to the left for the answer: 63 rounds yielded a score at or below 47.

---

[1]To be perfectly accurate, I should say that 5 people earned a score somewhere between 43.5 (which rounds off to 44) and 44.4 (which also rounds off to 44). Similarly, 20 persons earned a score between 45.5 and 46.4. This way of looking at a range of scores, rather than a single point, isn't very important when we're talking about this set of anxiety test scores, but when we talk about other distributions (like measurement in inches, which we'll be doing in a minute), it can be very important indeed.

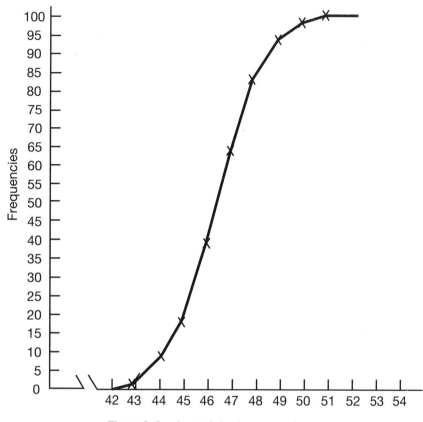

Figure 2–2. A cumulative frequency polygon.

This cumulative graph is typical of a learning curve: The learning rate is relatively slow at first, picks up speed in the middle, and levels out at the end of the set of trials, producing a flattened S shape.

THE NORMAL CURVE

Around 1870, Quetelet, a Belgian mathematician, and Galton, an English scientist, made a discovery about individual differences that impressed them greatly. Their method was to select a characteristic, such as weight or acuteness of vision, obtain measurements on large numbers of individuals, and then arrange the results in frequency distributions. They found the same pattern of results over and over again, for all sorts of different measurements. Figure 2–3

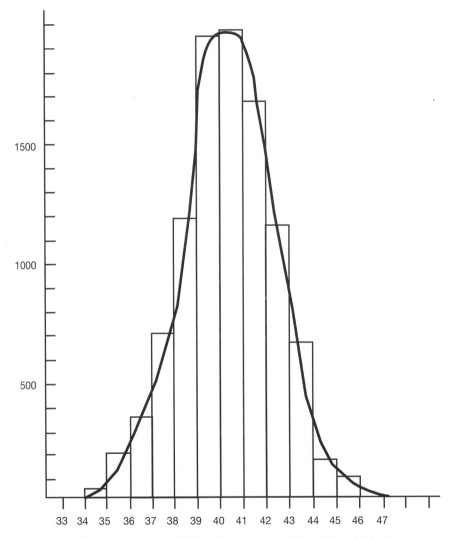

Figure 2-3. Chest sizes of 5,738 soldiers. Francis Galton, Natural Inheritance. London: Macmillan and Co., 1889.

is an example that depicts the results of measuring chest size of over 5000 soldiers.

The rectangles in this graph are called bars (it's a bar graph, or *histogram*), and the bars represent the number of folks who fell into each respective range. About 50 soldiers had chest sizes between 33.5 and 34.4 inches. If we were to put a mark at the top of each bar and draw straight lines between the marks, we'd have a frequency polygon of the sort we drew earlier. The curve that's drawn over the bars doesn't follow that polygon shape exactly, however; it's what we'd get if we measured thousands and thousands more soldiers and plotted the bar graph or frequency polygon for all of them, using narrower measurement intervals—maybe tenths or even hundredths of an inch, instead of whole inches.

The symmetrical, bell-shaped curve that results from plotting human characteristics on frequency polygons closely resembles a curve, familiar to mathematicians, known as the normal probability curve. The normal curve is bell-shaped and perfectly symmetrical and has a certain degree of "peaked-ness." Not all frequency distributions have this shape, however. Let's digress for a moment, and talk about skewed curves.

SKEWED CURVES

Skewed curves are not symmetrical. If a very easy arithmetic test were administered to a group of graduate students, for example, chances are that most students would earn high scores and only a few would earn low scores. The scores would tend to "bunch up" at the upper end of the graph, as if you'd taken a normal curve and pulled its bottom tail out to the left. When scores cluster near the upper end of a frequency polygon, so that the left side is "pulled down," the graph is said to be *negatively skewed.* An example of a negatively skewed curve is shown in Figure 2–4.

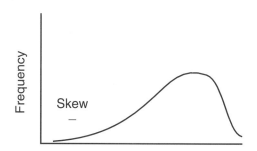

Figure 2–4.   A negatively skewed distribution.

On the other hand, if the test were too difficult for the class, most people would get low scores. When graphed as a frequency polygon, these scores would be said to be *"positively skewed,"* as shown in Figure 2–5.

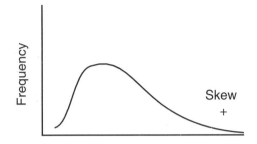

Figure 2–5. A positively skewed distribution.

When a distribution is skewed, the mean is the most strongly affected. A few scores far out in the tail of a distribution will "pull" the mean in that direction. The median is somewhat "pulled" in the direction of the tail, and the mode is not "pulled" at all. To see what I mean, look at the three distributions shown in Figure 2–6.

The first distribution (*X*) is perfectly symmetrical. Its mode, mean, and median are equal. In unimodal symmetrical distributions,

$$M = \text{Md} = \text{Mo}. \quad \textit{Always}$$

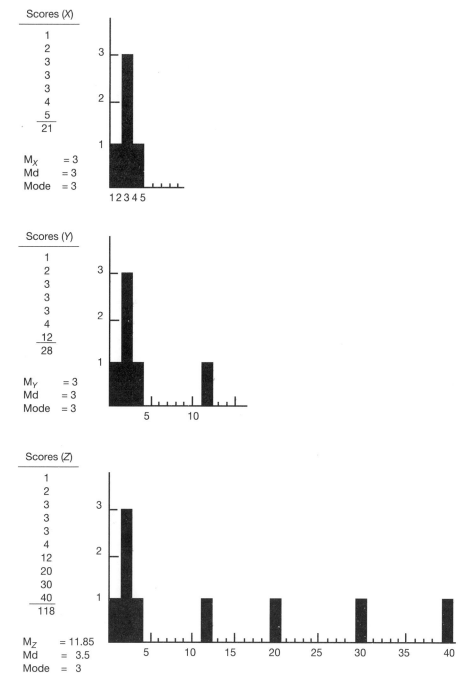

Figure 2–6. Symmetrical and skewed distributions.

Distribution *Y* has been skewed by changing the largest score, 5, to 12. Skewing it to the right like this shifted the mean from 3 to 4, but it didn't change either the mode or the median.

Finally, in distribution *Z*, we have not only shifted the 5 out to 12, but we have further skewed the distribution to the right by adding scores of 20, 30, and 40. The mean is again most sensitive to these changes. And this time, Md shifts too, just a bit, from 3 to 3.5. But the mode remains unchanged.

Now, after this fascinating discussion, let's get back to our major concern: the normal distribution. Data derived from measurement of human characteristics will never fit the normal probability curve exactly, because the normal probability curve is a hypothetical distribution—it doesn't exist in the real world. But graphs based on frequency distributions of many human characteristics, including psychological test results, often *resemble* the normal curve, at least to some extent, as can be seen in Galton's graph of soldiers' chest measurements.

Since many actual distributions approximate the normal curve so closely, we can use what mathematicians know about it to help us interpret test results and other data. Notice that, in the graph of chest measurements, large numbers of scores cluster near the middle of the distribution, and there are relatively small numbers of scores near the extremes: Most of the scores cluster around 40, and the percentage of persons who score lower than 36 or higher than 43 is quite small. When a set of scores is distributed approximately like the normal curve, mathematicians can provide us with a great deal of information about those scores, especially about proportions of scores in different areas of the curve.

PROPORTIONS OF SCORES UNDER THE NORMAL CURVE

In the next few paragraphs, I am going to show you how the mean, median, mode, standard deviation, and the normal probability curve all are related to each other. If you are still confused when you finish this section, at least you'll be confused at a higher level.

Consider the following example.

Test Scores (X)	Frequency
110	1
105	2
100	3
95	2
90	1

If you were to calculate the mean, median, and mode from the data in this example, you would find that $M_X = 100$, Md = 100, and Mo = 100 (go ahead and do it, just for practice). The three measures of central tendency always coincide in any group of scores that is symmetrical and unimodal.[2]

Recall that the median is the middle score, the score that divides a group of scores exactly in half. For any distribution, you know that 50% of the remaining scores are below the median and 50% above. In a normal distribution, the median equals the mean, so you know that 50% of the scores also are higher than and 50% lower than the mean. Thus, if you know that the mean of a group of test scores is 70, and if you know that the distribution is normal, then you know that 50% of the persons who took the test (and who didn't get a score of exactly 70) scored higher than 70 and 50% lower.

Now let's see how the standard deviation fits in. Suppose again that you had administered a test to a very large sample, that the scores earned by that sample were distributed like the normal probability curve, and that the mean equaled 70 ($M_X = 70$) and the standard deviation equaled 15 ($s = 15$). Mathematicians can show that in a normal distribution, exactly 68.26% of the scores lie between the mean and one standard deviation away from the mean. (You don't need to know why it works out that way; just take it on faith.) In our example, therefore, about 34.13% of the scores would be between 70 and 85 (85 is one standard deviation above the mean: $M_X + s = 70 + 15 = 85$). We know that the normal curve is symmetrical, so we know that about 34.13% of the scores will also be between 70 and 55 ($M_X - s = 70 - 15 = 55$). Thus, if we administered our test to 100 persons, approximately 34 would have scores between 70 and 85, and about 68 would have scores between 55 and 85 (34.13% + 34.13%). Most students find it helpful (necessary?) to see a picture of how all of this works; use the graph in Figure 2–7 to check it out.

[2]I almost said that mean and median and mode are always the same in any symmetrical distribution. Then I realized—you could have a symmetrical bimodal distribution, like this one: 1, 2, 2, 2, 3, 4, 5, 6, 6, 6, 7. The mean and the median would be the same, but the mode(s) would be 2 and 6. However, this kind of distribution is relatively rare. For all symmetrical unimodal distributions, M = Md = Mo. This implies, of course, that in a normal distribution M = Md = Mo.

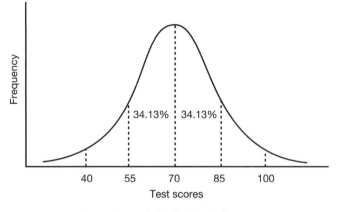

Figure 2–7. A distribution of IQ scores.

To take another example, suppose that grade-point averages (GPAs) were calculated for 1000 students and that $M_{GPA} = 2.5$ and $s = .60$. If our sample of GPAs was drawn from a normal distribution, you would know that approximately 500 students had GPAs higher and 500 had GPAs lower than 2.5.[3] You would also know that approximately 683 of them (34.13% + 34.13% = 68.26%; 68.26% of a thousand is approximately 683) had GPAs somewhere between 1.90 and 3.10 (plus and minus one standard deviation). Here's what the graph would look like:

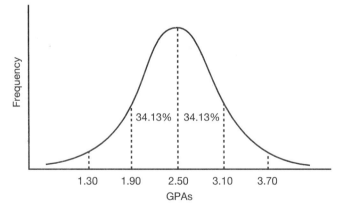

Figure 2–8. A distribution of GPAs

[3]Well, that would be true if nobody had a GPA of exactly 2.5. To be quite accurate, we'd have to say that once you've taken out all the folks who score exactly at the median, half of those who are left will score below, and half above, the median.

Mathematicians can tell us the proportion of the population between any two points under the normal curve. The following figure presents information about some selected points.

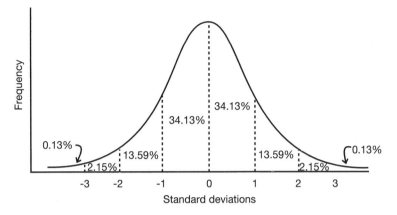

Figure 2-9. Percentage of scores between selected points under the normal curve.

The numbers on the base line of the figure represent standard deviations (*s*), where −1 represents one standard deviation below the mean, +2 represents two standard deviations above the mean, and so on.

Given the information in the graph, you can answer some interesting questions. For example, suppose again that you administered a test to 100 people, that the scores were distributed approximately normally, and that $X = 70$ and $s = 15$.

You know from the preceding discussion that about half of the 100 people scored lower than 70 and 50 higher. And you know that approximately 68 scored between 55 and 85. The graph also tells you the following:

1. About 13.59% of the scores are between −1*s* and −2*s*. In our example, therefore, around 14 people scored between 40 (two standard deviations below the mean) and 55 (one standard deviation below the mean). Of course, 13.59% (approximately) of the cases also are between +1*s* (85) and +2*s* (100).
2. About 95.44% of the cases fall between −2*s* and +2*s* (13.59% + 34.14% + 34.13% + 13.59%), so we know that approximately 95 out of 100 people scored between 40 (−2*s*) and 100 (+2*s*).
3. About 99.74% of the cases fall between −3*s* and +3*s*. Virtually all persons in our example scored between 25 (+3*s*) and 115 (+3*s*).
4. About 84.13% had scores lower than 85. How do we know this? 50% of the persons scored below 70 (the mean and median, remember?), and an-

other 34.13% scored between 70 and 85. Adding the 50% and the 34.13%, you find that 84.13% of the scores are predicted to fall below 85.

The following problems will test your understanding of the relationships among the mean, median, mode, standard deviation, and the normal probability curve. Remember that these relationships hold only if the data you are working with are distributed normally. When you have a skewed distribution or one that is more or less peaked than normal, what you have just learned does not hold true.

PROBLEMS

Suppose that a test of math anxiety was given to a large group of persons, the scores are assumed to be from a normally distributed population, that $M = 50$ and $s = 10$. Approximately what percentage of persons earned scores:

1. below 50?
2. above 60?
3. below 30?
4. above 80?
5. between 40 and 60?
6. between 30 and 70?
7. between 60 and 70?
8. below 70?
9. below 80?
10. A major pharmaceutical company has published data on effective dosages for their new product, FeelWell. It recommends that patients be given the minimum effective dose of FeelWell, and reports that the mean effective minimum dose is 250 mg, with a standard deviation of 75 mg (dosage effectiveness is reported to be normally distributed). What dose level will be effective for all but 2% of the total population? What dose level can be expected to be too low for all but 2%?
11. Dennis the Druggie has decided to grow marijuana in his basement. He has learned from friends (who wish to remain nameless) that the average marijuana plant grows to a height of 5′4″, with a standard deviation of 8″. Within what range can he expect 2/3 of his plants to grow? (*Hint:* Convert everything to inches, and then convert back to feet when you're done.)
12. New American cars cost an average of $17,500, with $s = 2000. (That's not really true; I just made it up for this problem.) If I'm only willing to spend up to $15,500, and if car prices are normally distributed, what percentage of the total number of new cars will fall within my budget?
13. Long-distance runners seem to be setting new records every year. If the current mean time for college athletes running the mile is 4 minutes and 32 seconds, with a standard deviation of 1 minute, figure out what the top 2% of runners can be ex-

pected to do. If your answer seems unreasonable to you (and it should), how do you explain what happened?

14. According to a survey carried out by the psychology department, students at the University of Oregon drink an average of 3.5 cups of coffee daily ($s = 1.2$). Assuming that coffee consumption is normally distributed, what percentage of students drink between 3.5 and 5.9 cups a day?

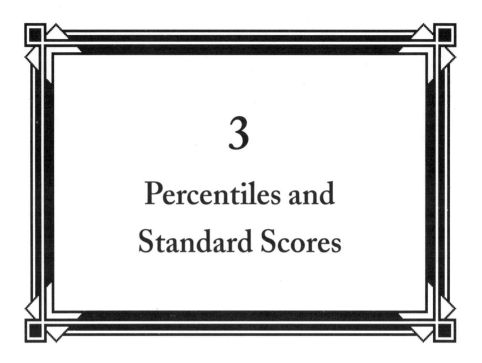

3

Percentiles and
Standard Scores

If you work as a teacher or a member of other helping professions, you frequently will be required to interpret material in student or client folders. Material in the folders typically will include several types of test scores. This chapter will introduce you to two common types of scores—percentiles and standard scores—as well as their major variations. Some of the material will appear complicated at first, but it's just a logical extension of what you've learned so far. You may not even find it particularly difficult!

Before discussing percentiles and standard scores, I want to point out some of the disadvantages of three types of scores with which you may be familiar from your school days: the raw score, the percentage correct score, and rank in class. Consider the following dialog:

Boy: Ma! I got 98 on my math test today!
Mother: That's very good, son. You must be very happy!
Boy: Yes, but there were 200 points on the test.
Mother: Oh! I'm sorry. I guess you didn't do too well.
Boy: Yes, but I got the second highest score in class.
Mother: Very good!
Boy: Yes, but there are only two of us in the class.

As you can see, the boy's raw score didn't communicate much information. But neither did his percentage correct score, because it didn't tell us whether the test was extremely difficult or very easy. Nor was his rank in class very helpful unless we knew how large the class was, and even when we found that out, we didn't know a whole lot because the class was small and our knowledge of the one person with whom he was being compared is nonexistent. When interpreting someone's test score, we would like to know, at a minimum, something about the group of persons with whom he or she is being compared (the *norm group*) and how he or she did in comparison with that group.

The norm group of a test usually will include large samples of people. For a standardized aptitude test, for example, the publishers will attempt to get a large representative sample of people in general. In their sample, they will usually include appropriate proportions of persons in the various age, gender, ethnic, and socioeconomic groups likely to be measured by that test. Test manuals often contain detailed descriptions of normative samples and the way in which they were obtained; a good textbook on tests and measurement can also give you that kind of information. Obviously, a test's usefulness to you is strongly influenced by the group(s) on which it was normed; if you intend to use a test with adolescents, for example, but the test was normed on adults, you would have no way of interpreting your clients' scores.

PERCENTILES

Percentiles are one of the most frequent types of measures used to report the results of standardized tests, and for good reason: They are the easiest kind of score to understand. An individual whose score is at the 75th percentile of a group scored higher than about 75% of the persons in the norm group.[1] Someone whose score is at the 50th percentile scored higher than about 50% of the persons in the norm group. And someone whose score is at the 37th percentile scored higher than about 37% of the persons in the norm group. And so on.

The *percentile rank* of a score in a distribution is the percentage of the whole distribution falling below that score, plus half the percentage of the distribution falling exactly on that score. That's why I said "about" just now—you can't tell for sure, from a percentile rank, how many folks in the norm group scored below that score and how many hit right on it. Consider the following two distributions:

[1]Why "about"? Read on to the next paragraph.

Distribution A	Distribution B
1	4
2	5
3	5
4	5
5	5
5	5
6	5
7	5
8	5
9	10

In both of these distributions, a score of 5 is at the 50th percentile; it has a percentile rank of 50. In distribution A, 40% of the scores are below 5, and 20% are at 5; $40 + (1/2)(20) = 40 + 10 = 50$. In distribution B, 10% of the scores are below 5, and 80% are at 5; $10 + (1/2)(80) = 10 + 40 = 50$. Fortunately, most scores are normed on very large groups in which the scores form an approximately normal distribution, so you can take a person's percentile rank as a very close estimate of how many folks could be expected to score lower than that person. If the percentile rank is based on a small group, or on one that isn't normally distributed, you will need to be more cautious in interpreting it.

No matter how large or small the group, though, or what the shape of the distribution, computing a score's percentile rank is always the same: the percentage of scores below the one in question, plus half the percent right at that score.

Pretty simple, huh?

STANDARD SCORES

On many published psychological tests, raw scores are converted to what are called standard scores. Standard scores are useful because they convert scores to a distribution that always has a mean of zero and a standard deviation of 1. This makes it possible to compare scores or measurements from very different kinds of distributions. Let's see how it works.

For any sample, the basic standard score (known as the Z score) is defined mathematically by

$$Z = \frac{X - M_X}{s}$$

where X = an individual's raw score
M_X = the mean raw score of the group with which the individual is being compared (usually a norm group of some kind)
s = the standard deviation of that group

Suppose you administered a test to a large number of persons and computed the mean and standard deviation of the raw scores with the following results:

$$M_X = 42$$
$$s = 3$$

Suppose also that four of the individuals tested had these scores:

Person	Score (X)
Jim	45
Sue	48
George	39
Jane	36

What would be the Z score equivalent of each of these raw scores? Let's find Jim's Z score first:

$$Z_{\text{Jim}} = \frac{\text{Jim's score} - M_X}{s_X} = \frac{45 - 42}{3} = \frac{3}{3} + 1$$

Notice that (1) we substituted Jim's raw score ($X = 45$) into the formula, and (2) we used the group mean ($M_X = 42$) and the group standard deviation ($s = 3$) to find Jim's Z score. Because lots of Z scores turn out to have negative values, we use the + sign to call attention to the fact that this one is positive.

Now for George's Z score:

$$Z_{\text{George}} = \frac{\text{George's score} - M_X}{s_X} = \frac{39 - 42}{3} = \frac{-3}{3} = -1$$

Your turn—you figure out Sue's and Jane's Z scores. Did you get $Z_{\text{Sue}} = +2$, and $Z_{\text{Jane}} = -2$? You did? Very good!

Here is some more practice. Suppose you administered a test to 16 persons who earned the following scores: 20, 19, 19, 18, 18, 18, 17, 17, 17, 17, 16, 16, 16, 15, 15, and 14. Start by finding the mean and the standard deviation. I'll give you the answers, but check yourself to see if you can get the same ones:

$$N = 16$$
$$\Sigma X^2 = 4664$$
$$(\Sigma X)^2 = 73{,}984$$
$$M_X = 17$$
$$s_X = 1.63$$

Fred was one of the two persons who scored 19; so for Fred, $X = 19$. To find Fred's Z score,

$$Z_{\text{Fred}} = \frac{19 - 17}{1.63} = \frac{2}{1.63} = +1.23$$

Sarah's raw score (X) was 14. Her Z score is—what? You figure it out.[2]

Notice that the sign in front of the Z score tells you whether the individual's score was above (+) or below (–) the mean.

Another example. Suppose a test was given to a large number of persons with the following results: $M = 47, s = 5$. Check your computation of Z scores.

Individual's Raw Score (X)	Z Score
57	+2.0
55	+1.6
52	+1.0
50	+.6
47	0
45	– .4
42	–1.0
40	–1.4
37	–2.0

What does a Z score of –1.4 tell us? First, the minus sign tells us that the score was below the mean. Second, the number 1.4 tells us that the score was 1.4 standard deviations below the mean.

What about a Z score of +2.0? The plus indicates that the score is above the mean, and the 2.0, again, tells us that the score is 2 standard deviations above the mean.

Notice that whenever a person's raw score is equal to the mean, his or her Z score equals zero. Take the person whose raw score (X) was 47, for example. That person's Z score = 0. If the score had been 1 standard deviation above the mean, the Z score would have been +1.0; if it had been 1 standard deviation below the mean, the Z score would have been –1.0.

To summarize, the Z score tells you if the raw score was above the mean (the Z score is positive) or if the raw score was below the mean (the Z score is negative), and it tells you how many standard deviations the raw score was above or below the mean.

Many people are uncomfortable with negative numbers; others don't like using decimals. Some don't like negatives *or* decimals! Since Z scores often involve both, these folks would rather not have to deal with them. Our

[2]That's right, –1.90.

mathematical friends have developed several ways to transform Z's into other measures that are always positive and usually can be rounded to whole numbers without distorting things too much. The most common of these is the T score, which always has a mean of 50 and a standard deviation of 10. We'll discuss T scores next.

T Scores

A number of published personality inventories report test results in a manner similar to that employed by the California Psychological Inventory (CPI). An example of a CPI profile is shown in Figure 3–1 on the following page. Along the top of the profile, you can see a number of scales designated with letters naming the psychological characteristics measured by the CPI, such as Sc (self-control) and To (tolerance). Under each scale name is a column of numbers. These are raw scores. More interesting to us are the numbers on the left- and right-hand edges. These are the standard score equivalents of the raw scores.

The standard score utilized by the CPI is a T score. The formula for T scores is

$$T = 10(Z) + 50$$

The Z in this formula is the Z you've just learned to compute. Remember that the formula for computing Z scores is

$$Z = \frac{X - M_X}{s}$$

To convert raw scores to T scores, you must do the following:

1. Calculate the M and s of the raw scores.
2. Find the Z score equivalent of each raw score.
3. Convert the Z scores to T scores by means of the formula $T = 10(Z) + 50$.

Imagine that you visited a large number of high school gym classes and counted the number of sit-ups that each student could do in 3 minutes. You computed the mean and standard deviation of these scores and found that $M_X = 40$ and $s = 13$. Matt, one of the students you tested, had a raw score of 46. What was his T score?

1. Step 1 has been done for you; we have found that $M_X = 40$ and $s = 13$.
2. Matt's Z score is

$$Z_{\text{Matt}} = \frac{\text{Matt's score} - M_X}{s_X} = \frac{46 - 40}{13} = \frac{6}{13} = +.46$$

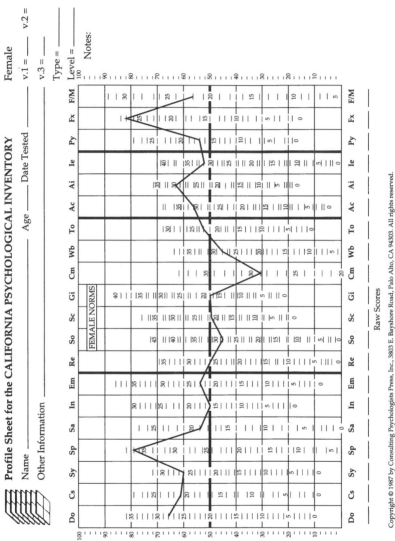

Figure 3-1.

42

3. Matt's T score is

$$T = 10 \times (+.46) + 50 = 4.6 + 50 = 54.6$$

Here are the Z and T score equivalents of seven more persons. See if you can get the same answers as I did.

Person	Raw Score	Z Score	T Score
Frank	49	+.69	56.9
Sam	40	0	50.0
Sharon	58	+1.38	63.8
George	35	−.38	46.2
Herman	20	−1.54	34.6
Fred	27	−1.0	40.0
Kate	67	+2.07	70.8

Notice that if a person's raw score is exactly at the mean of the group (see Sam's score), then his or her T score is 50; if the raw score is one standard deviation below the mean (see Fred's score), then his or her T score is 40, and so on.

Look at the sample CPI profile again. Notice that the score on the Sc scale has a *T* score equivalent of almost exactly 50. This *T* score lets you know that, relative to the norm group, this person's score was at or near the mean. On the other hand, look at the Sp (social presence) score. The *T* score is 80, so we know that it is 3 standard deviations above the mean. Very few people in the norm group score that high—the graph in Chapter 2 indicates that well under 1% are up there—so we can conclude that this person had an extremely elevated Sp score. Finally, imagine that someone had a score of 20 on both Sp and Py. Even though their raw scores are the same, they are well below the mean on Sp (their *T* score would be just under 40) and well above the mean on Py (*T* = 61).

Converting scores to *T* scores makes it possible to compare them meaningfully. But it doesn't end there—we can do lots more!

CONVERTING STANDARD SCORES TO PERCENTILES

The choice of what kind of test score will be used by a test publisher is somewhat arbitrary. Some types of scores are relatively easy for anyone to understand, whereas others can be really understood only by those who are sophisticated statistically (like you). My own preference of test-score type is the percentile. Percentile rank tells us exactly where a person stands relative to their norm group, without any need for further translation. A percentile rank of 50 means that the score is exactly in the middle of the norm group—at the median. A percentile rank of 30 means that the score is at the point where 30% of the remaining scores are below it and 70% above it. A percentile rank of 95 means that only 5% of the norm group scores were higher. Don't you just love it when you can score at the 99th percentile on an achievement test?

Figure 3–2 will help you to see the relationship between standard scores (*T*'s, *Z*'s), IQ scores, percentiles, and the normal curve. If all those numbers look a little threatening to you, don't worry; just take it slowly and it will make perfect sense. With a ruler or other straightedge to guide you, you can use the figure to make a rough conversion from one kind of score to another. In a moment, we're going to talk about how to do these conversions mathematically. For now, though, let's just look at the figure.

To use Figure 3–2 to move among different kinds of scores, you first need to convert a raw score to a *Z* score. Having done that, you can easily go to any of the other scores. For example, Fred's sit-up score was 1 standard deviation below the mean. This is equivalent to the following:

a *Z* score of –1

a *T* score of 40

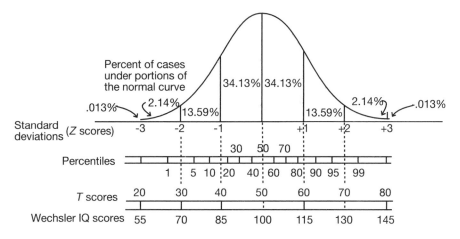

Figure 3–2. Relationships among areas under the normal curve, standard deviations, percentiles, and Z and T scores.

a percentile rank of about 16 (15.87)

a Wechsler IQ of 85[3]

Similarly, a raw score 2 standard deviations above the mean is equivalent to the following:

a Z score of +2

a T score of 70

a percentile rank of about 98 (97.72)

a Wechsler IQ of 130

Chances are that it will be helpful at some time in your work to translate standard scores into approximate percentiles. For example, if you know that a person's MMPI Depression score is 70, and if you know that MMPI scores are T scores, then you also know that he or she scored higher than almost 98% of the norm group on that scale. Similarly, if he or she earned an IQ of 85, you will know that the score is at approximately the 16th percentile.

What is the percentile equivalent of someone whose Z score is +.5? You can answer that question by looking down from the Z score scale to the

---

[3]Does it make any sense at all to say that one's ability to do sit-ups is "equivalent" to some IQ score? Of course not. A bushel of oranges tastes very different from a bushel of turnips, even though they have the same measurement. Being able to make a mathematical comparison doesn't necessarily imply that the comparison is meaningful!

percentile score on Figure 3–2 and making a rough approximation (a Z score of +.5 is about the 69th percentile). A more precise answer can be obtained by consulting Appendix C, concerned with proportions of area under the standard normal curve.

Don't be nervous; I'll tell you how to use that appendix. First, though, remember what you already know: If scores are distributed normally, the mean equals the median. Therefore, the mean is equal to the 50th percentile. Recall also (you can check it on Figure 3–2) that a raw score equal to the mean has a Z score equal to zero. Putting these facts together, you can see that $Z = 0 =$ 50th percentile.

You may also recall from Chapter 2 that a score 1 standard deviation above the mean is higher than 84.13% of the norm group, which is another way of saying that a Z score of +1 is at about the 84th percentile.

Now let's see how to use Appendix C. Look at the following example. Suppose you gave a test to a large group of people, scored their tests, and computed the mean and standard deviation of the raw scores. Assume that the population of scores was distributed normally and that $M_X = 45$ and $s = 10$. Cory had a raw score of 58. What is his percentile rank?

Procedure for Finding Percentile Ranks Given Raw Scores

First, convert the raw score to a Z score by using

$$Z = \frac{X - M_X}{s}$$

In our example,

$$X = 58 \text{ (Cory's raw score)}$$
$$M_X = 45 \text{ (given)}$$
$$s = 10 \text{ (given)}$$

Therefore,

$$Z_{\text{Cory}} = \frac{58 - 45}{10} = \frac{13}{10} = 1.3$$

At this point, I always draw a picture of a normal (approximately) curve, mark in 1 and 2 standard deviations above and below the mean, and put a check mark where I think the score I'm working with ought to go, as shown in Figure 3–3.

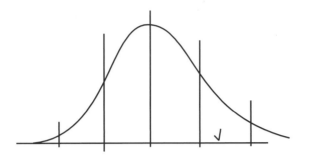

Figure 3–3.

As you can see, it doesn't have to be a very perfect figure. But it gives me an idea of what the answer is going to be. In this case, I know from my picture that the percentile is more than 84 and less than 98[4]; it's probably somewhere in the late 80's. Knowing that helps me to avoid dumb mistakes like reading from the wrong column of the table. If this step helps you, do it. If not, don't.

Now look in the Z columns of Appendix C until you find the Z score you just obtained ($Z = +1.3$), and write the first number to the right (in our example, .4032).

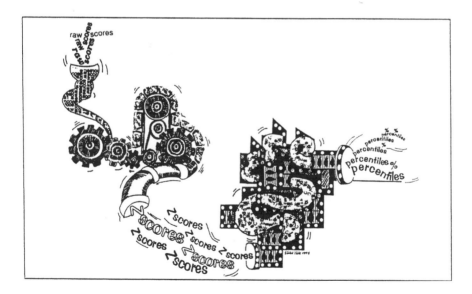

[4]Do you know why? One standard deviation above the mean (in a normal distribution, of course) is at the 84th percentile; two above the mean is at the 98th percentile. Our score is in between those two benchmarks.

This number indicates that between the mean and a Z score of +1.3, you will find a proportion of .4032, or 40.32% of the whole distribution (to convert proportions to percents, move the decimal two places to the right). You know that 50% of the cases in a normal curve fall below the mean, so a Z score of +1.3 is as high or higher than .50 + 40.32% = .9032, or 90.32% of the cases. A raw score of 58, therefore, corresponds to a percentile rank of 90.32. That's pretty close to my guess of "late 80's"!

A more accurate picture of what we just did is shown in Figure 3–4.

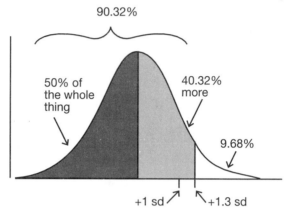

Figure 3–4.   Relationship between a raw score of 58, the corresponding Z score of +1.30, and the percentile rank of 90.32.

Another example: In Appendix C, locate a Z score of +.89. The table indicates that 31.33% of the cases fall between the mean ($Z = 0$) and $Z = +.89$, and that 18.67% of the cases fall *above* +.89. As in the previous problem, the percentile equivalent of $Z = +.89$ is 50% + 31.33% = 81.33%, a percentile rank of approximately 81. See Figure 3–5.

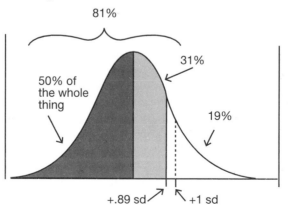

Figure 3–5.   Relationship between a Z score of .89 and the corresponding percentile rank of 81.

Remember that the standard normal curve is symmetrical. Thus, even though Appendix C shows areas above the mean, the areas below the mean are identical. For example, the percentage of cases between the mean ($Z = 0$) and $Z = -.74$ is about 27%. What is the corresponding percentile rank? Appendix C indicates that beyond $Z = .74$, there are 23% of the cases (third column). Therefore, the percentile rank is 23. See Figure 3–6.

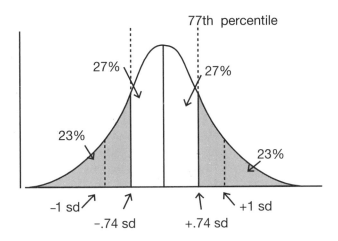

Figure 3–6.   Relationship between a Z score of –.74 and the corresponding percentile rank of 23.

I find that when I sketch a distribution, and use it to get the sense of what I'm looking for, problems like this are easy. When I don't make a sketch, I very often get confused. That's why I recommend that—unless you're very good at this indeed—you always draw a picture. Enough advice, now—back to business!

What percent of cases fall between $Z = +1$ and $Z = -1$? Appendix C indicates that 34.13% fall between the mean and $Z = +1$. Again, since the standard normal curve is symmetrical, there are also 34.13% between the mean and $Z = -1$. Therefore, between $Z = -1$ and $Z = +1$, there will be 34.13% + 34.13% = 68.26% of the cases.

Verify for yourself that 95% of the cases fall between $Z = \pm1.96$ (i.e., between $Z = +1.96$ and $Z = -1.96$) and that 99% of the cases lie between $Z = \pm2.58$.

You can use Appendix C to go backwards: to find out what Z score corresponds to a given percentile. What Z score marks the point where 2/3 of the scores are below, and 1/3 above? Well, that would be at the 66.67th percentile. Before you go to Appendix C and look in the second column for 66.67, and get all frustrated because you can't find it, draw a picture, as shown in Figure 3–7.

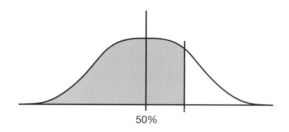

50%

Figure 3-7.   Relationship between Z score and the 66.67th percentile.

I've shaded in about 2/3 of this distribution, just to see what's going on. Below the mean is 50%; the lighter shaded area above the mean is 16.7%, because the whole shaded part is 66.67%. That's the number I have to find in the table, in the middle column. (The little diagrams at the top of the columns in Appendix C show you what part of the curve is being described in that column.) In this case, we find the number closest to .1667 (.1664) in the far-right column of the first page of Appendix C; reading over to the left, we see that this value corresponds to a Z score of +.43.

Working in the lower half of the distribution is just a bit more complicated, but using a sketch makes it easy. What Z score corresponds to a percentile rank of 30? Picture first: See Figure 3–8.

Since the curve is symmetrical (or it would be if I could draw), you can flip it over and work with its mirror image: See Figure 3–9 on the following page.

Thirty percent of the distribution was in the shaded tail of the first picture, so 30% is in the upper unshaded tail of the second, leaving 20% in the lower part of the top half. Looking up that 20%, we find that it corresponds to a Z of .52—that is, .52 standard deviation above the mean. What we want is the Z score that is .52 standard deviation *below* the mean—hey, we know how to do that; that's just $Z = -.52$!

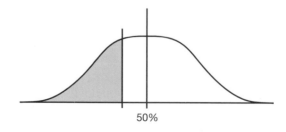

50%

Figure 3-8.   Relationship between Z score and the 30th percentile.

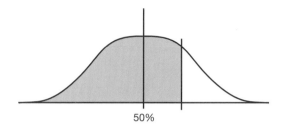

50%

Figure 3–9. Another way to look at the Z score–30th percentile relationship.

If you draw the picture, and use common sense to figure out what you're looking for, you should zip right through these kinds of problems.

WARNING

Remember that all the material in this chapter assumes that the scores you are interpreting are from normal (or nearly normal) distributions.. If the distribution is skewed, then conversions from standard scores to percentiles will not be accurate. (However, conversions from raw scores to standard scores can always be done. If you feel really ambitious, find a friend and explain why this is so.)

PROBLEMS

1. The following is a hypothetical set of anxiety scale scores from a population of students being seen at a college counseling center:

5	16	47
6	18	50
9	25	50
10	46	50
12	47	78

What are the Z and the T scores of the person who scored 6? 18? Of the two people who scored 47? Of the person who scored 78? Why is it not a good idea to use Appendix C to compute percentiles for these scores?

2. SAT scores are normally distributed, with a mean of 500 and sd of 100. Find the Z, T, and percentile equivalents of the following scores: 500, 510, 450, 460, 650, and 660.

3. Jack, Jill, James, and John all took a math aptitude test. The test was normed on a group that had a mean score of 70, $s = 15$; the scores were normally distributed. Complete the following table.

Name	Raw Score	Z Score	T Score	Percentile Rank
Jack	73	—	—	—
Jill	—	−1.2	—	—
James	—	—	60	—
John	—	—	—	23

4. Draw a diagram that shows the relationship of a raw score of 20 to Z, T, and percentile in a distribution with the following:
   (a) $M = 20, s = 5$
   (b) $M = 40, s = 7$
   (c) $M = 15, s = 4$
   (d) $M = 25, s = 10$

4

Correlation

Up to now, we have been dealing with one variable at a time. In this chapter, we will discuss how to measure the relationship between two variables. With such a measure, we will be able to answer important questions such as: Are achievement test scores related to grade-point averages? Is counselor empathy related to counseling outcome? Is student toenail length related to success in graduate school?

The relationship between two variables can be depicted by means of a scatter diagram. Suppose a group of students has taken an aptitude test. We'll use a scatter diagram to look at the relationship between Z scores and T scores on this test. We designate their Z scores as the X variable (the X variable is always plotted on the horizontal axis, or "X–axis" of a scattergram) and their T scores will be the Y variable (plotted on the vertical, or "Y–axis"). Each student has two scores. We find a given student's position on the graph by drawing an invisible line out into the center of the graph from the vertical-axis value (the Y value, in this case, the student's T score) and drawing another invisible line up into the graph from the X–axis value (the student's Z score). Put an X where the two lines cross, and you've plotted that student's location.

As you can see in Figure 4–1 on the following page, all the X's representing the relationship between Z scores and T scores fall on a straight line. When two variables have this kind of relationship, we say that they are *perfectly correlated*. This means that if we know the value of something on one of the variables, we can figure out exactly what its value is on the other. If we

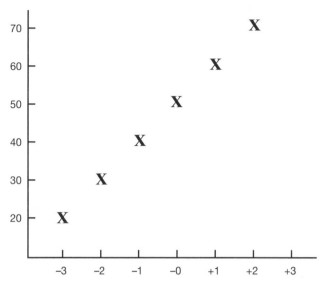

Figure 4–1. Relationship between Z and T scores.

know that someone has a T score of 35, her or his Z score has to be −1.5. Exactly. Every time.

Graphs that show relationships like this in picture form are useful, but often we need a more numerical way of expressing the same thing. In the next few pages, you'll learn how to compute a *correlation coefficient,* which is a quantitative measure of relationship. The relationship between Z scores and T scores has a correlation of +1.00, a perfect positive relationship. Here are some facts about correlation coefficients:

1. The values of correlation coefficients range from −1.00 to +1.00, representing perfect negative and perfect positive correlations, respectively. A coefficient of 0.00 represents no relationship at all.[1]
2. A positive correlation coefficient indicates that those individuals who scored high on one variable also tended to score high on the other (in our example, a high Z score means a high T score). When you plot the relationship between two positively correlated variables, the dots tend to fall around a line that runs from the lower left of the graph to the upper right.

---

[1]Not quite true, actually—a correlation coefficient of 0 means no *linear* relationship at all. Two variables could be *curvilinearly* related (we're going to talk about this later) and have a correlation coefficient of 0.

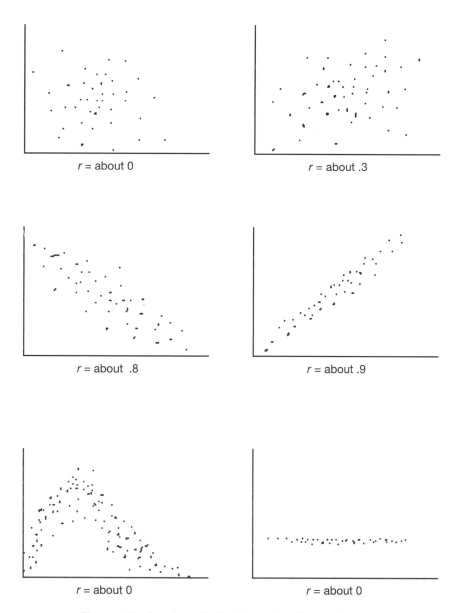

Figure 4–2. Sample graphs depicting various degrees of correlation.

3. A negative correlation indicates that when the value for one of the variables is high, the value of the other will be low. As in, for example, the number of cookies eaten in midafternoon (variable X) and the amount of meat, potatoes, and spinach eaten at dinner (variable Y). Two negatively correlated variables tend to plot out around a line running from the upper left of the graph to the lower right.
4. When the correlation is either +1.00 or –1.00 (an unlikely event in educational or psychological research), all the points in the plot fall on a straight line. As the correlation gets farther from 1.00 (toward 0), the points *scatter* out away from the line. That's why such graphs are known as *scatter plots*.

Figure 4–2 on the previous page shows sample scatter plots depicting various degrees of correlation.

THE PEARSON PRODUCT–MOMENT CORRELATION COEFFICIENT (r)

Many measures of correlation have been developed by statisticians for different purposes. The most common measure is the Pearson product-moment correlation coefficient, designated by lowercase r. Try to relax as much as you can before you look at the next computational formula, because it looks horrendous. Smile. We'll do it together, following the indicated steps, one at a time. It isn't as bad as it looks.

$$r = \frac{N\Sigma XY - (\Sigma X)(\Sigma Y)}{\sqrt{[N\Sigma X^2 - (\Sigma X)^2][N\Sigma Y^2 - (\Sigma Y)^2]}}$$

Suppose you wanted to compute the correlation between intelligence test scores (designated as X) and grade-point averages (Y) earned by a group of fifth-graders:

Student	IQ Score (X)	GPA (Y)
1	118	3.6
2	113	3.4
3	131	3.6
4	126	3.6
5	124	4.0
6	109	4.0
7	118	3.7
8	122	3.7
9	127	4.0
10	115	3.5

If you'll look closely at the formula for the Pearson product-moment correlation coefficient *r*, you'll notice that many of the values and computations are the same as for the variance. You might want to go back and review the last part of Chapter 1 now. Only one term in this formula is new: the $N\Sigma XY$ term found in the numerator. N is, of course, the number of pairs of measurements. In our example, $N = 10$. The rest of the term, ΣXY, directs you, first, to multiply each person's X score by his or her Y score, and then to sum the products. I'll add an XY column to the preceding data so you can see what I mean:

Student	IQ Score (X)	GPA (Y)	IQ × GPA (XY)
1	118	3.6	424.8
2	113	3.4	384.2
3	131	3.6	471.6
4	126	3.6	453.6
5	124	4.0	496.0
6	109	4.0	436.0
7	118	3.7	436.6
8	122	3.7	451.4
9	127	4.0	508.0
10	115	3.5	402.5

Now you have everything you need to compute *r*.

1. Look at the numerator of the formula for *r* first:
   (a) Find $N\Sigma XY$. In our example, $N = 10$ and $\Sigma XY = 4464.7$.

$$N\Sigma XY = (10)(4452.3) = 44,647$$

   (b) Find $(\Sigma X)(\Sigma Y)$. $\Sigma X = 1203$ and $\Sigma Y = 37.1$.

$$(\Sigma X)(\Sigma Y) = (1203)(37.1) = 44,631.3$$

   (c) $N\Sigma XY - (\Sigma X)(\Sigma Y) = 44,647 - 44,631.3 = 15.7$.
2. Now let's look at the denominator:
   (a) Look inside the square-root sign at the left-hand side of the denominator first. Notice that it is exactly the same as the numerator in the formula for the variance of X:

$$N\Sigma X^2 - (\Sigma X)^2 = (10)(145,149) - 1,447,209 = 4281$$

   (b) Now look at the right-hand side of the denominator, and, again, notice that it is the same as the numerator for the variance of Y:

$$N\Sigma Y^2 - (\Sigma Y)^2 = (10)(138.07) - 1376.41 = 4.29$$

(c) Now notice that you are directed to multiply the left-hand side of the denominator by the right-hand side:

$$[N\Sigma X^2 - (\Sigma X)^2](N\Sigma Y^2) = (4281)(4.29) = 18{,}365.49$$

(d) Your next step is to calculate the final value of the denominator. To do this, take the square root of the value you just got in step 2c. The square root of 18,365.49 is 135.52.

3. You're (finally) ready to calculate r! All you have to do is divide the numerator [the value you found in step 1(c)] by the denominator [step 2(d)]:

Numerator = 15.7
Denominator = 135.52

Dividing the numerator by the denominator gives you r:

$$r = \frac{15.7}{135.52} = .12$$

Before going on to discuss the meaning of the Pearson product-moment r just obtained, check your computational skills on the following data:

Student	5th-Grade IQ (X)	9th-Grade GPA (Y)
1	104	2.9
2	92	2.8
3	108	3.2
4	99	2.0
5	95	2.7
6	102	3.0
7	117	3.6
8	90	2.6
9	107	3.1
10	119	3.8
$N = 10$	$\Sigma X = 1033$	$\Sigma Y = 29.7$
	$\Sigma X^2 = 107{,}573$	$\Sigma Y^2 = 90.55$
	$\Sigma XY = 3104.4$	
	$r = .81$	

In our two examples of correlations between intelligence test scores (X) and GPA (Y), you obtained $r = .12$ and $r = .81$. What do these values mean? There are a number of possible interpretations:

1. You will recall that a perfect correlation between two variables would result in $r = 1.00$, whereas if there were no correlation at all between X and Y, then $r = 0$. Since both r's are positive and neither of the obtained r's equals either 1.00 or 0.00, we can say that there may be some correlation between the variables X and Y, but the relationship is not perfect.

2. How high are these correlations? Relative to what? Relative to the first correlation ($r = .12$), the second ($r = .81$) is quite high. Relative to correlations usually obtained between intelligence test scores and GPA, .12 is quite low, and .81 is a bit higher than usual ($r = .60$ would be more typical for this grade level). The point I'm trying to make here is that one way to judge whether or not an obtained r is high or low is to compare it with correlation coefficients typically obtained in similar studies. For example, if you have studied psychological measurement, you know that .60 as a predictive validity coefficient would be fairly high, but as a measure of split-half reliability, it might be relatively low. (And if you haven't studied measurement and don't know what those big words mean, don't worry—this just wasn't a good example for you.)

3. It is important not to confuse correlation with causation. In the second example, $r = .81$, the two variables are fairly closely related. But that doesn't prove that intelligence causes achievement, any more than achievement causes intelligence. There probably is a positive correlation between the number of counselors and the number of alcoholics in a state, but one does not necessarily cause the other. Two variables may be correlated with each other due to the common influence of a third variable.

On the other hand, if two variables do not correlate with each other, one variable cannot be the cause of the other. If there is no difference in counseling outcome between, for example, "warm" and "cold" counselors, then "warmth" cannot be a factor determining counseling outcome. Thus, the correlational approach to research can also help us to rule out variables that are not likely to be important to our theory or practice.

This point is so important that it bears repeating: If two variables are correlated, it is still not necessarily true that one causes the other. However, if they are *not* correlated, one can*not* be the cause of the other.

4. The Pearson product-moment r is a measure of linear relationship between two variables. Some variables are related to each other in a curvilinear fashion. For example, the relationship between anxiety and some kinds of performance is such that moderate levels of anxiety facilitate performance, whereas high levels interfere with it. A scatter diagram showing the relationship between the two variables would show the dots distributing themselves along a curved line (curvilinear), rather than a straight line (linear). Product-moment r is not an appropriate measure of relationship between two variables that are related to each other in a curvilinear fashion. If you are interested in the relationship between two variables measured over a large number of subjects, it's a good idea to construct a scatter diagram for 20 or so of these subjects before calculating r, just to get a general idea of whether the relationship (if any) might be curvilinear.

5. Another common way to use r is to calculate what is known as the coefficient of determination, which is the square of the correlation coefficient. For example, if the obtained r between intelligence test scores and GPA were $r = .60$, squaring would give you .36 (I know that it seems wrong when you see that the square of a number is smaller than the number being squared, but it's true. Try it.) The obtained square of the correlation coefficient (in our example, .36) indicates that 36% of the variability in Y is "accounted for" by the variability in X. "Why is it that some people achieve more in school than others?" some might ask. If intelligence were one cause of variability in achievement and if the correlation between intelligence and achievement were $r = .60$, then 36% (squaring .60 and converting it to a percentage) of the variability in achievement among people would be "accounted for" by intelligence, the other 64% being independent of intelligence. Another way of saying the same thing is that if $r_{XY} = .60$, variables X and Y have 36% of their variability "in common."

   6. When presenting statistical data in textbooks or professional journals, the author often will indicate whether or not the r obtained in the study was "significant" or "statistically significant." You will be exposed to an extended discussion of the concept of statistical significance when you study inferential statistics in later chapters in this book, but I will introduce one explanation now.

   I own a pocket calculator that will compute r's at the push of a button. If I wish, I can sit and punch in random numbers representing fictitious X and Y variables, press the appropriate button, and get the correlation between X and Y. Even though the numbers entered were random, the obtained r is almost never exactly zero. Just by chance, the numbers usually come out as if there were some slight relationship among them. The point of this digression is that when you compute r and it comes out to some number other than zero, how do you know it wasn't the result of "chance"?

   Enter the concept of statistical significance. Perhaps you have read studies that said things like, "The obtained results are significant at the .05 or the 5% level." What the author is saying is that only 5 times out of 100 could you expect to get a result as extreme as the one obtained in the study by chance alone. If you and 999 other students sit and punch random numbers into your calculators and then press the "correlate" button, about 50 of you will get a value of r that is "significant at the .05 level." The rest of you will get values closer to zero. About 10 of the 50 who got .05 significance will get a value big enough to be "significant at the .01 level," meaning that only 1 time in 100 would you get a result like that just by chance.

   Fortunately for us, we don't have to do any mathematics to determine if our obtained r is statistically significant. Statisticians have done that for us. Turn now to Appendix D, the table of r values. To enter the table, you will need first to locate the appropriate degrees of freedom (df) for your study. You'll learn more about df when you get to inferential statistics, too, but for now, all you'll need to know is that df = $N - 2$, where N is the number of pairs of measurements in your study. If, in calculating a correlation coefficient, you have 10 subjects and 2 measurements from each subject, then $N = 10$ pairs of measurements. Since $N = 10$ for both of the r values we computed, df = $N - 2 = 8$ for both.

   Now that you know your df, move down the df column until you get to 8, and then look across. If you want to know whether or not your obtained r is significant at the .05 level, go to the column headed with .05. For df = 8, r's of .6319 or larger are significant at the .05 level. That is, an r as large as or larger than .6319 will turn up just by chance only 5 times in 100. The r of the first example (r = .12) does not meet this standard. In the second sample, though, the r (r = .81) is greater than .6319, and we can say that the probability of its occurring just by chance is less than 5% (p < .05).

Notice also that the correlation coefficient obtained in the second example (r = .81) is significant at the .01 level, indicating that you would expect to get an r that size or larger by chance alone only 1 time in 100 (p < .01).

If you had 20 subjects in your study (N = 20), then df = 18 and an obtained r of .4438 would be significant at the .05 level, and an r of .5751 would be significant at the .01 level. The more subjects (pairs of observations) in your sample, the less likely it is that you'll get a high value of r just by chance.

When your df falls between tabled values, use the values for the next lower df. For example, if N = 60 and df = 58, you would use the significance values for df = 50 (an r = .2732 would be significant at the .05 level).

Many years ago, when I was a graduate student, significance level was considered to be enormously . . . well . . . significant. If your data showed that two variables had a statistically significant level of correlation (generally taken to be .05, or a result that would occur by chance only 5 times in a hundred), you set off fireworks, blew trumpets, and wrote it into your thesis. Now, however, scientists have learned to be a bit more pragmatic: Even if your results are statistically significant, what do they really mean? Is the size of the relationship large enough to get excited about? For instance, with a sample of 102 pairs, a correlation of .19 is significant at the .05 level. It almost certainly didn't occur just by chance; the two variables *are* related. But how strongly? The coefficient of determination tells us that less than 4% of the variability in one of the measures can be accounted for or predicted by variability in the other. A 4% overlap isn't much—is it enough to be useful? The answer, of course, depends on what we are trying to accomplish. There's no neat "yes or no" formula for the "how much is enough" question, as there is for statistical significance. But it's an important consideration, nevertheless.

One last bit of information: There are a number of other correlational techniques in addition to the Pearson product–moment r. Pearson's correlation assumes that both of the sets of values being looked at come from distributions that are roughly normal in shape. When the deviation from normality is slight, and/or when your samples are very large, violating this assumption won't be very serious. But with a strongly skewed distribution and a small sample size, Pearson's r just isn't appropriate, and you must use a different correlational formula. One of these, the Spearman correlation for ranked data, is presented later, along with a discussion of which measure of correlation is most appropriate for your particular data.

PROBLEMS

1. Given the following N's (where N is the number of pairs of observations) and obtained r's, indicate whether the result is significant at the .05 level:
   (a) $N = 100, r = .22$
   (b) $N = 100, r = .60$
   (c) $N = 9, r = -.70$
   (d) $N = 36, r = .23$
   (e) $N = 100, r = -.19$

2. Given the following data, what are the correlation and the coefficient of determination between
   (a) IQ scores and anxiety test scores?
   (b) IQ scores and statistics exam scores?
   (c) anxiety test scores and statistics exam scores?
   Indicate whether the obtained r is statistically signicant, and, if so, at what level. Also, would you consider the magnitude of the relationship large enough to be useful in making predictions about student achievement? (You may want to save your work on this one; we'll be using the same data for problems at the end of Chapter 5.)

Student	IQ (X)	Anxiety (Y)	Statistics Exam Scores (Z)
1	140	14	42
2	130	20	44
3	120	29	35
4	119	6	30
5	115	20	23
6	114	27	27
7	114	29	25
8	113	30	20
9	112	35	16
10	111	40	12

3. Feel like more arithmetic? Here's another set of measurements; again, find the value of r, whether that value is significant at the .05 level, and the coefficient of determination for each possible pair.

Name	Height (inches)	Weight (pounds)	Shoe Size	Ring Size
George	72	200	12	8
Herman	70	160	10	6
Alfie	68	170	11	7.5
Brent	70	150	$8\frac{1}{2}$	6.5
Donald	66	150	8	6
Kareem	72	185	11	$7\frac{3}{4}$
Graham	66	135	$7\frac{1}{2}$	6
Chaco	69	165	9	7.5

5
Other Correlation Topics

REGRESSION

Statisticians and researchers and teachers and weather forecasters and all sorts of other folks are interested in making predictions. A prediction, in this sense, is simply a best guess as to the value of something. We try to make our predictions so that, over the long run, the difference between the value we predict and the actual value (what the thing really turns out to be) is as small as possible.

If we have no additional information, the best guess that we can make about a value is to predict that it will equal the mean of the distribution it comes from. If I want to predict John's score on a test, and I know that the average score students like John have received on that test is 50, my best prediction of John's score is 50. Over time, across lots and lots of predictions, always predicting that somebody's score will equal the mean of the distribution will give me the best chance of coming close to a correct answer.

Making predictions with no extra information is not very useful. If the weatherperson always made exactly the same forecast (variable clouds, possibility of showers) day after day, people would quickly stop paying attention. Most often, though, we do have additional information, and we use that information to improve the accuracy of our prediction.

You know from Chapter 4 that when there is a positive correlation between two variables, X and Y, those persons who score high on the X variable also tend to score high on the Y variable, and those who score low on X tend to score low on Y. For example, suppose you know that there is a positive correlation between shoe size and weight. Given a person's shoe size, you can improve your guess about his weight. If you knew that John's shoe size was 12, you would predict that he weighs more than Jim, whose shoe size is $7\frac{1}{2}$. You can increase the accuracy of predictions of this sort considerably if you use what statisticians call a regression equation:

$$Y_{\text{predicted}} = M_Y + b(X - M_X)$$

The predicted value of Y is the mean of the Y distribution (no surprise here) plus something that has to do with the value of X. Part of that "something" is easy—it's how far X is from its own mean. That makes sense: Having a shoe size way above the mean would lead us to predict that weight would also be above the mean, and vice versa.

That takes care of the $(X - M_X)$ part. But what's the "b"? Well, b is a term that adjusts our prediction so as to take into account differences in the means and the standard deviations of the two distributions with which we're working, as well as the fact that they aren't perfectly correlated. In our example, if IQ scores and achievement test scores had a correlation of 1.0, and if they had the same means and the same standard deviations, the value of b would turn out to be 1 and we could just ignore it.

It isn't necessary to go into the details of where b comes from or why it works—all we need to know for now is how to calculate it, and we can make our predictions. Fortunately, it's fairly easy to calculate:

$$b = r_{XY} \frac{s_Y}{s_X}$$

when you are predicting values of Y based on knowledge about X. So to make a prediction about Y, based on knowing the corresponding value of X, you need to know the correlation between X and Y (that's the Pearson product-moment correlation that you learned how to compute in Chapter 4), the standard deviations and the means of both distributions, and the value of X.

Let's work it out with an example. A researcher has been collecting information about teenage school achievement and family life. She has discovered that the average high-schooler in her community spends an average of 5.3 hours a week on homework, with $s = 1.4$; she also learned that the parents of these students pay an average of \$1.32 for each A their kids earn, with $s = \$.35$. And, finally, she has calculated that there is a correlation of .43 between money paid for A's and time spent on homework. Putting all that in table form, we have

$$M_{\text{hours}} = 5.3 \qquad M_{\text{payment}} = 1.32 \qquad r_{HP} = .43$$
$$s_{\text{hours}} = 1.4 \qquad s_{\text{payment}} = .35$$

This researcher happens to have a teenage son, Marty, whom she pays a dollar and a half for every A he brings home. Can you predict how many hours per week Marty will study next term?

First, find the value of b:

$$b = r\frac{s_{\text{hours}}}{s_{\text{payment}}}$$

$$= .43\left(\frac{1.4}{.35}\right)$$

$$= 1.72$$

Now we can plug all the values into the basic regression equation:

$$Y_{\text{Marty}} = M_Y + b(X - M_X)$$
$$= 5.3 + 1.72(1.50 - 1.32)$$
$$= 5.3 + .31$$
$$= 5.61$$

We would predict that Marty will spend 31 minutes more time studying than the average kid does, and his mom was paying him a little more than the average kid was paid. How about Kindra, who doesn't get any money at all for the A's she earns?

$$Y_{\text{Kindra}} = M_Y + b(X - M_X)$$
$$= 5.3 + 1.72(0 - 1.32)$$
$$= 5.3 + (-2.27)$$
$$= 3.03$$

Kindra, we predict, will spend a lot less time studying than most of her classmates.

Once you've calculated the value of b, everything is easy. The basic formula, $Y = M_Y + b(X - M_X)$, is always the same. The only thing that changes is the X value for each person.

Now, do these numbers mean that Marty will study exactly 5.61 hours every week, and Kindra will always put in only 3.03 hours of book time? Well, no—for one thing, I cheated a little when I made up that example. The regression calculation is based on some mathematical assumptions that may or may not be true for these data.[1] But even if the assumptions were met, our predic-

[1]It's important, too, to remember that regression equations don't imply anything about causality—even though they may appear to do so. Just because we can predict number of hours of studying on the basis of amount paid for A's doesn't mean that paying for grades improves study habits. We could just as easily go the other way, and predict the amount parents pay for a kid's grades on the basis of how many hours that kid studies per week. Regressions, like correlations, simply reflect the fact that two variables are linked, so that changes in one will be accompanied by changes in the other.

tions wouldn't be perfectly accurate. We will overestimate the amount some kids study and underestimate others. On the average, we'll be right, but there will be errors when we look at individuals. Is there any way to know ahead of time just how much error we can expect? Well, yes, there is. Unfortunately, though, this isn't a simple problem; it will require some explanation.

STANDARD ERROR OF THE ESTIMATE

Schools and employers use a variety of measures to predict how well people will do in their settings. Although such predictions usually are more accurate than those made by nonmathematical methods (guesstimation), there is some danger in using the results of predictions in a mechanical way.

Suppose, for example, that the University of Michifornia uses an admissions test to predict the expected GPA of incoming students. Over the years, it has been established that this test has a correlation of .7 with freshman GPAs, and that the distributions of test scores and GPAs have the following characteristics:

$$M_{test} = 50 \qquad M_{GPA} = 2.4$$
$$s_{test} = 10 \qquad s_{GPA} = .6$$
$$b = .7\left(\frac{.6}{10}\right) = .7(.06) = .042$$

Denny, a 12th-grader, took the admissions test and got a score of 34. His predicted GPA is

$$Y_{Denny} = 2.4 + .042(34 - 50) = 2.4 + (-.67) = 1.73$$

Since his predicted GPA is less than a C average, it might be tempting to conclude that Denny is not "college material." Before jumping to that conclusion, however, it is wise to remember that predictions about individual performance aren't perfectly accurate. Not everyone who has a predicted GPA of 1.73 achieves exactly that: Some do better than predicted (overachievers?), and others do worse (underachievers?).

In fact, if you took 100 persons, all of whom had a predicted GPA of 1.73, their actual GPAs would vary considerably—they would form a distribution. If you could look into a possible future and actually see how well these students did, you could compute a mean and standard deviation of the distribution of their GPAs. Theoretically, the scores would be distributed normally, would have a mean equal to the predicted GPA of 1.73, and a standard deviation of

$$\sigma_{\text{est}} = \left(s_Y\sqrt{1 - r_{XY}^2}\right)\sqrt{\frac{N - 1}{N - 2}}$$

where N = the number of pairs of observations
          σ_{est} = the standard error of the estimate
          r_{XY}^2 = the squared correlation between the X and Y variables

Now this is a very important idea. We're talking about a group of people selected out of probably thousands who took the college admissions test—selected because that test predicted that they would get a 1.73 GPA. But they *don't* all get a GPA of 1.73: Some do better than predicted and some not so well. Their GPAs cluster around the predicted value. If there were enough of them (it would probably take more than 100 in order to smooth out the curve), the distribution would be normal in form, would have a mean equal to the predicted value, and would have a standard deviation of

$$\sigma_{\text{est}} = .6\sqrt{1 - .7^2} = .6\sqrt{1 - .49} = .6\sqrt{.51} = .6(.71) = .43$$

Notice that the term $\left(\sqrt{\dfrac{N - 1}{N - 2}}\right)$ evaluates to 1 and drops out of the equation. This term doesn't matter much when your sample is large; it can matter a lot with a small sample.

You will recall from Chapter 3 that approximately 68% of the scores in a normal distribution fall between plus and minus one standard deviation from the mean. In this example, the standard deviation of our distribution of GPA scores from those low test-score students is .43. That value, .43, is known as σ_{est}, the standard error of the estimate. So 68% of the GPAs in this distribution can be expected to fall between 1.73 − .43, and 1.73 + .43, or between 1.30 and 2.16. In other words, 68% of the scores fall between ±1 standard error of the estimate from the mean.

In Figure 5–1, I've shaded the area that represents GPAs of 2.0 and above. If you define someone who graduates from college with a C average as "college material," then you can see that a fairly good percentage of those who were predicted to have a 1.73 GPA (less than a C average) actually would do all right (i.e., have a GPA higher than 2.0). In fact, using the table in Appendix C, you can figure out exactly how many students are likely to fall into this category:

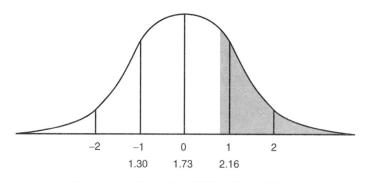

Figure 5–1. Proportion of GPAs of 2.0 and above.

1. A GPA of 2.0 is .27 grade point above the mean (2.0 − 1.73).
2. That's .27/.43 of a standard deviation, or .63 standard deviation above the mean.
3. Going to the table, we find that .26 of the distribution lies above a Z score of .63: More than a quarter of the GPAs in this distribution will be 2.0 or better.
4. About 26% of the total population of students would be mislabeled if we used a cutting point of exactly 1.73.

It's all very logical if you just take it one step at a time.

Using the standard error of the estimate, we can report predictions in a way that tells others how accurate the prediction is. If we were to say that a student who scores 34 on the admissions test will have a GPA of 1.73 ± .43, we would be right 2/3 of the time. (If that confuses you, better go back to Chapter 3 and read about proportions of scores under the normal curve.) And that means, of course, that we'd still be wrong about 1/3 of the time—about 17% of folks getting that score on the test would do *better* than a 1.73 GPA, and about 17% would do worse.

Do you see now why σ_{est} is called the standard *error* of the estimate? It gives us a way of estimating how much error there will be in using a particular prediction formula—a particular regression equation.

Look at the formula one more time:

$$\sigma_{est} = s_Y\sqrt{1 - r_{XY}^2}$$

Notice that if $r = 1.00$, $\sigma_{est} = 0$, which is another way of saying that if the correlation between X and Y were perfect, there would be no errors in predicting performance on Y from our predictor X. Unfortunately (or fortunately?), there are virtually no perfect correlations between predictor and predicted variables in measuring human beings. We are not able to predict individual human performance with anything near perfection at this time—nor do I believe that we ever will.

MULTIPLE CORRELATION

Suppose you are the dean of admissions at Michifornia U, and you want to predict the grade-point average of admissions applicants using *two* predictors, SAT verbal and SAT math scores. You've collected lots of data over the years, and you know the following facts about these variables among people who come to your school (we'll call the variables X, Y, and Z):

$$M_{X(verbal)} = 500 \qquad M_{Y(math)} = 475 \qquad M_{Z(GPA)} = 2.5$$
$$s_{X(verbal)} = 110 \qquad s_{Y(math)} = 140 \qquad s_{Z(GPA)} = .8$$
$$r_{XY} = .60 \qquad r_{XZ} = .61 \qquad r_{YZ} = .58$$

What we need to do is combine our two predictors, verbal and math SAT scores, in the mathematically best way, and then find out how well this combination correlates with college GPA. The result of all this calculation is known as a multiple R. In this case, it will be designated $R_{Z.XY}$, which indicates that X and Y are predictors and Z is the predicted variable.

Theoretically, you can combine as many predictor variables as you want in order to predict the value of some other variable. At one time, some psychologists believed that if, in addition to variables like test scores and high school performance, they added other variables as predictors, such as motivation to learn, interest, and personality factors, each new predictor would improve the prediction. Eventually, they thought, they would be able to achieve multiple R's approaching 1.0. So far, they haven't been able to do this; the improvement in prediction tends to drop very rapidly as each new predictor is added.

Here is the formula and a worked-out example for multiple R based on the preceding data: two predictor variables, SAT math and verbal scores, predicting a third variable, and college GPA. Note that the formula yields R^2, not R. You will need to take the square root of R^2 to end up with $R_{Z.XY}$.

$$R^2_{Z.XY} = \frac{r^2_{XZ} + r^2_{YZ} - 2(r_{XZ})(r_{YZ})(r_{XY})}{1 - r^2_{XY}}$$

In our example,

$$R^2_{Z.XY} = \frac{(.58)^2 + (.61)^2 - 2(.58)(.61)(.60)}{1 - (.60)^2} = .44 \qquad R_{Z.XY} = .67$$

As you can see, when you combined X and Y predictors to get a multiple R, the correlation was slightly higher than that obtained by using either predictor alone. This value can be interpreted in much the same way as a Pearson product-moment r, except that you enter Appendix D with $N - 3$ degrees of freedom, rather than $N - 2$. Methods are available for using three or more variables as predictors, but you would do best to consult with a friendly computer person if you want to use them.

PARTIAL CORRELATION

Suppose that you were interested in the effect of counselors' touching their clients during counseling sessions. You observed a large number of counselors and counted the number of times each counselor touched his or her client (call this variable X); at the end of the session, you asked each client to fill out a client satisfaction measure (call this variable Y). And you got a significant positive correlation—hurrah! But when you announced to your fellow counselors that your data indicated that frequent counselor touch contributed to greater client satisfaction, a skeptic argued that perhaps the correlation was not due to counselor touch at all, but rather to counselor empathy. The skeptic went on to say that more empathic counselors also tend to touch more—clients like those counselors not because they touch, but because they are empathic and understanding. The correlation between satisfaction and touch is just an irrelevant side effect of the relationship between touching and empathy.

To answer this criticism, you might well choose to use the statistical technique known as *partial correlation*. Partial correlation allows you to measure the degree of relationship between two variables (X and Y) with the effect of a third variable (Z) "partialed out" or "controlled for."

Here's how it would work in our example. First, you need a way of measuring each variable with which you are concerned. You've already measured client satisfaction and touching (you did that in order to get your first correlation); let's say you also ask independent raters to observe the counselors at work and rate them for "degree of empathy."

You've collected your data on all three variables and have found that the correlation between counselor touch (X) and client satisfaction (Y) is $r_{XY} = .36$; the correlation of empathy (Z) and counselor touch (X) is $r_{XZ} = .65$; and the relationship between empathy (Z) and client satisfaction (Y) is $r_{YZ} = .60$. The formula for finding the relationship between X and Y, with Z partialed out is

$$r_{XY.Z} = \frac{r_{XY} - (r_{XZ})(r_{YZ})}{\sqrt{(1 - r_{XZ}^2)(1 - r_{YZ}^2)}}$$

Now we can use this formula to compute the correlation of touch and client satisfaction, with empathy "controlled for":

$$r_{XY.Z} = \frac{.36 - (.65)(.60)}{\sqrt{[1 - (.65)^2][1 - (.60)^2]}} = -.05$$

This result would tend to support the hypothesis of your skeptical friend: There doesn't seem to be a very strong relationship, if any, between counselor touch and client satisfaction when empathy is partialed out.

PROBLEMS

1. Here are some interesting (and imaginary) facts about cockroaches: The average number of roaches per home in the United States is 57; $s = 12$. The average number of packages of roach killer purchased per family per year is 4.2; $s = 1.1$. The correlation between roaches in the home and roach killer bought is .5.
   (a) The Cleanly family bought 12 packages of roach killer last year. How many roaches would you predict they have in their home?
   (b) The Spic-Spans have 83 roaches at their house. What would be your best prediction of how many boxes of roach killer they bought?
2. A developmental psychologist found that a sample of babies born in 1996 said their first sentences at 12.3 months ($s = 4.3$). Their mothers, born between 1956 and 1976, said *their* first sentences at age 11.5 months ($s = 4.1$). The correlation between these two variables was .61.
   (a) If we know that baby Leigh said her first sentence at 10.8 months, what is our best guess as to when her mom first strung words together?

(b) Jake's mother began to talk at 15.8 months. When should she expect Jake to say his first sentence?

3. Some standard error of the estimate problems for you:
(a) Find the standard error of the estimate for the prediction of the amount of roach killer bought, based on the number of roaches in the home (Problem 1), and assuming that the data are from a sample of 1,000 homes.
(b) Find the standard error of the estimate for the prediction of when a baby will start to talk, based on when its mom started to talk (Problem 2), and assuming that the data are from a sample of 25 babies.
(c) Find the range of ages at which baby Jake can be expected to start to talk, with an approximately 67% chance of being correct. (Problem 2, same sample size).

4. A personnel director of a large computer firm gave all employees "quickie" IQ tests as well as questionnaires to measure their job satisfaction. She reported that job satisfaction was clearly related to IQ, since the two measures had a correlation of .42. A company executive pointed out, however, that the correlation might really have more to do with salary than with IQ—that smart people tend to be paid more, and people who get more money tend to like their jobs better. Given the following values, compute the correlation between IQ and job satisfaction, with salary effects partialed out: $r_{IQ, \text{satisfaction}} = .42$; $r_{IQ, \text{salary}} = .46$; and $r_{\text{salary, satisfaction}} = .63$

5. A researcher tested 2nd-grade children for their reading skills. He used a test that had three subscales: decoding, vocabulary, and comprehension. Here's what he found:

$M_{\text{decoding}} = 29.97$ $M_{\text{vocab}} = 11.93$ $M_{\text{comprehension}} = 42.87$
$S_{\text{decoding}} = 7.93$ $S_{\text{vocab}} = .37$ $S_{\text{comprehension}} = 23.19$

$r_{\text{decoding/vocab}} = .60$ $r_{\text{decoding/comprehension}} = .77$ $r_{\text{vocab/comprehension}} = .56$

Find the value of **b** in the regression equation that predicts
(a) decoding score, if you know the student's vocabulary score.
(b) vocabulary score, if you know the student's comprehension score.
(c) comprehension score, if you know the student's decoding score.
(d) decoding score, if you know the student's comprehension score.

6. Compute the multiple correlation for the data in Problem 5, using
(a) decoding and vocabulary to predict comprehension.
(b) decoding and comprehension to predict vocabulary.
(c) vocabulary and comprehension to predict decoding.

7. Farmer Zeke calculated the correlation between the amount of food his chickens ate and their peak weight. He also calculated the correlation between weight and water consumed and (since he loved his pocket calculator) the correlation between food and water. Here are his data:

$r_{\text{food,weight}} = .82$ $r_{\text{water,weight}} = .53$ $r_{\text{food,water}} = .75$

(a) What is the partial correlation between food and weight, controlling for the contribution of water?

(b) What is the partial correlation between water and weight, controlling for the contribution of food?

(c) What is the correlation between food and water, controlling for the contribution of weight?

(d) If you were Farmer Zeke, what conclusions might you draw from all this information?

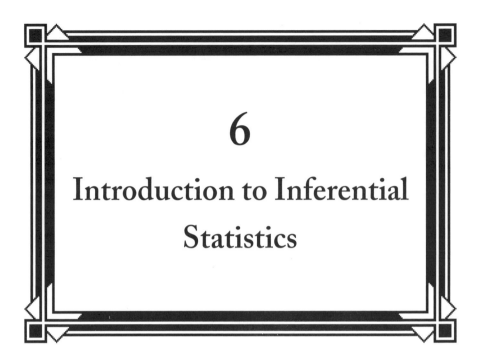

6

Introduction to Inferential Statistics

We've all had the experience of flipping on the evening news and getting the weather forecast. In Chapter 5, we talked about the kind of forecast the weatherperson would have to make if he or she had no information at all except the most common weather situation that occurs in that location. For Oregon, that would likely be "tomorrow it will rain." But the weatherperson doesn't say that; the forecast is more like "tomorrow there is an 80% chance of showers." What, exactly, does that "80% chance of showers" mean? Will it will rain 80% of the time tomorrow? Or, maybe, 80% of us will get rained on? Or, we'll have 80% of a full rainstorm sometime during the day? Those are pretty silly interpretations; we all know that a "80% chance of rain" means that it's very likely to rain—but then again, maybe it won't. More precisely, it means that in the past, with conditions like this, there was rain the next day 80% of the time. And, one time out of five, the rain didn't happen.

"There's an 80% chance of rain tomorrow" is a *probability* statement. Such statements tell us how likely—how probable—it is that a particular event will occur. Probability statements are statistical statements, but, unlike the kind of statistics we've been looking at so far, they go beyond simply describing a set of data that we have in hand. They represent ways of describing and predicting what we *don't* know, on the basis of current data.

As we'll see in later chapters of this book, probability statements play an important role in research. The whole notion of statistical significance rests on probability statements. "Significance" here, and as we used it in Chapter 5, has a very specific meaning, but I think I'll wait to give you the formal definition later, when it will make more sense. For now, I just want to introduce you to some of the concepts of simple probability.

Almost every explanation of probability starts with a description of the process of flipping coins, and this will be no exception. I'm tired of "heads" and "tails," though. My coin will be a Canadian $1 coin, generally known as a "loony" because it has a picture of a loon on one side—the other side depicts the Queen. So, instead of "heads" and "tails," we'll be talking about "loons" and "Queens."

If I flip my coin 600 times, and if it's a fair coin (equally likely to come up either way), how many of those times should I expect it to come up loons? Right, half the time—300 loons. And 300 Queens. We would say that the probablility of getting a loon is 50%, or .5. What if I'm throwing a die instead of flipping a coin? A die has six sides, and if it's a fair die, each side is equally likely to come up. So I would expect that my 600 throws would yield 100 ones, 100 twos, 100 threes, and so on.

Will I always get the same numbers if I repeat the coin-tossing experiment over and over again? Nope, there'll be some randomness in the data I generate. I might get 305 loons and only 295 Queens in one set of coin flips, or 289 loons and 311 Queens in another. And there would be similar fluctuations if I repeated the die-throwing experiment over and over again. But, over many many sets of coin flips or die throws, the deviations would even out. The more often I repeated the experiment, the more closely my total data would approximate the predicted percentages. Over an *infinite* number of experiments, the numbers of loons and Queens, or of ones–twos–threes–fours–fives–sixes, would be exactly as predicted. Probability statements don't tell us exactly what will happen, but they are our best guess about what will happen. Making our predictions about events based on known probabilities will, over the long run, result in less error than making them any other way.

There are a couple of things that I'd like you to notice about those two situations, flipping the coin or throwing a die. First, each throw comes out only one way—it's an all-or-nothing situation. You can't flip a coin and have it come out half loon and half Queen (unless it stands on edge, and I won't let that happen); you can't throw a die and get 2.35 as a result. Second, each possible outcome is known. There are only two ways that my coin can land; there are exactly six possible outcomes when we throw a die. And we know exactly what those possible outcomes are.

Okay, I'm going to flip that loony again. This time, though, I want you to tell me the probability of getting *either* a loon or a Queen. Silly question, you say—I'll always get one or the other. Exactly right—the probability of getting either a loon or a Queen is 100%, or 1.0. The probability of getting a loon is .5, the probability of getting a Queen is .5, and the probability of getting a loon *or* a Queen is 1.0. Do you see a rule coming? When two mutually exclusive[1] outcomes have known probabilities, the probability of getting either the one or the other in a given experiment is the sum of their individual probabilities. What's the probability of our die throw yielding either a 5 or a 6? If you added $\frac{1}{6}$ and $\frac{1}{6}$ and got $\frac{2}{6}$, or $\frac{1}{3}$, or .33, you've got the idea!

Let's do just one more loony experiment (yes, I really said that), and then move on to something more interesting. This time we're going to flip *two* coins. How many possible outcomes are there, and what is the probability of each? Before you answer, let me warn you that this is a trick question. The most obvious answer is that there are three possible outcomes: 2 loons, or 2 Queens, or a loon and a Queen. So far, so good. But if you go on to say that since the coins are all fair coins and that loons and Queens are equally likely, the probability of each of those three outcomes is .33, then you've fallen for the trick. Look at the possible outcomes more closely:

	Coin A	Coin B
Outcome 1	loon	loon
Outcome 2	loon	Queen
Outcome 3	Queen	loon
Outcome 4	Queen	Queen

Even though it looks, on the surface, as if only three different things can happen, there are actually four possible outcomes. And each is equally likely. Knowing that, we can easily determine the probabilities of tossing 2 loons, 2 Queens, or a Queen and a loon. The probability of two loons is 1 in 4, or .25. The probability of 2 Queens is the same, .25. And the probability of a loon and a Queen is the sum of the probabilities of the two ways of getting that outcome: Loon on coin A and Queen on coin B has a probability of .25; Queen on coin A and loon on coin B has a probability of .25; the probability of getting exactly one loon and one Queen when we toss two coins is .25 + .25, or .50. Putting it in standard symbols,

$$p_{L,Q} = .50$$

The Sampling Experiment

Most of the time, in the kinds of research that call for statistical procedures, we aren't able to look at the total population in which we are interested. We use relatively small samples to represent much larger populations. If I do an experiment that involves testing the reading skills of 3rd-graders, I might

---

[1]"Mutually exclusive" is a fancy way of saying that you can have one or the other, but not both at the same time.

work with a sample of 50 or 100 3rd-graders. But I'm not really interested in just those 50 or 100 children; I want to say something that will hold true for all 3rd-graders. Agriculturists who test the usefulness of fertilizers or pesticides want to make predictions about how those fertilizers or pesticides will work for all the crops on which they might be used, not just describe the small sample they've tested. And looking at the effects of a new vaccine on a sample of 20 volunteers would be pretty useless unless we expected to generalize those results to lots and lots of other folks. Sampling, and predicting outcomes on the basis of those samples, is a fundamental idea in research. That's why we need to understand the concept of probability in sampling.

We'll start with some definitions. I've already used the words, and I hope you've understood what they mean, but it's a good idea to get the precise definitions out on the table.

population: a large (sometimes infinitely large) group about which some information is desired.

    Examples: 3rd-grade children in the United States
                     wheat crops in North America
                     height of men entering basic training in the armed forces
                     all the beans in a 5-gallon jar

sample: a subset of a population; a smaller group selected from the population.

    Examples: the 3rd-grade children in Mrs. Lane's room at McCornack School
                     the southernmost acre of wheat in each farm in Ayres County
                     the height of the first 100 men entering Army basic training in North Carolina in the month of January 1998
                     the first 10 beans drawn from a 5-gallon jar of beans

random sample: a sample selected in such a way that (1) every member of the population from which it is drawn has an equal chance of being selected, and (2) selection of one member has no effect on the selection of any other member.

    Examples: these are hard to find! How could you get a sample of 3rd-graders, or wheat crops, or brand new soldiers, such that every single member of the overall population had an equal chance of getting in? In the world of the social sciences, the art of random sampling—or of getting a sample that can be treated as if it were random—is a complicated one. You'll learn much more about it when you study how to design research. For now, we'll let somebody else put our samples together for us, and we'll just assume that the samples are truly random.

The randomness of a sample is very, very important, because everything we are going to say about samples and populations only holds (for sure) when the sample is truly random. That's why I put that jar of beans in as an example: If we stir the beans up very thoroughly, and then pull out a sample with our eyes shut, then every bean has an equal chance of ending up in our sample. Jars of beans are favorite tools for statistics teachers, because they do yield random samples.

Our jar of beans, by the way, has two colors of beans in it, red and white. Exactly half of the beans are red and exactly half are white. Okay, stir them up, close your eyes, and pull one out. Don't look at it yet! Before you open your eyes, what color bean do you think you drew? Of course, you can't make a very good guess—since half of the beans are red and half are white, you have an equal chance of drawing a red bean or a white one. Over in jar 2, 80% of the beans are red. Mix them up, close your eyes, draw one, and guess its color. You'll guess red, of course, and in the long run that guess will be correct 80% of the time. The probability of getting a red bean is equal to the proportion of red beans in the total population. For jar 1, p_{red} = .5; for jar 2, p_{red} = .8.

If you drew a random sample of not 1 bean, but 10 beans, from each jar, what would those samples look like? Intuitively, we know the answer: The sample from jar 1 would have about half red and half white beans; the sample from jar 2 would have about 80% red beans. Samples resemble the populations from which they are drawn. More specifically, over time, the proportions of the sample (for the characteristic of interest) approximate more and more closely the proportions of that characteristic in the parent population. And the bigger the sample, the more likely it is to resemble the parent population. The more experiments we do with jar 1, the more the number of red and white beans will tend to equal out. The larger the samples we draw from jar 2, the closer our samples will come to having exactly 80% red and 20% white beans. If we had a magic jar, with an infinite supply of beans, these statements would be true whether or not we put each sample back into the jar before we took another. This basic characteristic of random samples, that over time and with increasing size they come to resemble the parent population more and more closely, is true for samples taken with or without replacement.

Sample Values (Statistics) and Population Values (Parameters)

You can easily see where all this is going, can't you? Since it's often difficult or even impossible to measure an entire population, it makes sense to get a sample from that population and measure it instead. What's the average weight of 10-year-olds? Get a sample of 10-year-olds, and weigh them. How much do North Americans spend on groceries every week? Get 50 or so folks to let you keep track of what they do in the supermarket. What's the effect of second-hand smoke on the water intake of white rats? Put a dozen rats in a cage and blow smoke at them, and measure what they drink. We can find the means and standard deviations of samples like this, and use them to estimate the same values in the populations from which they came. Or can we?

There are a couple of problems that must be overcome in order to use sample values (technically, these are called "statistics") to estimate population values (called "parameters"). One has to do with the *representativeness* of the sample: If we are going to use sample measurements to estimate population values, the sample has to be truly representative of the population. The experiment with the 10-year-olds wouldn't yield very useful data, for instance, if we got the children in our sample from a group of young gymnasts. Kids involved in gymnastics tend to be thinner than the general population of kids. The easiest way to ensure that our sample is representative is to select it randomly.[2] That way, even though it may not be exactly like the parent population, the differences will at least tend to even out over a large number of samples, or as a single sample gets larger. Samples that are truly representative of their parent population are said to be *unbiased*. Perhaps the most notorious biased sample was taken inadvertently in 1936, when the *Literary Digest* predicted on the basis of its sample of automobile and telephone users that Alf Landon, the Republican candidate, would win the presidential election by a landslide. In 1936, many voters didn't have telephones or cars, and the ones who didn't have them were more likely to be Democrats than Republicans. And, of course, Alf Landon didn't win by a landslide; he lost to Franklin Roosevelt.

Even with an unbiased sample, however, bias can creep into some estimates of population values. Some statistics—mathematical descriptions—are inherently biased, and some aren't. The two statistics that are most important to us at this point are the mean and the standard deviation. The mean of a sample is an unbiased estimate of the mean of the population from which it came. Hmm . . . that's a complicated-sounding sentence. Let's introduce a couple of new symbols to simplify things. The mean of a population is designated by μ, the Greek letter mu. (If we're talking about samples, we use our standard English "M"; and if we're talking about populations, we use the Greek "m," μ. Similarly with variance and standard deviation: For samples, we use the English "s^2" and "s"; and for populations we use the Greek lowercase "s": σ^2 and σ.) Now, getting back to business—if we take lots and lots of samples from a given population, the means of those samples (M) will form a distribution that clusters around the mean of the population (μ). What's more, that distribution will be normal—but that's another story, one we'll save for later.

Remember, back when we first talked about the variance, I promised to explain why we divide the squared deviations from the mean by $n-1$ instead of by n, in order to get s^2? Well, now we're ready to talk about that. When we compute the variance of a sample, we are actually estimating the variance of the population from which the sample was drawn. If we just divided by n—that is, if we found a true "average squared deviation" by using the formula $s^2 = \dfrac{\Sigma(X - M_X)^2}{n}$ —we'd get the variance of the sample itself, but this value would *not* be an unbiased estimate of the population variance. The value would tend to be smaller than the population variance. The smaller the sample, the greater this error is likely to be. Dividing by $n-1$ instead of by n is a way of

---

[2]One of the easiest ways to get an (approximately) random sample is by using a random-number table. Such a table, together with instructions for how to use it, is found in Appendix E.

correcting the problem—of correcting for bias in estimating the population value. When the sample is very large, the difference between n and $n-1$ is negligible; little correction is made, and little is needed. With small samples, the correction is larger. Just as it should be.

Perhaps looking at two extreme situations will help you see how this works. What's the smallest sample you could draw? That's right, just one case, $N=1$. If we were to find s without correcting for bias, we'd get

$$s^2 = \frac{\Sigma(X - M_X)^2}{N} = \frac{\Sigma(0)^2}{1} = 0$$

No matter how large the population variance might be, this "sample" wouldn't reflect any of it all.

What's the biggest sample you could draw? Right again, one the size of the whole population. And its variance (again, uncorrected) would be exactly the same as σ^2. So we have this situation shown in Figure 6–1.

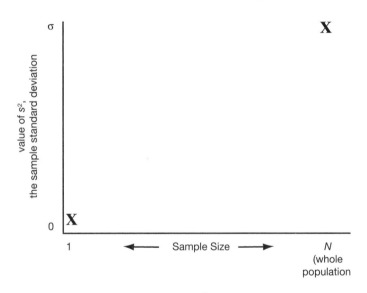

Figure 6–1.   Uncorrected values of s^2 for small and large samples.

It turns out, by the way, that the points in between those two check marks don't fall in a straight line—s^2 and σ^2 aren't linearly related. Instead, s^2 and σ^2 can be quite different when the sample is small, but the difference levels out relatively quickly, something like that shown in Figure 6–2.

This situation leads to a very handy fact. Since the amount of bias in using s^2 to estimate σ^2 is proportional to the size of the sample (N), we can correct for that bias by substituting $N-1$ for N in the formula for the variance:

$$s = \frac{\Sigma(X - M_X)^2}{N - 1}$$

The computational formula becomes

$$s^2 = \frac{N\Sigma X^2 - (\Sigma X)^2}{N(N - 1)}$$

—and this is exactly what we have been doing all along.

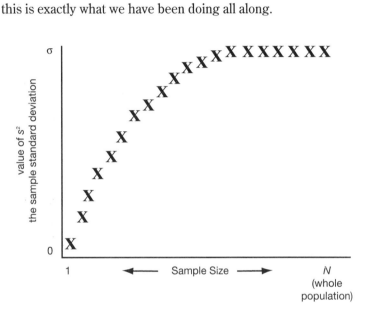

Figure 6–2. Uncorrected values of s^2 for a range of sample sizes.

THE NULL HYPOTHESIS

Ordinarily, researchers are interested in demonstrating the truth of some hypothesis of interest: that some relationship exists between two variables; that two groups differ in some important way; that population A is bigger, stronger, smarter, more anxious, and so on, than population B. We need statistical procedures to test such hypotheses. The problem is, though, that it's almost impossible (with most statistical techniques) to demonstrate that something is *true.* Statistical techniques are much better at demonstrating that a particular hypothesis or statement is *false,* that it's very unlikely that the hypothesis could really hold up.

So we have an interesting dilemma. We want to show that something is true, but our best tools only know how to show that something is false. The solution is both logical and elegant: State the exact opposite of what we want to demonstrate to be true, disprove that, and what's left—what hasn't been disproved—must be true.

In case you are now thoroughly confused, here's an example. A researcher wants to show that boys, in general, have larger ears than girls. (I know, it's a dumb idea, but grants have been awarded for stranger things.) She knows that her statistical tools can't be used to demonstrate the truth of her hypothesis. So she constructs what's known as a *null hypothesis,* which takes in every possibility except the one thing she wants to prove: Boys' ears are either smaller or just the same size as girls' ears. If she can use her statistical techniques to disprove or reject this null hypothesis, then there's only one thing left to believe about boys' and girls' ears—the very thing she wanted to prove in the first place.

This whole blob represents all the possible ways the world might be.

The little white patch represents the thing you'd like to prove is true.

And the big gray area represents everything that *isn't* what you'd like to prove.

So, if you can rule out all the gray parts, the only thing left (the thing that must be true) is the white part—exactly what you wanted to prove in the first place.

Figure 6–3.   A blob diagram of the world

So, if you can rule out all the gray parts, the only thing left (the thing that must be true) is the white part—exactly what you wanted to prove all along. See Figure 6–3.

The hypothesis that the scientist wants to support or prove is known as the *research hypothesis,* symbolized H_1; the "everything else" hypothesis is called the *null hypothesis* and is symbolized as H_0. A primary use of inferential statistics is that of attempting to reject H_0.

Okay, time for an example. Suppose we wanted to compare the math anxiety of male and female graduate students in the United States. We could, theoretically, administer a math anxiety test to all female and male graduate students in the country, score the tests, and compare the μ's for the two populations. Chances are good, however, that our resources would not allow us to conduct such a study. So we decide to use statistics. If we suspect that there is a difference in the two populations, and that's what we want to demonstrate, then our H_0 is that there is *no* difference. In statistical notation,

$$H_0: \quad \mu_{\text{Females}} = \mu_{\text{Males}}$$

The purpose of our study is to decide whether H_0 is probably true or probably false.

Suppose we drew 50 subjects (using a random sampling method, of course) from each of the two populations, male graduate students and female graduate students, and tested them for math anxiety. Suppose also that the mean of our female sample was 60 and the mean for our male sample was 50:

$$M_{\text{Females}} = 60 \qquad M_{\text{Males}} = 50$$

Obviously, the mean of our female sample was higher than that for males. But how do we use this fact to justify throwing out—rejecting—the null hypothesis, so as to be left with the hypothesis we are trying to prove?

There are two possible explanations for our observed difference between male and female sample means: (1) There is, in fact, a difference in math anxiety between the male and female population means, that is, $\mu_{\text{Female}} \neq \mu_{\text{Male}}$, and the difference we see between the samples reflects this fact; or (2) there is no appreciable difference in anxiety between the means of the male and female graduate student populations, that is, $\mu_{\text{Female}} = \mu_{\text{Male}}$, and the difference we observe between the sample means is due to chance, or sampling error (this would be analogous to drawing more white beans than red even though there is no difference in the proportion of the two in the jar from which the sample was drawn).

If the null hypothesis really is true, then the differences we observe between sample means is due to chance. The statistical tests you will study in later chapters, such as the t test or analysis of variance, will help you to decide if your obtained result is likely to have been due to chance or if there probably is a difference in the two populations. If the result of your study is that the difference you observe is "statistically significant," then you will reject the null hypothesis and conclude that you believe there is a real difference in the two populations. Of course, even after concluding that the difference was real, you would still have to decide whether it was large enough, in the context of your research situation, to have practical usefulness. Researchers call this the "magnitude of effect" question.

TYPE I AND TYPE II ERRORS

Your decision either to reject or not to reject the null hypothesis is subject to error. Because you have not studied all members of both populations and because statistics (such as M and s) are subject to sampling error, you can never be completely sure whether H_0 is true or not. In drawing your conclusion about H_0, you can make two kinds of errors, known (cleverly) as Type I and Type II errors. Rejection of a true null hypothesis is a Type I error, and failure to reject a false null hypothesis is a Type II error. Perhaps the following table will help you to understand the difference.

| | The Real Situation (unknown to the investigator) | |
Investigator's Decision	H_0 is true	H_0 is false
Reject H_0	Investigator makes a Type I error	Investigator makes a correct decision
Do not reject H_0	Investigator makes a correct decision	Investigator makes a Type II error

If the real situation is that there is no difference in math anxiety between males and females, but you reject H_0, then you have made a Type I error; if you do not reject H_0, then you have made a correct decision. On the other hand, if there *is* a real difference between the population means of males and females and you reject H_0, you have made a correct decision, but if you fail to reject H_0, you have made a Type II error.

The primary purpose of inferential statistics is to help you to decide whether or not to reject the null hypothesis and to estimate the probability of a Type I or Type II error when making your decision. Inferential statistics can't tell you for sure whether or not you've made either a Type I or a Type II error, but they can tell you how likely it is that you have made one.

One last point: Notice that you do not have the option of *accepting* the null hypothesis. That would amount to using your statistical test to "prove" that the null hypothesis is true, and you can't do that. Your two possible decisions really amount to either (1) I reject the null hypothesis, and so I believe that there really are important differences between the two populations, or (2) I can't reject the null hypothesis, and I still don't know whether there are important differences or not. For this reason, Type I errors are generally considered to be more serious than Type II errors. Claiming significant results when there really are no differences between the populations is a more serious mistake than saying that you don't know for sure, even when those differences might exist. As you will see, statistical decisions are usually made so as to minimize the likelihood of a Type I error, even at the risk of making lots of Type II errors.

STATISTICAL SIGNIFICANCE AND THE TYPE I ERROR

Suppose that a colleague of yours actually did the study of math anxiety that we've been talking about and concluded that the difference between male and female sample means was "statistically significant at the .05 (or the 5%) level."

Type I error

Type II error

This statement would mean that a difference as big or bigger than he observed between the sample means could have occurred only 5 times out of 100 by chance alone. Since it could have happened only 5 times out of 100 just by chance, your colleague may be willing to bet that there is a real difference in the populations of male and female graduate students and will reject the null hypothesis.

You must realize, however, that whenever you reject the null hypothesis, you may be making an error. Perhaps the null hypothesis really is true, and this is one of those 5 times out of 100 when, by chance alone, you got this large a difference in sample means. Another way of saying the same thing is that, if the null hypothesis were true, 5 times out of 100 you would make a Type I error when you use this decision rule. You would reject the null hypothesis when it was, in fact, true 5% of the time.

You might say, "But, I don't want to make errors! Why can't I use the .01 (or 1%) level of significance instead of the .05 level? That way, I reduce the likelihood of a Type I error to 1 out of 100 times." You can do that, of course, but when you do so, you increase the probability of a Type II error. That's because you reduce the probability of a Type I error by insisting on more stringent conditions for accepting your research hypothesis—that is, you fail to reject H_0 even when H_0 is fairly unlikely. Reducing the probability of a Type I error from .05 to .01 means that you'll fail to reject H_0 even if the odds are 98 out of 100 that it is untrue. In educational and psychological research, it is conventional to set the .05 level of significance as a minimum standard for the rejection of the null hypothesis. Typically, if an obtained result is significant at, say, the .08 level, an author will conclude that he or she was unable to reject the null hypothesis or that the results were not statistically significant.

Making a Type II error, failing to reject the null hypothesis when it's really not true, is rather like missing your plane at the airport. You didn't do the right thing this time, but you can still catch another plane. Making a Type I error is like getting on the wrong plane—not only did you miss the right one, but now you're headed in the wrong direction! With a result significant at the .08 level, the odds still suggest that the null hypothesis is false (you'd only get this large a difference by chance 8 times in 100). But researchers don't want to get on the wrong airplane; they'd rather make a Type II error and wait for another chance to reject H_0 in some future study.

Remember our discussion about magnitude of effect, when we were looking at correlation coefficients? Just because an observed difference may be significant (i.e., may represent real differences between populations), it is not necessarily useful. We might reject the null hypothesis with regard to differences between male and female math anxiety scores, but if the real difference were only one or two points, with means of 50 and 60, would those differences be worth paying attention to?

Magnitude of effect is often ignored in media reports of medical discoveries. "Using toothpicks linked to the rare disease archeomelanitis!" trumpet the headlines, and the news story goes on to say that researchers have shown that people who use toothpicks are 1.5 times more likely to get archeomelanitis than people who don't. But if you look at the actual numbers, the likelihood of getting archeomelanitis (with no toothpicks) is one in a million, and so using a toothpick increases those odds to $1\frac{1}{2}$ in a million. Are you going to worry about raising your risk from .00001 to .000015? I'm not.

PROBLEMS

1. **(a)** What is the difference between M and μ? Between s and σ?
   (b) Which of the four preceding symbols represents a value that has been corrected for bias? Why not the others?
2. Which of the following would *not* be a truly random sample and why?
   (a) To get a sample of children attending a particular grade school, the researcher numbered all the children on the playground at recess time and used a random-number table to select 50 of them.
   (b) Another researcher, at a different school, got a list of all the families who had kids in that school. She wrote each name on a slip of paper, mixed up the slips, and drew out a name. All kids with that last name went into the sample; she kept this up until she had 50 kids.
   (c) A third researcher took a ruler to the school office, where student files were kept. She used a random-number table to get a number, measured that distance into the files, and the child whose file she was over at that point was selected for the sample. She did this 50 times and selected 50 kids.
   (d) A fourth researcher listed all the kids in the school and numbered the names. He then used a random-number table to pick out 50 names.
3. What is the appropriate H_0 for each of the following research situations?
   (a) A study to investigate possible differences in academic achievement between right- and left-handed children
   (b) A study to find out if left-handed people have more artistic ability than right-handed people
   (c) A study to find out if 20- to 25-year-olds have poorer vision than 15- to 20-year-olds.
   (d) A study to determine if registered nurses give a different level of patient care than LPNs
   (e) A study exploring whether dogs that were raised in kennels have different training patterns than dogs raised in homes
4. Assume that each of the following statements is in error: Each describes a researcher's conclusions, but the researcher is mistaken. Indicate whether the error is Type I or Type II.
   (a) "The data indicate that there are significant differences between males and females in their ability to perform task 1."
   (b) "There are no significant differences between males and females in their ability to perform task 2."
   (c) "On the basis of our data, we reject the null hypothesis."

   (d) "On the basis of our data, we accept the null hypothesis."

   (e) "On the basis of our data, we cannot reject the null hypothesis."

5. **(a)** Explain, in words, the meaning of the following: "The difference between group 1 and group 2 is significant at the .05 level."

   (b) When would a researcher be likely to use the .01 level of significance rather than the .05 level? What is the drawback of using the .01 level?

7

Differences Between the Means of Two Groups

THE *t* TEST

The *t* test is one of the most commonly used statistical tests. Its primary purpose is to determine whether the means of two groups of scores differ to a statistically significant degree. Here's an example: Suppose that you randomly assigned 12 subjects each to group 1, a counseling group, and to group 2, a waiting-list control group. Suppose also that after those in group 1 had been counseled, you administered a measure of psychological adjustment to the two groups, with results as follows:

Counseled Group Scores	Control Group Scores
25	14
14	11
23	13
21	9
24	15
17	12
19	9
20	11
15	8
22	13
16	12
21	14
$M = 19.75$	$M = 11.75$
$N = 12$	$N = 12$
$s_1^2 = 12.93$	$s_2^2 = 4.93$

Since you hope to show that the two groups are really different, your null hypothesis is

$$H_0: \quad \mu_1 = \mu_2$$

The null hypothesis states that there is no difference in mean adjustment level between those who receive counseling and those who don't. As you can see, there is a difference in the two sample means, but it may be that these observed differences occurred by chance. We need to find out if the difference is statistically significant. If the difference between M_1 and M_2 is statistically significant, you will reject the null hypothesis and conclude that there is a difference in adjustment level between people who have had counseling and those who have not.

There are two kinds of t tests, those appropriate for two groups whose members are paired in some way (like pretreatment and posttreatment measures, for instance, or pairs of siblings), and groups whose members are independent of each other. Since the counseled and control groups in our hypothetical study were not paired in any way, we would use the t test for independent samples. Here we go!

THE t TEST FOR INDEPENDENT SAMPLES

The t test, like most other statistical tests, consists of a set of mathematical procedures that yields a numerical value. In the case of the t test, the larger the absolute value of t, the more likely it is to reflect a significant difference between the two groups under comparison. We'll learn how to compute the value of t in the next few pages; first, though, let's think about what a t test really explores.

A major application of the t test for independent samples is found in experimental research like the study in our example. Researchers often draw a sample from one population and randomly assign half of the subjects to an experimental and the other half to a control group, or to some other comparison group (see Appendix E for a method of assigning subjects at random to two or more groups). They then administer some sort of treatment to the experimental group. Since the subjects were assigned to their two groups by chance (i.e., at random), the means of the two groups should not differ from each other at the beginning of the experiment any more than would be expected on the basis of chance alone. If a t test were done at the beginning of the experiment, the difference between the means would probably not be statistically significant.[1] After the treatment, the means of the two groups are compared using

---

[1]If we are to be very precise here, we would say that the difference between the means would be significant at the .05 level only 5 times out of 100 or would be significant at the .01 level only once in 100 such experiments.

the *t* test. If the absolute value of *t* is large enough to be statistically significant, the experimenter rejects H_0. Since the two groups have now been shown to differ more than would be expected on the basis of chance alone, and since the only difference between them (that we know of) is the experimental treatment, it is reasonable to conclude that this treatment is responsible for the differences we have observed.

The formulas for the *t* test look pretty horrendous at first. Just remember to relax and work on one step at a time. When you look closely, you will see that you learned how to do most of the computations in earlier chapters.

Formulas for the *t* Test for Two Independent Samples

$$t_{obt} = \frac{M_1 - M_2}{s_{M_1 - M_2}}$$

$$s_{M_1 - M_2} = \sqrt{\frac{s_p^2}{N_1} + \frac{s_p^2}{N_2}}$$

$$s_p^2 = \frac{(N_1 - 1)s_1^2 + (N_2 - 1)s_2^2}{N_1 + N_2 - 2}$$

where

t_{obt}	= the value of *t* obtained through your data
N_1, N_2	= the number of subjects in each of the two groups
s_1^2, s_2^2	= the estimates of the variances of the two populations
M_1, M_2	= the means of the two groups
$s_p^2, s_{M_1 - M_2}$	= values you need in order to arrive at t_{obt} [2]

Next, I'll give you a worked-out example using the data of the counseling and no-counseling groups. You might want to see if you can do it on your own before you look at the example. Notice that you have to compute the bottom-most formula first and then work your way up through the three formulas until you can solve for t_{obt}. And don't get discouraged if you can't do it on the first try, because I'll go through the computations with you a step at a time.

---

[2] $s_{M_1} - M_2$ does have a logical meaning. If you took thousands of pairs of samples from these two populations, and found $M_1 - M_2$ for each pair, those differences between means wouldn't all be the same. They would form a distribution; the mean of that distribution would be the difference between the means of the populations ($\mu_1 - \mu_2$), and its standard deviation would be $s_{M_1 - M_2}$.

COMPUTATION OF t_{obt} FOR COUNSELED AND CONTROL GROUPS

Each successive formula of the three formulas I gave you provides some value to plug into the earlier one. Therefore, we begin at the bottom, with the formula for s_p^2

Notice that this computation requires that you know the number of subjects (N) and the variance (s^2) for each of your groups. If you go back to the beginning of this chapter, you will see that both N_1 and $N_2 = 12$, $s_1^2 = 12.93$, and $s_2^2 = 4.93$. If you were doing your own study, you would, of course, have to compute both of those variances. But you know how to do that, right?

Go ahead now and do the arithmetic indicated in the formula for s_p^2 (remember that multiplying and dividing are done before adding and subtracting, unless parentheses indicate otherwise). Your answer should come out to 8.93.

$$s_p^2 = \frac{(N_1 - 1)s_1^2 + (N_1 - 1)s_2^2}{N_1 + N_2 - 2}$$

$$= \frac{[(12 - 1) \times 12.93] + [(12 - 1) \times 4.93]}{12 + 12 - 2} = 8.93$$

Next comes the middle formula. Use the value that you got in the first computation, 8.93, to plug into this one. Unless you make an arithmetic error, you'll get 1.22 as your answer.

$$s_{M_1 - M_2} = \sqrt{\frac{s_p^2}{N_1} + \frac{s_p^2}{N_2}} = \sqrt{\frac{8.93}{12} + \frac{8.93}{12}} = \sqrt{\frac{17.86}{12}} = \sqrt{1.49} = 1.22$$

Finally, you're ready for the last step, the formula that gives the value of t_{obt}. Again, in your own study, you would have to do some preliminary work this time to get the means of the two samples. In our example, this has been done for you: $M_1 = 19.75$ and $M_2 = 11.75$. Note that these values go into the numerator of the formula. The value of t_{obt} is 6.56.

$$t_{obt} = \frac{M_1 - M_2}{s_{M_1 - M_2}} = \frac{19.75 - 11.75}{1.22} = 6.56$$

Notice, by the way, that the decision of which sample mean is subtracted from the other is purely arbitrary; we could just as well have used $M_2 - M_1$ for the numerator of that last equation. Had we done so, the value of t_{obt} would have been negative rather than positive. When the direction of the difference we are interested in is unimportant, the t test is *nondirectional* and we use the absolute value of t_{obt}: With a negative value, we would just drop the negative sign and proceed as if we had subtracted in the other direction.

THE CRITICAL VALUE OF t: t_{crit}

"Okay," you might say, "I've done all the computations. Now what does my t_{obt} mean?" Good question. To find out whether your t_{obt} is statistically significant—that is, if it is large enough so that it probably reflects more than chance or random differences between the two samples—you will have to compare it with what is known as the critical value of t (I'll designate the critical value of t as t_{crit}). To find t_{crit}, go to Appendix F. Look at the left-hand set of values (labeled "Two-Tailed or Nondirectional Test") and notice that the farthest column to the left is headed with the letters df.[3] The abbreviation df means

---

[3]Don't worry too much about what "two-tailed" means; we'll get back to it after you've learned how to do this first kind of t test.

"degrees of freedom." To find the degrees of freedom for a t test for independent samples, just subtract 2 from the total number of subjects in your study. In our example, df $= n_1 + n_2 - 2 = 12 + 12 - 2 = 22$.

t_{crit} is determined by df and by your selected level of significance. Suppose you selected the .05 level of significance (the most commonly chosen value). Go down the df column to 22, the number of df in our example, and across to the value in the column to the right (headed with .05). There you will see the number 2.074. That is the critical value of t, or t_{crit}, for the .05 level of significance when df $= 22$. If your t_{obt} is equal to or greater than t_{crit}, your results are statistically significant at the .05 level. Another way of saying this is that there are fewer than 5 chances out of 100 that a t value this large could have occurred by chance alone. The statistician's way of saying it is $p < .05$.

The t_{obt} in our example was 6.56 This is obviously larger than $t_{crit} = 2.074$; therefore, your results are significant at the .05 level. In fact, if you go across the df $= 22$ row, you will see that your $t_{obt} = 6.56$ is greater than the t_{crit} for the .01 level (2.819) and for the .001 level (3.792). You cannot claim that your results are significant at the .001 level, though; to do that, you'd have to say ahead of time that you would only reject H_0 if you got such an extreme value. You must decide what level of significance will justify rejecting H_0 *before* you look at your data; that's the rule. Bummer. But you're still okay; you got what you were looking for, a t_{obt} that will allow you to reject H_0 at the .05 level. You conclude that the differences between your samples of counseled and control subjects reflect a real difference in the populations of counseled and noncounseled people.

Let's do one more example, going through each step in a typical study comparing two groups. Suppose you wanted to test the hypothesis that men and women differ in the degree of empathy that they show to a stranger. You could select representative samples of men and women, tape record their conversations with your research associate, and use some sort of test to measure their degree of empathy. Imagine that your results were as follows (the higher the score, the greater the degree of empathy shown):

Group 1 (Men's Empathy Scores)	Group 2 (Women's Empathy Scores)
7	7
5	8
3	10
4	7
1	

Step 1: State Your Hypothesis. The statistical hypothesis you will be testing is the null hypothesis. In this example, the null hypothesis is that there is no difference between populations of men and women in the level of empathy that they offer to a stranger. In statistical terms,

$$H_0: \quad \mu_1 = \mu_2$$

Sometimes hypotheses are stated as alternative or research hypotheses, which represent the thing you want to show to be true. Alternative or research hypotheses are the opposite of the null hypothesis. In this case, the alternative hypothesis would be that there *is* a difference between populations of men and women in the degree of empathy that they offer to a stranger:

$$H_1: \quad \mu_1 \neq \mu_2$$

Step 2: Select α, Your Significance Level. The level of significance chosen is known as α (alpha). Why α, rather than p? It's a pretty niggling difference, but α is the probability of a Type I error, and p refers to the probability of getting the actual results you got just by chance. The most typical alpha level for social science research is $\alpha = .05$. As indicated in Chapter 6, you might choose $\alpha = .01$ if you want to be supercareful to avoid committing a Type I error. If a significant result would commit you to investing a great deal of money in program changes, or would lead to other important policy decisions, for example, then a Type I error would be quite dangerous and you would want to be very cautious indeed in setting your α level.

Step 3: Compute t_{obt}

(a) Find N, M, and σ^2 for each group:

$$\text{Group 1 (males): } N_1 = 5, M_1 = 4, \sigma^2 = 5$$
$$\text{Group 2 (females): } N_2 = 4, M_2 = 8, \sigma^2 = 2$$

(b) Plug these values into the formulas:

$$\sigma_p^2 = \frac{(N_1 - 1)\sigma_1^2 + (N_2 - 1)\sigma_2^2}{N_1 + N_2 - 1}$$

$$= \frac{[(5 - 1) \times 5] + [(4 - 1) \times 2]}{5 + 4 - 2} = 3.71$$

$$\sigma_{M_1 - M_2} = \sqrt{\frac{\sigma_p^2}{N_1} + \frac{\sigma_p^2}{N_2}} = \sqrt{\frac{3.71}{5} + \frac{3.71}{4}} = 1.29$$

$$t_{obt} = \frac{M_1 - M_2}{\sigma_{M_1 - M_2}} = \frac{4 - 8}{1.29} = -3.10$$

Step 4: Find t_{crit}. Entering Appendix F with df $= n_1 + n_2 - 2 = 5 + 4 - 2 = 7$, and with $\alpha = .05$, you can see that $t_{crit} = 2.365$.

Step 5: Decide Whether or Not to Reject the Null Hypothesis. As I pointed out earlier, the sign of t_{obt} will depend on which sample mean you happened to label M_1 and which one you labeled M_2. For the hypothesis you are testing now, it doesn't really matter which sample mean is larger; you're only interested in whether or not they're different. For this reason, use the absolute value of t_{obt}: If you get a negative value for t_{obt}, just change the sign to positive before comparing it to the tabled value. If t_{obt} has an absolute value equal to or greater than t_{crit}, you will reject H_0. Comparing $t_{obt} = 3.10$ with $t_{crit} = 2.365$, we decide to reject the null hypothesis. Our results are significant at the .05 level. Not only is t_{obt} significant, but the actual values of the means look quite different—the magnitude of effect is large. It is reasonable to conclude on the basis of our study that female counselors offer a higher level of empathy to their clients than do male counselors, and that this difference may be of practical interest.

Requirements for Using the *t* Test
for Independent Samples

The *t* test you have just learned requires that you have two independent samples, which means that the subjects for one group were selected independently from those in the second group. That is, the measurements from the two groups aren't paired in any way; a given measurement from group 1 doesn't "go with" a particular measurement from group 2. Sometimes you want to do a study in which this is not the case; for paired data you will use the *t* test for nonindependent groups.

Also, *t* tests assume that both of the populations being considered are essentially normally distributed. I say "essentially" because a really close fit to the normal distribution isn't necessary. The *t* test is considered "robust" with respect to this assumption—that is, we can violate the assumption without putting too much strain on our findings, especially if we have large samples. If you have only small samples (as in the last example we worked), and if the populations they came from are likely to be quite skewed, then you should not use a *t* test—you should use one of the tests we'll talk about in Chapter 10.

THE *t* TEST FOR NONINDEPENDENT
(MATCHED) SAMPLES

Suppose you gave a group of 10 subjects a test both before and after a movie intended to influence attitudes toward public schools. You had two sets of scores, one from the pretest and the other from the posttest, and you wanted to find out if attitudes as measured by the tests were more or less favorable after seeing the movie than they were before. You now have pairs of scores, a score for each subject on the pretest and another score from each subject for the posttest. You have two groups of scores, but they are not independent of each other; they are matched.

Table 8–1

Subject	Pretest Scores	Posttest Scores	Posttest − Pretest = D	D^2
1	84	89	+5	25
2	87	92	+5	25
3	87	98	+11	121
4	90	95	+5	25
5	90	95	+5	25
6	90	95	+5	25
7	90	95	+5	25
8	93	92	−1	1
9	93	98	+5	25
10	96	101	+5	25

The results are shown in Table 8–1 (pretest and posttest scores are in columns 2 and 3, column 4 is the difference between each pair of scores, and column 5 is the square of that difference).

The most important thing to notice about these data, when deciding what statistical test to use, is that the scores are *paired*. The pretest score of 84 goes with the posttest score of 89, and it is the fact that subject 1 raised his or her score by 5 points that is important, rather than the values of the two scores by themselves. It wouldn't make sense to scramble the posttest scores and then look at the *D* (the difference between pretest and posttest) scores. Each pretest score is logically linked to one, and only one, posttest score. That's the definition of nonindependent samples; whenever that condition holds, then a nonindependent samples test is appropriate.

You will probably be pleased to discover that this nonindependent samples *t* test is easier to compute than the independent samples one. Here we go, step by step:

Step 1: State Your Hypothesis.   Your null hypothesis is that there is no difference between attitudes before the movie and attitudes after the movie; that is,

$$H_0: \quad \mu_1 = \mu_2$$

Your alternative, or research, hypothesis is that there is a difference between attitudes before and after the movie:

$$H_1: \quad \mu_1 \neq \mu_2$$

Step 2: Select Your Level of Significance.   For this example, we arbitrarily select the .05 level of significance, $\alpha = .05$.

Step 3: Compute t_{obt}. The formula, with appropriate numbers plugged in, is

$$t_{obt} = \frac{M_D}{\sqrt{\dfrac{n\Sigma D^2 - (\Sigma D)^2}{n(n-1)}}} = \frac{5}{\sqrt{\dfrac{10(322) - (50)^2}{10(10-1)}}} = \frac{5}{2.83} = 1.77$$

where | ΣD | = | the sum of the D column, the column of differences between pretest and posttest scores. In our example, $\Sigma D = 50$. Note that here we *do* pay attention to the sign of the differences; that value of -1 has to be subtracted, not added. Note also that the formula calls for $(\Sigma D)^2$, which is not the same as ΣD^2. Remember? In our example, $(\Sigma D)^2 = (50)^2 = 2500$. Finally, notice that I subtracted each subject's pretest score from his or her posttest score. I could have subtracted posttest from pretest scores, in which case most of my D values would have been negative and my t_{obt} would also have been negative. It wouldn't have made any difference, however, as long as I did it the same way for every pair. If the absolute value of t_{obt} is greater than t_{crit}, then the difference between the two groups is statistically significant.

n = the number of *pairs* of scores. In our example, $n = 10$. Don't confuse n with N, the number of subjects in a sample!

M_D = the mean difference, computed by dividing ΣD by n. In our example, $M_D = 5$.

ΣD^2 = the sum of the D^2 column. In our example, $\Sigma D^2 = 322$.

Step 4: Find t_{crit}. As was true for the t test for independent samples, we enter the table in Appendix F to find t_{crit}. In the case of the t for noninde-pendent samples, however, df $= n - 1$, where n is the number of subjects (the number of pairs of scores, not the total number of scores). Thus, in our example, df $= 10 - 1 = 9$ and $t_{crit} = 2.262$ at the .05 level of significance.

Step 5: Decide Whether to Reject H_0. As was the case with independent t tests, we compare our t_{obt} with t_{crit}. If t_{obt} (either positive or negative) is equal to or greater than t_{crit}, then we reject H_0 and conclude that our results are significant at the chosen level of α. Since in our example t_{crit} is greater than t_{obt}, we cannot reject the null hypothesis and conclude that the movie appeared to have a positive effect on attitudes toward public schools. We don't conclude that attitudes were unchanged—that would be accepting H_0, and we can't do that. The data failed to confirm our hypothesis, but they did not disconfirm it.

DIRECTIONAL VERSUS NONDIRECTIONAL TESTS

When you as a researcher are quite confident, on the basis of previous research or theory, that the mean of one group should be higher than that of some other group (or that you are only interested in demonstrating that it is higher), and you predict the direction of the difference before you collect your data, you can then use what is called a one-tailed, or directional, t test. When conducting a one-tailed test, the t_{obt} formulas will be the same, but the value of t_{crit} will be different.

Suppose you predicted in advance that the mean weight of a group who had participated in a Weight Watchers program ($n = 12$) would be lower than the mean of a control group who hadn't been in Weight Watchers ($n = 12$). Suppose also that $t_{obt} = 2.0$. If you were conducting a two-tailed test, you would look up t_{crit} with 22 degrees of freedom (do you know why df = 22 and not 11? Because these data are not paired; a given subject in the treatment group isn't logically linked to some particular subject in the control group). But this time you'd look in the column labeled "One-Tailed or Directional Test" and the value of t_{crit} would be 1.717 at the .05 level of significance. Since t_{obt} is larger than t_{crit}, the result is statistically significant.

If you had not predicted the direction of the difference in advance of your study, you would have to use a two-tailed test and use the t_{crit} values from

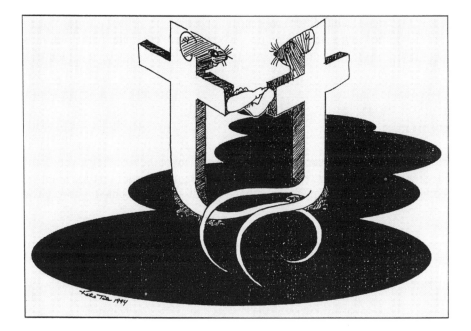

the left-hand side of Appendix F. As you can see from that table, with df = 22, t_{crit} = 2.074 for a two-tailed test. t_{obt} is still 2.0, but your results would not be statistically significant at the .05 level.

The diagrams at the top of Appendix F show how a value of t_{obt} can be significant for a one-tailed test but not for a two-tailed test. In a one-tailed test, we are only interested in differences in one direction—out in one tail of the distribution. If a t_{obt} is large enough to fall beyond the value of t_{crit} in that tail, t_{obt} is significant. With a two-tailed test, differences in *either* direction are important, and so we have to split the value of α and put half into each tail of the distribution. With α = .05, t_{crit} will mark off .025 at either end. Because the area marked off is smaller, t_{crit} must "slide" farther out away from 0, the mean,[4] and the farther it slides away from the mean, the bigger it gets. With everything else equal, the value of t_{crit} will always be larger for a two-tailed test than for a one-tailed test. It's easier to get significant results with a one-tailed test, because t_{obt} doesn't have to be so large.

So why not always use a one-tailed test? To use the one-tailed test legitimately, you must make your predictions prior to data collection. To do otherwise would be analogous to placing your bets after you see the outcome of an event. When in doubt, it is better to do two-tailed tests, if only to avoid temptation. However, doing a two-tailed test does increase the likelihood of a Type II error, that is, of not rejecting the null hypothesis when it should be rejected. If a significant outcome of your research would make sense *only* if the observed differences are in a particular direction (if you'd dismiss anything else as chance or random differences, no matter how unlikely), then do a one-tailed test. Remember, though, that if you choose to do a one-tailed test and your data show "significant" differences in the opposite direction, you may not reject H_0. By choosing a one-tailed approach, you have committed yourself to assuming that *any* differences in the nonpredicted direction are due to chance or error.

PROBLEMS

For each problem, be sure to specify the null hypothesis being tested, and whether you will use a *t* test for independent samples or a *t* test for nonindependent samples; also, specify whether you will use a one-tailed or two-tailed test.

[4]Why is the mean taken to be zero? Because the table is giving values for the null hypothesis, that there is no difference between the two groups. If there is no difference, the differences between sample means will form a distribution that has some negative values (group A will, by chance, be slightly smaller than group B) and some positive values (group B will, by chance, be slightly smaller than group A), with a mean of zero. We talked about this distribution in an earlier footnote; its name (if you care to know) is the *sampling distribution of the differences*.

1. In a study designed to discover whether men or women drink more coffee, a researcher (working on a *very* limited budget) observes five men and five women randomly selected from her university department. Here's what she found:

Number of Cups of Coffee
in 1 Day at Work

Men	Women
5	8
1	3
4	7
2	3
3	5

(a) Run the appropriate test, assuming that both men and women were originally part of one random sample, with $n = 10$, and were then divided into men's and women's groups.
(b) Use the same data, but this time assume that the men were randomly selected and then women were selected so that each man could be matched with a woman of the same age, job classification, and overall health status.

2. Using hospital and agency records, you locate six pairs of identical twins, one of whom was adopted at birth and the other of whom was in foster care for at least 3 years. All the twins are now 5 years old. You want to show that early adoption leads to better intellectual ability, so you test all the twins with the Wechsler Intelligence Scale for Children (WISC). Your results are as follows:

WISC Score

Twin Pair No.	Adopted Twin	Foster-Care Twin
1	105	103
2	99	97
3	112	105
4	101	99
5	124	104
6	100	110

3. The following table contains scores on an index of depression for three groups of clients at a college counseling center. Group 1 clients have received six sessions of counseling; group 2 clients were put on a waiting list for 6 weeks and asked to keep a personal journal during that time; group 3 clients were put on the waiting list with no other instructions. Use a t test to decide whether:
(a) group 2 (journal) clients scored differently from group 3 (control) clients.
(b) group 1 (counseled) clients scored differently from group 2 (journal) clients.
(c) group 1 (counseled) clients scored higher than group 3 (control) clients.

Group 1 (Counseled)	Group 2 (Journal)	Group 3 (Control)
22	6	8
16	10	6
17	13	4
18	13	5
	8	2
	4	

4. A researcher tests the high-frequency hearing acuity of a group of teens 2 days before they attend a rock concert; 2 days after the concert, she tests them again. Here are her results; she hopes to show that the teens hear better before the concert than afterward (the *higher* the score on this test, the poorer the hearing).

Subject	Scores (Preconcert)	Scores (Postconcert)
Tom	12	18
Dan	2	3
Sue	6	5
Terri	13	10
Karen	10	15
Lance	10	15
Christy	5	6
Jan	2	9
Lenora	7	7
Roberta	9	9
Dave	10	11
Victoria	14	13

5. Cindy, who has had several autumn outings spoiled by bad weather, is convinced that it rains more on weekends than on weekdays in the fall. To test this hypothesis, she randomly selects 10 weekdays and 10 weekend days from last fall, and finds out how much rain fell on each. Her data follow. (With such small numbers, roundoff errors can make a big difference. Best carry your work in this problem out to four places, instead of the usual two.)

Rainfall on Weekdays	Rainfall on Weekend Days
0	.5
.3	0
.2	0
0	0
.15	.2
0	0
0	.1
0	.07
.05	0
.03	.12

6. Do dogs who are fed twice a day eat more in the morning or more in the evening? Here are data from 15 healthy pets; what do you conclude?

Dog	Morning Feeding (oz)	Evening Feeding (oz)
Rover	5.9	5.8
Spot	9.9	7.6
Zachary	1.3	1.9
Cagney	8.6	7.2
Clem	7.1	7.3
Claudia	6.0	4.2
Johann S. Bark	7.3	7.2
Tigger	3.3	3.2
Beelzebub	11.9	10.0
Whiskers	5.4	5.2
Him	8.8	9.0
Chiggers	6.9	6.3
Sam	6.5	6.5
Lucy	5.4	5.1
Frisky	5.8	7.2

7. You really are interested in dogs, so you decide to test another hypothesis: Male dogs generally eat more than females. In the data in Problem 6, Rover, Spot, Zachary, Clem, Johann Bark, Beelzebub, Him, and Sam are males. Is your hypothesis supported?

8. The registrar at Cow Catcher College is interested in the relationship between academic achievement and early choice of major. She randomly selects 20 students from the sophomore class at CCC, and records their GPAs and whether they've decided on a major yet. Given the following data, what can she conclude?

GPA When Major Is Chosen	GPA When Major Not Chosen
3.5	3.2
3.1	2.5
2.9	2.0
4.0	3.7
3.8	1.5
3.2	2.9
3.7	3.4
3.5	3.3
2.9	
3.4	
3.6	
3.0	

8

Analysis of Variance

In Chapter 7, you learned how to determine if the means of two groups differ to a statistically significant degree. In this chapter, you will learn how to test for differences among the means of three or more groups.

Suppose you assigned subjects to one of three groups: a peer support group (group 1), an exercise/diet group (group 2), and a no-treatment control group (group 3), with posttreatment adjustment test scores as follows:

Group 1 (Peer Support)	Group 2 (Exercise/Diet)	Group 3 (Control)
22	6	8
16	10	6
17	13	4
18	13	5
	8	2
	4	

You could test for the differences between pairs of means with the t test: You could test for the significance of difference for M_1 versus M_2, M_1 versus M_3, and M_2 versus M_3. There are at least two reasons why it would not be a good idea to do this kind of analysis.

1. It's tedious. If you do t tests, you will have to compute $k(k-1)/2$ of them, where k is the number of groups. [In our example, $3(3-1)/2 = 3$. This

isn't too bad, but if you were comparing means among, say, 10 groups, you would have to compute $10(10 - 1)/2 = 45$ t tests!]

2. More importantly, when you select, for example, the .05 level of significance, you expect to make a Type I error 5 times out of 100 by sampling error alone. If you performed 20 t tests and one of them reached the .05 level of significance, would that be a chance occurrence or not? What if 3 of the 20 were significant—which would be chance and which would be a "real" difference? With multiple t's, you really don't know what is the probability of a Type I error, but it almost surely is greater than .05.

You can take care of both of these problems by using an *analysis of variance* (ANOVA) to test for statistical significance of the differences among the means of three or more groups. It may be important to note here that, even though the name of this statistic has the term "variance" in it, it is used to test for significant differences among means. The test looks at the amount of variability (the differences) between the means of the groups, compared with the amount of variability among the individual scores in each group—that is, the variance between groups versus the variance within groups—and that's where the name comes from. The ANOVA starts with the total amount of variability in the data and divides it up (the statisticians call it "partitioning") into various categories. Eventually, the technique allows us to compare the variability among the group means with the variability that occurred just by chance or error—and that's exactly what we need to be able to do.

Perhaps you recall the formula for the variance of a sample, given to you in Chapter 2:

$$s^2 = \frac{\Sigma(X - M_X)^2}{N - 1}$$

More precisely, this is the formula for estimating the variance of the population from which the sample was drawn, since that's what we are really interested in. And that's why we use $N - 1$ in the denominator of the fraction, rather than just N: just getting the average of the sample members' deviations around the mean would yield a biased estimate of the population value. $N - 1$, one less than the number of things in the sample (scores, people, hot fudge sundaes) is known as the sample's *degrees of freedom*.

Degrees of freedom is a concept you may not yet understand, although we've used the term several times already. The basic idea has to do with the number of scores in a group of scores that are free to vary. In a group of 10 scores that sum up to 100, you could let 9 of the scores be anything you wanted. Once you had decided what those 9 scores were, the value of the tenth score would be determined. Let's say we made the first 9 scores each equal to 2. They'd add up to a total of 18; if the sum has to be 100, then the tenth score has to be 82. The group of 10 scores has only 9 degrees of freedom, 9 scores that are free to vary, 9 df. Why is this important? Because the calculations for an ANOVA involve degrees of freedom, and you need to be able to figure out what those df are. But we need to do a few other things first.

The first step in carrying out an analysis of variance is to compute the variance of the total number of subjects in the study—we put them all together, regardless of the group to which they've been assigned, and find the variance of the whole thing. We do this using $N_T - 1$ (the total degrees of freedom) for the denominator of the formula:

$$s_T^2 = \frac{\Sigma(X - M_T)^2}{N_T - 1}$$

Nothing new so far—this is just our old friend, the formula for estimating a population variance based on a sample drawn from that population. We do have a couple of new names for things, though. The numerator of this formula is called the "total sum of squares," abbreviated SS_T—"total" because it's calculated across the total number of scores, combining all the groups. SS_T is the basis for all the partitioning that will follow. Notice, too, that the formula uses M_T as the symbol for the overall mean of all scores (some authors use "GM," for "grand mean"), and N_T, the total number of subjects. The denomina-

tor of the formula is known as the total degrees of freedom, or df_T. Translating the old variance formula to these new terms, we get

$$s_T^2 = \frac{\Sigma(X - M_X)^2}{N_T - 1} = \frac{SS_T}{df_T}$$

In ANOVA calculations, this pattern—dividing a sum of squares by an associated df—is repeated again and again. The number that you get when you divide a sum of squares by the appropriate df is called a mean square (MS). So

$$s_T^2 = MS_T = \frac{SS_T}{df_T}$$

I want to pause here to remind you of something I said way back at the very beginning of this book: Mathematical formulas take much longer to read and understand than do most other kinds of reading. You struggled through a lot of formulas in Chapter 7, and we're going to be dealing with lots more of them here. So, please, remember to take your time! Pause, translate the formula into words, and make sure you understand how it relates to what went before. This last formula, for instance, says that the total mean square of a group of scores is the sum of squares for that group, divided by the degrees of freedom. And what are the sum of squares, and the degrees of freedom? Go back, read again, and put it together in your head. Understand each piece before you go on to the next. Reading in this way will actually prove to be a faster way to learn, in the long run.

In a simple ANOVA, the total sum of squares (SS_T) is broken down into two parts: (1) a *sum of squares within groups*, SS_W, which reflects the degree of variability within groups but is not sensitive to overall differences between the groups; and (2) a *sum of squares between groups*, SS_B, which reflects differences between groups but is not sensitive to variability within groups. The total sum of squares is the sum of the sum of squares within and the sum of squares between: $SS_T = SS_W + SS_B$. The total degrees of freedom can be broken down similarly: $df_T = df_W + df_B$. To find df_W, add up the df's within all the groups: $(n_1 - 1) + (n_2 - 1) + \ldots + (n_{last} - 1)$. And df_B is the number of groups minus 1: $k - 1$.

For the groups in our example,

$$df_W = (4 - 1) + (6 - 1) + (5 - 1) = 3 + 5 + 4 = 12$$
$$df_B = 3 - 1 = 2$$

If we did our math right, $df_W + df_B$ should equal df_T:

$$[(4 - 1) + (6 - 1) + (5 - 1)] + [3 - 1] = (4 + 6 + 5) - 1$$
$$12 \qquad\qquad + \quad 2 \quad = \qquad 14$$

Dividing SS_W by df_W gives us what is known as the mean square within, a measure of the variability within groups:

$$MS_W = \frac{SS_W}{df_W}$$

And dividing SS_B by df_B gives us the mean square between, a measure of variability between groups:

$$MS_B = \frac{SS_B}{df_B}$$

I know you haven't been told how to find SS_W and SS_B yet—that comes next. For now, just look at the logic of the process.

With MS_B, we have a measure of variability between the groups, that is, a measure that reflects how different they are from each other. And our MS_W is a measure of the variability inside the groups, variability that can be attributed to chance or error. Ultimately, of course, we want to know if the between-group differences are significantly greater than chance. So we will compare the two by computing their ratio:

$$F_{obt} = \frac{MS_B}{MS_W}$$

F is the ratio of a mean square between groups to a mean square within groups. (It's named after Sir Roland Fisher, who invented it.) The "obt" subscript means that, as usual, we will compare this obtained value of F with some critical value (F_{crit}), which will tell us how likely it is that our F_{obt} could have happened just by chance. The values of F_{crit} are found in Appendix G (I'll show you how to do this later). If F_{obt} is equal to or greater than F_{crit}, then we reject the null hypothesis.

You may have guessed that when comparing three group means the null hypothesis is

$$H_0: \quad \mu_1 = \mu_2 = \mu_3$$

The only hard part about ANOVA is learning how to compute SS_W and SS_B. You can do it, though. It's no harder than some of the other computations we've done.

The scores from our hypothetical study are shown again in Table 8–1. Under the scores, you'll see some rows of computations, which I'll explain as we go along. In this computational table, we'll end up with intermediate values, which I've labeled I, II, and III, which we'll use to compute our SS_W and SS_B.

Computation Steps

Step 1.   Find N_T. N_T stands for the total number of subjects in the entire study. Under each column of scores, you will see the number of subjects (N) for each group. In the last column in row 1, you will see N_T, which is the total number of subjects in the study. You get that, of course, by adding the N's for the columns:

$$N_T = N_1 + N_2 + N_3 = 4 + 6 + 5 = 15$$

Step 2.   Find ΣX_T. ΣX_T stands for the grand total of all the scores. Start by finding ΣX for each column. For example, $\Sigma X = 73$ for group 1. Then find ΣX_T by adding the totals, the sums of the scores, for each column:

$$\Sigma X_T = 73 + 54 + 25 = 152$$

Table 8–1.   Computation of values for 1-way ANOVA

Step		Group 1	Group 2	Group 3	
		22	6	8	
		16	10	6	
		17	13	4	
		18	13	5	
			8	2	
Step			4		
1	N	4	6	5	$N_T = \Sigma N = 15$
2	ΣX	73	54	25	$\Sigma X_T = 152$
3					$\mathrm{I} = \dfrac{(\Sigma X_T)^2}{N_T}$ $\mathbf{I = 1540.27}$
4	ΣX^2	1353	554	145	$\mathbf{II = \Sigma\Sigma X^2 = 2052}$
5	$\dfrac{(\Sigma X)^2}{N}$	$\dfrac{(73)^2}{4}$	$\dfrac{(54)^2}{6}$	$\dfrac{(25)^2}{5}$	$\mathrm{III} = \Sigma\dfrac{(\Sigma X)^2}{N} = \dfrac{\Sigma(\Sigma X)^2}{N}$ $\mathbf{III = 1943.25}$
6	M	18.25	9	5	

Step 3.   Find **I**. **I** is the first intermediate value we will compute. As the formula indicates, **I** is found by squaring ΣX_T (found in row 2) and dividing that by N_T (found in row 1).

$$\mathbf{I} = 1540.27$$

Step 4.   Find **II**. **II** is the total sum of X^2 for the entire set of numbers. First, find ΣX^2 for each column (square each score first, then find the sum of the squares—remember?), and then compute **II** by adding those sums of squares.

$$\mathbf{II} = 1353 + 554 + 145 = 2052$$

Step 5.   Find **III**. To find **III**, square ΣX for each column and divide it by N for that column; then find the sum of those values.

$$\mathbf{III} = 1332.25 + 486 + 125 = 1943.25$$

Step 6.   Find the mean of each group. This is an "extra" step that I added because you're going to need the group means shortly.

Now use the intermediate values to compute the sums of squares with the following formulas:

$$SS_B = \mathbf{III} - \mathbf{I} = 1943.25 - 1540.27 = 402.98$$
$$SS_W = \mathbf{II} - \mathbf{III} = 2052 - 1943.25 = 108.75$$

We will also need to know the degrees of freedom for both between and within groups. In the following formulas, k stands for the number of groups. In our example, $k = 3$. Also, remember that N_T is the total number of subjects in the study:

$$df_B = k - 1 = 3 - 1 = 2$$
$$df_W = N - k - 15 - 3 = 12$$

(Here's a chance for another quick arithmetic check. Since the total df is $N_T - 1$ (in our study, $15 - 1$, or 14), the df_B and the df_W should add up to that number. And they do: $12 + 2 = 14$.

Now we can fill in what is known as an ANOVA summary table (see Table 8–2).

As was true for the t test, to find out whether your F_{obt} is statistically significant, you will need to compare it with F_{crit}. You find F_{crit} in Appendix G. Go across the table until you come to the column headed by the df_B for the F_{obt}

Table 8–2.   ANOVA summary table.

Source of Variation	Degrees of Freedom (df)	Sum of Squares	Mean Squares	F
Between (B)	$k - 1 = 3 - 1 = 2$	$SS_B = III - I$ $= 402.98$	$MS_B = \dfrac{SS_B}{df_B}$ $= \dfrac{402.98}{2}$ $= 201.49$	$F_{obt} = \dfrac{MS_B}{MS_W}$ $= 22.24**$
Within (W)	$N_T - k = 15 - 3$ $= 12$	$SS_W = II - III$ $= 108.75$	$MS_W = \dfrac{SS_W}{df}$ $= \dfrac{108.75}{12}$ $= 9.06$	
Total	$N - 1 = 14$	$SS_T = 511.73$		

you are interested in (in our example, there is only one F_{obt} to worry about, and $df_B = 2$). Follow down that column until you are directly across from your df_W (in our example, $df_W = 12$). Appendix G includes critical values of F for both the .05 and the .01 levels of significance; the .01 level is in boldface type. As you can see, for $df_B = 2$ and $df_W = 12$, F_{crit} at the .05 level of significance is 3.88, and at the .01 level, F_{crit} is 6.93. Since your $F_{obt} = 22.24$ is obviously larger than F_{crit} for either the .05 or the .01 levels of significance, you reject the null hypothesis (that there is no difference among means) and conclude that at least one of the means is significantly different from at least one of the others. Conventionally, a value of F that exceeds F_{crit} for the .05 level is followed by a single asterisk; if it exceeds F_{crit} for the .01 level it gets two asterisks (see Table 8–2).

Looking at the means of the three groups in our example, it appears that the mean of group 1, the peer support group ($M_1 = 18.25$) is significantly different from that of group 3, the control group ($M_3 = 5$). We might wonder if it is also significantly different from group 2, the exercise/diet group ($M_2 = 9$), or if the exercise/diet group is significantly different from the control group. To answer these types of questions, you will need to learn how to do what is known as post hoc analysis. One method of doing this kind of analysis is found in the next section.

POST-HOC ANALYSIS

The procedure in this section is designed to be used after an ANOVA has been done and the null hypothesis of no difference among means has been rejected. Let's look at another example. Consider a study of five different teaching methods. Five groups of students were taught a unit, each group being exposed to a different teaching method, and then the groups of students were tested for how much they had learned. Even if an ANOVA were to show the differences among the five means to be statistically significant, we still would not know which of the pairs of means were significantly different: Is M_1 significantly different from M_2? How about the difference between M_2 and M_3? If we looked at each possible combination, we would have $5(5 - 1)/2 = 10$ pairs of means to analyze. You will recall from the discussion at the beginning of this chapter that it is not good practice to analyze differences among pairs of means with the t test because of the increased probability of a Type I error; the same criticism can be leveled at any large set of independent comparisons.

Many procedures have been developed to do what is called post hoc analysis (tests used after an F_{obt} has been found to be statistically significant in an ANOVA). This book will present only one of these methods, the Scheffé, which can be used for groups of equal or unequal N's.

THE SCHEFFÉ METHOD OF POST-HOC ANALYSIS

The statistic you will compute in the Scheffé method is designated as C. A value of C is computed for any pair of means that you want to compare; unlike the t test, C is designed to allow multiple comparisons without affecting the likelihood of a Type I error. Moreover, if all the groups are the same size, you don't have to compute C for every single pair of means; once a significant C has been found for a given pair, you can assume that any other pair that is at least this far apart will also be significantly different. (With a t test, this is not necessarily true; nor is it always true for C when the group N's are unequal.)

As is the usual procedure, you will compare your C_{obt} with a C_{crit}; if C_{obt} is equal to or greater than C_{crit}, you will reject the null hypothesis for that pair of means. In the Sheffé test, you don't look up C_{crit} in a table; I'll show you how to compute it for yourself. First, though, we'll deal with C_{obt}.

$$C_{obt} = \frac{M_1 - M_2}{\sqrt{MS_W\left(\frac{1}{N} + \frac{1}{N_2}\right)}}$$

where M_1, M_2 = the means of two groups being compared
         N_1, N_2 = the N's of those two groups
         MS_W = the within-group mean square from your ANOVA

Now let's go back to our original three groups, peer support (group 1), exercise/diet (group 2), and control (group 3). Since we were able to reject H_0, we know that at least one group is significantly different from one other group; but we don't know which groups they are. And there may be more than one significant difference; we need to check that out. We'll start with the first pair, group 1 versus group 2.

$$C_{obt} = \frac{M_1 - M_2}{\sqrt{MS_W\left(\frac{1}{N_1} + \frac{1}{N_2}\right)}} = \frac{18.25 - 9}{\sqrt{9.06\left(\frac{1}{4} + \frac{1}{6}\right)}} = \frac{9.25}{1.95} = 4.74$$

For group 1 versus group 3,

$$C_{obt} = \frac{M_1 - M_3}{\sqrt{MS_W\left(\frac{1}{N_1} + \frac{1}{N_2}\right)}} = \frac{18.25 - 5}{\sqrt{9.06\left(\frac{1}{4} + \frac{1}{5}\right)}} = \frac{13.25}{2.02} = 6.56$$

And for group 2 versus group 3,

$$C_{obt} = \frac{M_2 - M_3}{\sqrt{MS_W\left(\frac{1}{N_1} + \frac{1}{N_2}\right)}} = \frac{9 - 5}{\sqrt{9.06\left(\frac{1}{6} + \frac{1}{5}\right)}} = \frac{4}{1.83} = 2.19$$

(Notice that, although it's still tedious to look at each possible pair, it's a lot less work than doing multiple t's!)

Now we are ready to compute C_{crit}. The general formula for C_{crit} is

$$C_{crit} = \sqrt{(k - 1)(F_{crit})}$$

where k is the number of groups.

At the .05 level of significance ($\alpha = .05$),

$$C_{crit} = \sqrt{(k - 1)(F_{crit})} = \sqrt{(3 - 1)(3.88)} = 2.79$$

and at the .01 level ($\alpha = .01$).

$$C_{crit} = \sqrt{(k - 1)(F_{crit})} = \sqrt{(3 - 1)(6.93)} = 3.72$$

Since it doesn't matter which group mean is subtracted from which in each computation of C_{obt}, the sign of the value you get doesn't matter either. Just treat C_{obt} as if it were positive. As you can see by comparing C_{crit} with C_{obt}, for both the .05 and the .01 levels of significance, the mean of the counseled group (group 1) is significantly larger than either the exercise/diet or the control groups. However, the mean of the exercise/diet group is not significantly greater than that of the control group.

Once you have determined that two groups are significantly different from each other, you will still have to decide if the differences are large enough to be useful in the real world. This is the "magnitude of effect" decision, which we discussed in relation to the *t* test. Unfortunately, there's no handy-dandy rule or formula to tell us whether or not we have a "large enough" magnitude of effect. It depends upon what's at stake: what's to be gained by a correct decision and what's to be lost by an incorrect one, and how much difference between groups is enough to be worth paying attention to. In our example, the mean of the peer support group is twice as high as the mean of the exercise/diet group, and more than three times the mean of the control group. For me, differences of that magnitude would play a very important part in treatment recommendations to students or clients. How about for you?

MORE COMPLEX ANALYSES

The analysis of variance is an extremely versatile tool. A one-way ANOVA, together with an appropriate post-hoc test, can be used to compare the means of any number of groups. But it doesn't stop there! To show you what I mean, let's look at another (hypothetical) researcher's data.

Ellen is interested in the social development of adolescents, and one of the things she is measuring in her young subjects is the number of phone calls they make to members of the opposite sex. After gathering her data, she divides the subjects up into four groups: younger (age 12–14) and older (age 16–18) boys, and younger and older girls. The mean number of calls to the opposite sex for these groups looks like this:

	Boys		Girls	
	12–14	16–18	12–14	16–18
Mean number of phone calls	6	15	5	3

Now, Ellen could simply do a one-way ANOVA to compare the four group means. But she wants to know more than just whether the four groups are different. She wants to know whether, overall, boys differ from girls. Similarly, she wants to know whether all the older subjects differ significantly from all the younger subjects. And she wants to know if there is an *interaction* between her two variables: Do boys, for example, make more calls when they are older, and girls make more calls when they are younger?

Hmmm. Well, lump all the boys' scores together, and all the girls' scores together, and do a *t* test. Then put all the younger kids' scores in one group, and all the older in another, and do a second *t* test. And then do the one-way ANOVA, and look at which of the four original groups are significantly different from each other. Will that work? Not very well—it's a lot of work, and you again have the problem of multiple independent comparisons. Enter our hero: the two-way ANOVA.

We aren't going to do the actual calculations for a two-way ANOVA, or for any of the other more complex ANOVAs. (I can almost hear your sigh of relief.) Computers can do that work faster and more accurately, and statistics software is available for almost every computer these days. The logic, though, is important for you to understand, and it is the same in all ANOVAs: Find the total MS, partition it out into MS_W plus the MS_B for each comparison you're interested in, and use those values to compute an F ratio.

Let's imagine that Ellen had 20 subjects in each of her four groups: 40 boys and 40 girls, with 20 younger and 20 older of each. Plugging her data in to the appropriate computer program, she might end up with a summary table that looks like:

Table 8–3.   Summary table for two-way ANOVA.

Source of Variation	Degrees of Freedom (df)	Sum of Squares	Mean Square	F
Age (12–14 vs. 16–18)	1	206.85	206.85	24.625**
Gender (Boys vs. Girls)	1	29.74	29.74	3.54
Interaction (Age × Gender)	1	126.59	126.59	15.07**
Within groups	76	9620.84	8.4	
Total	79	9984.02		

Look first at the "Source of Variation" column. Here's where you find a list of all the comparisons that will be made, together with the "Within groups" and the "Total" designations. That "Within groups," by the way, is also called an *error term*, and in more complex ANOVA designs there may be several error terms, each assigned to different comparisons. If you're wildly curious about that, consult a textbook on research design. Otherwise, read on.

The next column is for degrees of freedom. Each "main effects" comparison—that is, each comparison that includes only levels within a single variable—has $(k - 1)$ df, where k is the number of groups involved in the comparison. There are two age groups, and two gender groups, so each of those comparisons uses 1 df. The "Within groups" df is the sum of the df within all the groups: $(20 - 1) + (20 - 1) + (20 - 1) + (20 - 1) = 76$. The total df is, of course, $N_T - 1$, or 79. The only tricky one here is that Age × Gender interaction. For interactions, the df is $(k - 1)$ *minus* the df's for the main effect variables involved in that interaction. In our example, there are four groups in the Age by Gender comparison; Age has 1 df and Gender has 1 df; the df for the interaction will be $(4 - 1) - 1 - 1$, or 1.

The arithmetic check: df's for all comparisons, plus df_W, should add up to df_T.

$$1 + 1 + 1 + 76 = 79$$

The SS column is the one we're going to skip over; our friendly neighborhood computer found those values for us. And from there on, it's simple: the MS is the SS divided by the df, and the F is the MS divided by the MS_W.

And what does it all mean? First of all, those asterisks by the F values tell us that the difference between the older and the younger subjects is significant at the .01 level. The F of 3.54, the one that goes with the Gender main effect comparison, is not significant: The overall difference between boys and girls might have occurred just by chance. And the interaction between Age and Gender is also significant at the .01 level.

Interaction effects are difficult to explain in words; I always find that graphing the group means helps me to understand what is going on. Here's such a graph of the mean phone calls made by each group:

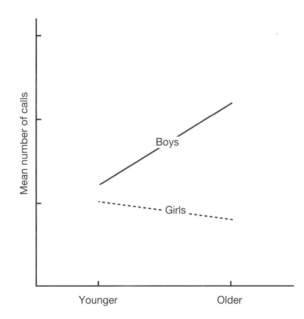

The graph makes it pretty clear: older boys made more opposite-sex phone calls than did younger boys, but older girls tended to make fewer calls than younger ones. That's what Ellen suspected, remember? Since the difference between younger and older boys is the largest, we can be sure that this difference is significant. To find out whether the others (younger vs. older girls; younger boys vs. younger girls; older boys vs. older girls) are significant, you would need to do a post-hoc test. And, as always, remember that even a statistically significant difference may not have a large enough magnitude of effect to be important in the real world!

In theory, ANOVAs can be done for designs with an unlimited number of variables and interactions among variables. In practice, though, there is usually a diminishing return: After a while, adding new variables doesn't generally yield enough information to justify the time and effort needed to gather all the extra data. The most elaborate ANOVAs that I am familiar with came from Carl Rogers's 1967 study of psychotherapy with schizophrenics. He and his team of researchers categorized his subjects as to age, gender, socioeconomic status, and diagnosis, yielding four independent variables. They also used repeated measures (yes, ANOVAs can do that, too), gathering data on their subjects every 6 months over a period of more than 2 years. But how would you graph or interpret a significant Age × Gender × Socioeconomic Status × Diagnosis × Time interaction, even if you got one?

PROBLEMS

1. A researcher is interested in differences among blondes, brunettes, and redheads in terms of introversion/extroversion. She selects random samples from a college campus, gives each subject a test of social introversion, and comes up with the following:

Blondes	Brunettes	Redheads
5	3	2
10	5	1
6	2	7
2	4	2
5	3	2
3	5	3

Use a simple ANOVA to test for differences among the groups.

2. A (hypothetical!) study of eating patterns among people in different occupations yielded the following:

	Bus Drivers ($N = 10$)	College Professors ($N = 10$)	U.S. Presidents ($N = 4$)
Mean junk food score	12	17	58.3

Source	df	Sum of Squares	Mean Square	F
Between	2	6505	3252.5	6.1**
Within	21	11197	533.2	

(a) What do you conclude?

(b) Perform the appropriate post-hoc analysis.

3. Farmer Hensh suspects that his chickens like music, because they seem to lay more eggs on days when his children practice their band instruments in the hen house. He decides to put it to a scientific test, and records the number of eggs collected each day for a month, along with the music provided on that day:

No Music	Mary (Piccolo)	Benny (Clarinet)	Satchmo (Trumpet)
11	12	35	52
26	17	42	78
31	19	31	16
18	25	33	41
15	32	44	25
	27	40	55
	30		57
			64
			20
			22
			73
			25

What does he conclude, and how does he explain it?

4. The college librarian at Harton University has been keeping track of who checks out library books. After 6 months of collecting data, he performed an ANOVA, scribbling his results on a sheet of paper. Unfortunately, his dog got into his briefcase and what you see below is all that could be resurrected. Assuming that his calculations were accurate, what could you conclude from his research? Draw a graph of the group means to make your explanation clear.

Compare # of books used by Math majors, psych majors, education majors Divide each into graduate students (G) and undergraduate (U).
    Group means look good—

	Math	Psych	Education
Undergrad	15	13	7
Grad	8	42	26

source	df	SS	MS	f
major	2			7.82
Level (u/g)	1			8.33
Interaction (MxL)	2			9.77
Within Groups	344			

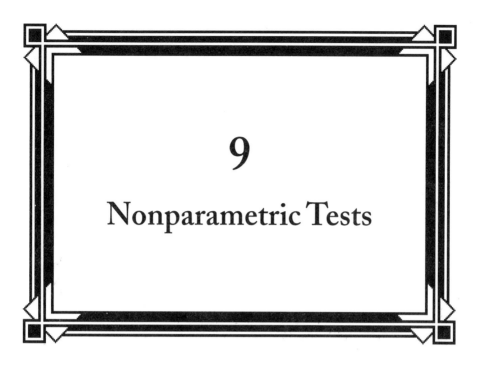

9
Nonparametric Tests

"Nonparametric"—oh, no! Is this something I should recognize from what has gone before? If we're going to look at *non*parametric things, what in the world are parametric ones? Relax—all these questions will be answered. You should know, though, first of all, that the things we will be doing in this chapter will be easier, not harder, than what you have already done.

All the statistical procedures that you have learned so far are *parametric* procedures. The idea of parametric involves a number of things, including the assumption that the data we work with are drawn from normally distributed populations, but the most important thing is that the data used in parametric tests or techniques must be scores or measurements of some sort. When comparing groups of people by means of a parametric test, we measure all the people and then use the test to determine whether the groups' measurements are significantly different from what could be expected just by chance.

But what if we are dealing with a situation in which we don't measure or test our subjects? That's not as unusual as you may imagine. Here's an example: A researcher wants to know if men and women college students differ in terms of their use of the college counseling center. She randomly selects 100 students and asks them if they have ever used the center. Here are her findings:

	Men	Women	Totals
Have used the center	12	16	28
Have not used the center	48	24	72

How should this researcher analyze her data? There are no scores, no means or variances to calculate. What she has is four *categories:* men and women who either used or did not use the center. Each person in the sample can be assigned to one, and only one, of these categories. What the researcher wants to know is whether the distribution she observed is significantly different from what she might expect, by chance, if the total populations of men and women didn't differ.

THE CHI-SQUARE TEST

Her question is quite easy to answer, using a procedure called the chi-square test. Chi square (symbolized by the Greek letter chi, squared: χ^2) is a nonparametric test. It doesn't require that its data meet the assumptions of the parametrics, and it most particularly doesn't require that the data be in the form of scores or measurements. Instead, it was specifically designed to test hypotheses about category data.

The null hypothesis for our example is that men and women don't differ significantly in their use of the counseling center:

$$H_0: \quad \text{Men's use of the center} = \text{Women's use of the center}$$

To test it using chi square, we first need to figure out the distribution that we would most often get just by chance if H_0 were true. Because there are not equal numbers of men and women in the total sample, we can't say that H_0 predicts that half of the center's clients will be male and half female. Rather, since 60% of the total sample are male, H_0 predicts that 60% of the people who used the counseling center should also be male and 40% female. Similarly, 60% of the people who didn't use it should be male and 40% female, if H_0 were true. We call these numbers the expected frequencies, or f_e. The observed frequencies, not surprisingly, are designated f_o.

f_e for men who have used the center is $.6(28) = 16.8$
f_e for men who have not used the center is $.6(72) = 43.2$
f_e for women who have used the center is $.4(28) = 11.2$
f_e for women who have not used the center is $.4(72) = 28.8$

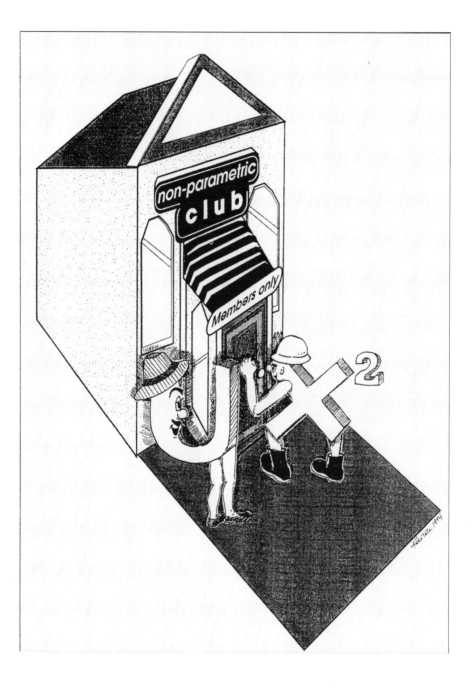

Notice that the f_e's yield the same row and column totals as the f_o's, providing you with a good way to check your math!

	Men	Women	Totals
Have used the center	$f_o = 12$ $f_e = 16.8$	$f_o = 16$ $f_e = 11.2$	28
Have not used the center	$f_o = 48$ $f_e = 43.2$	$f_o = 24$ $f_e = 28.8$	72
Totals	60	40	100

The formula for those f_e's is

$$f_e \text{ of cell } i, j = \frac{T_{\text{column } j}}{GT}(T_{\text{row } i})$$

where　$T_{\text{column } j}$　=　the total number of people in column j
　　　　$T_{\text{row } i}$　=　the total number of people in row i
　　　　GT　　=　the grand total, the number of people in the whole study

And notice that this formula will work no matter how many rows and columns you have: It would be perfectly fine to use it with data collected on blondes, brunettes, and redheads who are majoring in physics, chemistry, psychology, P.E., or English literature. Come to think of it, that would be an interesting problem. I think I'll set it up for you at the end of the chapter.

Once the f_e's have been calculated, it is a simple matter to find the value of χ^2:

$$\chi^2 = \Sigma \frac{(f_o - f_e)^2}{f_e}$$

1. Within each cell, find the value of $(f_o - f_e)$.

$$12 - 16.8 = -4.8$$
$$48 - 43.2 = 4.8$$
$$16 - 11.2 = 4.8$$
$$24 - 28.8 = -4.8$$

(Are you wondering why all of those differences have the same absolute value? It will always be that way in a 2×2 χ^2 design; if they don't come out equal, you've made an arithmetic error. Not so with larger designs, though—in the larger ones, the f_e's will not have equal absolute values.)

2. For each of the differences, square and divide by f_e.

$$\frac{(-4.8)^2}{16.8} = 1.37$$

$$\frac{(4.8)^2}{43.2} = .53$$

$$\frac{(4.8)^2}{11.2} = 2.06$$

$$\frac{(-4.8)^2}{28.8} = .80$$

3. Add up your answers.

$$\chi^2 = 1.37 + .53 + 2.06 + .80 = 4.76$$

As has been the case with all our statistics, we must compare the calculated value of chi square with a critical value. To do so, enter Appendix H with df = $(r - 1)$ $(c - 1)$: the number of rows minus 1 times the number of columns minus 1. In our example, $r = 2$ and $c = 2$, so

$$df = 1 \times 1 = 1$$

You can see from the table that for $\alpha = .05$,

$$\chi^2_{crit} = 3.84$$

Since our observed value of χ^2 (4.76) is greater than the critical value, we reject the null hypothesis. It is reasonable to conclude that men and women do differ in their use of the counseling center. Note, though, that this result does not imply any sort of causal relationship: We cannot say that gender "causes" the differences in counseling center behavior, any more than we could say that use of the counseling center "causes" people to be either male or female. Also—aren't you tired of having me say this? Statistical significance does not guarantee magnitude of effect. Evaluation of magnitude of effect involves qualitative, as well as quantitative, considerations.

Here's another example: Suppose that you wished to evaluate the effectiveness of three different methods of teaching basketball skills to elementary school children, methods A, B, and C. Also suppose that the best measure of outcome that you could get was a categorization of "improved" or "not improved." Sixty kids were randomly assigned to and taught by each method, with results as follows:

	Method A	Method B	Method C	Totals
Improved	10	18	12	40
Not Improved	10	2	8	20

Begin by calculating the values of f_e, using the same formula as before. I'll give you the first one:

$$f_e \text{ of cell } 1,1 = \frac{T_{\text{column 1}}}{GT} (T_{\text{row 1}}) = \frac{20}{60}(40) = 13.3$$

Do the rest of them yourself before looking at the following table.

	Method A	Method B	Method C	Totals
Improved	$f_o = 10$ $f_e = 13.33$	$f_o = 18$ $f_e = 13.33$	$f_o = 12$ $f_e = 13.33$	40
Not improved	$f_o = 10$ $f_e = 6.67$	$f_o = 2$ $f_e = 6.67$	$f_o = 8$ $f_e = 6.67$	20
Totals	20	20	20	60

Now, compute chi square:

$$\chi^2 = \Sigma \frac{(f_o - f_e)^2}{f_e} = .83 + 1.64 + .13 + 1.66 + 3.27 + .27 = 7.8$$

In this example, we have two rows and three columns, so

$$df = (2 - 1)(3 - 1) = (1)(2) = 2$$

Appendix H shows $\chi^2_{\text{crit}} = 5.99$ for an α of .05; and 9.21 for an α of .01. You can reject the null hypothesis at the .05 level and conclude that there are significant differences in the success rates among the three teaching methods.

The last chi-square example: The school at which the basketball research was done has two P.E. teachers. These teachers arranged their classes

	Mrs. Pick			Mr. Dunk			
	Method A	Method B	Method C	Method A	Method B	Method C	Totals
Improved	$f_o = 6$	$f_o = 10$	$f_o = 2$	$f_o = 4$	$f_o = 8$	$f_o = 10$	40
Not improved	$f_o = 4$	$f_o = 0$	$f_o = 8$	$f_o = 6$	$f_o = 2$	$f_o = 0$	20
Totals	10	10	10	10	10	10	60

so that they could each use all three methods, but with different students. Taking into account this new variable, here are the data:

You did a χ^2 to check on overall differences between the two teachers, and it showed no significant differences (check it out, if you'd like; it would be good practice!). But you still think there's something important going on, so you decide to do another χ^2, but this time you'll do it across all those separate cells. I'd like you to try your hand at this one, and I'm going to put my own results in Table 9–1 so you won't be tempted to peek until you've got your own answer.

A χ^2 of 24.13, with df = (5)(1) = 5, is highly significant—but what does it mean? Before you even try to answer that question, you need to recognize that you have again run into the old problem of multiple comparisons. You've done three separate tests on the same set of data, just divided up in different ways, and two of them yielded "significant" values. But "significant" at the .05 level means that this single value would occur only 5 times in a hundred just by chance. Two results that were significant at α = .05—does that mean that either might occur just by chance once in 10 times? With multiple comparisons, the likelihood of a Type II error is unknown.

In the example of the two teachers, you are pretty safe in concluding that the differences you analyzed in that last χ^2 are significant, because the value of χ^2 far exceeds the level needed for significance even at the .01 level. What you have tested is essentially an interaction effect, similar to the interaction effects we worked with in the analysis of variance. And, as with those interactions, the best way I know to understand what's happening is to draw a graph. Since the "improved" and the "unimproved" frequencies will just be mirror images of each other, we only need to graph one of them (see Figure 9–1 on p. 127).

Now we can see the relationships much more clearly. Method B was better than method A for both Mrs. Pick and Mr. Dunk. But Mr. Dunk's students did best of all with method C, while for Mrs. Pick, method C was a disaster.

Generally, studies utilizing chi square will require a relatively large number of subjects. Many statisticians recommend a certain minimum *expected* frequency (f_e) per cell. A very conservative rule of thumb is that f_e must always be equal to or greater than 5. When you don't meet this requirement, the values of χ^2_{crit} in the table won't apply to your data, and so you won't know whether or not your is χ^2_{obt} is significantly different from chance.

THE MANN-WHITNEY *U* TEST

Not infrequently, researchers find themselves collecting data in the form of ranks rather than scores: We can say whether a particular person did better/more/longer than another, but not *how much* better/more/longer. The members of the sample can be put in rank order, from top to bottom, but can't be given actual score values. Parametric tests should not be used with ranked

Table 9–1 Calculation of a $6 \times 2\ \chi^2$

	Mrs. Pick			Mr. Dunk			Totals
	Method A	Method B	Method C	Method A	Method B	Method C	
Improved	$f_o = 6$ $f_e = 6.7$	$f_o = 10$ $f_e = 6.7$	$f_o = 2$ $f_e = 6.7$	$f_o = 4$ $f_e = 6.7$	$f_o = 8$ $f_e = 6.7$	$f_o = 10$ $f_e = 6.7$	40
Not improved	$f_o = 4$ $f_e = 3.3$	$f_o = 0$ $f_e = 3.3$	$f_o = 8$ $f_e = 3.3$	$f_o = 6$ $f_e = 3.3$	$f_o = 2$ $f_e = 3.3$	$f_o = 0$ $f_e = 3.3$	20
Totals	10	10	10	10	10	10	60

$\chi^2 = .07 + 1.63 + 3.30 + 1.09 + .25 + 1.63 + .15 + 3.3 + 6.69 + 2.21 + .51 + 3.3 = 24.13$

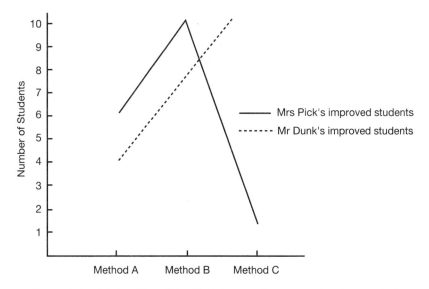

Figure 9–1.   Mr. Dunk's and Mrs. Pick's improved students, using three methods of teaching.

information like this; parametrics require that each score be a direct measurement of the subject, rather than just an indication of where that subject stands relative to the others. To determine whether two groups of ranked data are significantly different from each other, we need to use a nonparametric technique. One of the most commonly used of these is the Mann-Whitney *U* test.

I'll use an example to show you how the *U* test works. A teacher was asked to rank his second-grade students in terms of their social skills, and he provided the following information:

Judith	1	(highest skill level)
Sam	2	
Kenny	3	
Lester	4	
Brian	5	
Marilyn	6	
Loice	7	
Elaine	8	
Holly	9	
Hope	10	
Grant	11	
Bobby	12	
Toni	13	
Meredith	14	
Wyatt	15	(lowest skill level)

Our researcher is interested in possible social skill differences between children who change schools versus children who stay in the same school. Of this class, seven children had transferred from other school districts: Lester, Elaine, Holly, Grant, Bobby, Meredith, and Wyatt.

The null hypothesis here is that the rankings of the transferred children are not significantly different from those of the nontransferred children, H_0: R_{trans} = $R_{nontrans}$. To test this hypothesis, we first divide the total class into transferred and nontransferred groups.

Nontransferred		Transferred	
Name	Rank	Name	Rank
Judith	1	Lester	4
Sam	2	Elaine	8
Kenny	3	Holly	9
Brian	5	Grant	11
Marilyn	6	Bobby	12
Loice	7	Meredith	14
Hope	10	Wyatt	15
Toni	13		
Sum of Ranks	47		73

Notice that we kept the ranks that were given when the children were in a single sample. If we had started out with two separate groups, we would have to combine them and assign ranks for the combined sample. Then we would re-separate them into their original groups, keeping track of each child's combined-group rank.

Next, choose one of the two groups (it doesn't matter which one) and add up its ranks; then plug that sum into the formula for U:

$$U_1 = N_1 N_2 + \frac{N_1(N_1 + 1)}{2} - T_1$$

where N_1, N_2 = the numbers of people in each group
         T_1 = the total of the ranks for the group you've chosen

Just for practice, let's compute the value of U for both of groups:

$$U_1 = (8)(7) + \frac{(8)(9)}{2} - 47 = 45$$

$$U_2 = (8)(7) + \frac{(7)(8)}{2} - 73 = 11$$

You will probably not be surprised to learn that we are going to compare our obtained value of *U* with a U_{crit} that we'll look up in a table. But which of our *U*'s do we use (*U*'s use? use *U*'s? forget it . . .)? We use the smaller of the two. If we don't want to compute both of them directly, we can find the value of the smaller by

$$U_2 = N_1 N_2 - U_1$$
$$= (8)(7) - 45 = 56 - 45 = 11$$

And this also provides us with a handy check of our arithmetic.

We use the smaller value of *U* because with the Mann-Whitney test, unlike the other statistical tests you've learned, a *smaller* obtained value is more likely to be significant. You use the table in Appendix I to find out if your obtained value of *U* is small enough to indicate that the two groups of children are more different from each other than would be expected by chance alone.

There are a number of different ways to organize a table of Mann-Whitney *U* critical values, none of which is completely satisfactory; I've chosen the one that seems easiest to use. But it's different from the other tables you've seen in this book, in three important ways:

1. It's really a series of tables, one for each possible value of N_2 (the size of the larger group). So you need to be sure you're entering the right subtable.
2. The body of the table contains the probability of obtaining a given *U* value just by chance.
3. It contains one-tailed values; that is, the values are appropriate only when you have been able to predict ahead of time which group will be ranked higher. If you haven't made a one-tailed prediction, you will need to double the probability values in the body of the table.

For our example, we'll want the subtable for $N_2 = 8$. Read across the top to find the column for the size of the other group ($N_1 = 7$); when you've found it, follow down to the row for the value of *U* that we calculated, *U* = 11. The probability of obtaining a value of *U* this small just by chance is only .027. Can we reject H_0 at the .05 level? We could if we were doing a one-tailed test. But we didn't predict ahead of time which group of children would do better, and so we must use a two-tailed test. Twice .027 is .054; we cannot reject the null hypothesis at the .05 level.

What if one of our groups has an *N* of more than 8? With larger groups, *U* converts to *z*, and we look in the normal-curve table for significance levels. Simply plug the smaller value of *U* into the formula

$$z = \frac{U_1 - \dfrac{(N_1)(N_2)}{2}}{\sigma_U}$$

where

$$\sigma_U = \sqrt{\frac{(N_1)(N_2)(N_1 + N_2 + 1)}{12}}$$

This is another one that looks hard, but isn't. Imagine, for instance, that you have two groups with N of 7 and 9, respectively. You've calculated that the value of the smaller $U = 15$.

$$\sigma_U = \sqrt{\frac{(7)(9)(17)}{12}} = \sqrt{\frac{1071}{12}} = \sqrt{89.25} = 9.45$$

and

$$z = \frac{15 - \left[\frac{(7)(9)}{2}\right]}{9.45} = \frac{15 - 31.5}{9.45} = -1.75$$

Looking in Appendix C, we find that a z of -1.7 or less, *or of* 1.7 *or more* (remember, since we didn't specify a predicted direction of difference, we must do a two-tailed test), will occur only $.0446 + .0446$ or $.0892$ of the time just by chance. Since $.0892 > .05$, we cannot reject H_0.

THE SPEARMAN CORRELATION FOR RANKED DATA

You have now been introduced to nonparametric techniques that allow you to test for differences between groups when your data are in the form of categories (chi square) and ranks (U test). The last nonparametric technique we will discuss is also used with ranked data, but it allows us to look directly at the degree to which two variables are related. It's called the Spearman correlation for ranked data, symbolized by r_S.

Remember when, a long time ago, we talked about correlations and learned to compute the value of r? That correlation coefficient, r, gave us a measure of the amount of relationship between two variables. But r, like all the parametric statistics, is based on the assumptions that the measurements within each group are independent of each other. It follows that r would be inappropriate to use with ranked data, since ranks are neither quantitative measurements nor independent. So what do you do when the variables you want to know about come in the form of rankings? Enter the Spearman correlation for ranked data, r_S.

Like r, r_S can range between -1.00 and $+1.00$. Also, like r, values of r_S near zero indicate little relationship between the two variables; values close to

−1.00 or 1.00 indicate a near-perfect relationship. And finally, like r, it is possible to determine whether an obtained r_S is large enough to reject the null hypothesis (i.e., that the variables are not related).

Our example: A researcher suspects that teachers tend to believe that physically attractive students have greater ability than less attractive students. To test this theory, the researcher selects 10 third-grade students (he's working on a very limited budget), takes their pictures, and has a panel of judges rank them according to physical attractiveness. He then asks their teacher to rank the same 10 students according to academic ability. Here is what he found:

Student	Ranking by Appearance	Ranking by Ability	D	D^2
Brad	1	2	−1	1
Homer	2	1	1	1
Lisa	3	8	−5	25
Danielle	4	3	1	1
Karin	5	6	−1	1
Michelle	6	4	2	4
Ernie	7	7	0	0
Kiko	8	5	3	9
Starburst	9	10	−1	1
Jane	10	9	1	1

Notice that we start with the students arranged in the order of their appearance rankings, from lowest ranking to highest. When we look at the ability rankings, things have shifted a bit; most noticeably, the student who was originally ranked third is now number 8. Nevertheless, the sets of rankings look awfully similar. Just how similar are they? We can compute r_S using the following formula:

$$r_S = 1 - \frac{6\Sigma D^2}{- n(n^2 - 1)}$$

where
D = the difference between each pair of ranks
D^2 = the square of those differences
n = the number of pairs of rankings

For our data,

$$r_S = 1 - \frac{(6)(44)}{10(100 - 1)} = 1 - \frac{264}{990} = 1 - .27 = .73$$

Although r_S is not an exact analog to r, we can still evaluate it in roughly the same way. A correlation of .73 seems quite respectable, whether it is an r or an r_S. But appearances can sometimes be deceiving. The "respectability" of a value of r or r_S depends on how likely it was to have happened just by chance, and that in turn depends on how many pairs of values have been considered (since smaller numbers of measurements can often produce high correlations just by chance). Appendix J gives the critical values for r_S. In this table, n again refers to the number of pairs. With $n = 10$ and $\alpha = .05$, any value of r_S greater than .564 is significant and allows us to reject the null hypothesis. We conclude that our original impression was correct, that rankings of attractiveness and ability are more closely related than would be expected by chance alone.

A BIT MORE

This chapter has been a sort of grab bag, a description of three tools for dealing with data that can't be handled by parametric techniques. There are lots more—three of them are just a teaser to whet your appetite! It's safe to say that a nonparametric test exists, or can be cobbled to fit, virtually any research situation. Additionally, nonparametric tests tend to have a relatively simple structure, to be based on less complex sets of principles and assumptions than their parametric brethren. For this reason, if you can't find a ready-made nonparametric test that fits your situation, a competent statistician can probably design one for you without much trouble.

At this point, you may be asking, "So why don't we always use nonparametrics? Why bother with parametric tests at all?" The answer is simple: Parametric tests are more powerful than nonparametrics. When the data allow, we prefer to use parametrics because they are less likely to invite a Type II error. Another way of saying this is that parametric tests let us claim significance more easily; they are less likely to miss significant relationships when such relationships are present. However, using a parametric test with data that don't meet parametric assumptions can cause even more problems—can result in Type I error—and we can't even estimate the likelihood of a Type I error under these circumstances. That's when we need the nonparametrics. Not only are they, by and large, easier to compute, but they fill a much needed spot in our statistical repertoire.

PROBLEMS

1. To explore differences in seating preferences between male and female college students, you count who is sitting where in a large introductory English class.

	Males	Females
Front part of the room	12	26
Back part of the room	35	20

Do a χ^2 test to determine if the differences are significant; use $\alpha = .05$.

2. Here's the one I promised you back on p. 122. A researcher randomly selects a sample of college students majoring in physics, chemistry, psychology, P.E., or English lit. He notes each student's major subject, and also whether that student is a blonde, a brunette, or a redhead. The data are as follows:

	Physics	Chem	Psych	P.E.	English	Total
Blonde	8	10	20	4	10	52
Brunette	10	8	30	3	10	61
Redhead	5	3	10	14	10	42
Totals	23	21	60	21	30	155

Can the researcher conclude that the relationship between major and hair color is greater than would be expected by chance alone?

3. You randomly selected 10 men and 10 women from a large college class, mixed up their names, and asked the professor to put them in order in terms of attentiveness. After some grumbling, the professor agreed; the next week, he arranged the names as follows (most attentive first):

1. Ann	6. Karen	11. Brad	16. Bruce
2. Sue	7. Darren	12. Jane	17. Ned
3. George	8. Christopher	13. Claire	18. Elaine
4. Mary	9. Emily	14. Harry	19. Rudy
5. Sam	10. Marie	15. Lucy	20. Alex

Why must you use a nonparametric test to determine whether there is a significant difference between the men and the women in terms of attentiveness? What test will you use? (You know what's coming. . . .) Do it!

4. You learn that these same 20 students are also taking a beginning math class. Is there a relationship between attentiveness level in the two classes? You ask the math professor to do the same kind of ranking as was done in the English class, and the data look like this:

1. Ann	6. Darren	11. Jane	16. Emily
2. Alex	7. Bruce	12. Karen	17. Harry
3. Brad	8. George	13. Lucy	18. Ned
4. Christopher	9. Elaine	14. Claire	19. Sam
5. Marie	10. Sue	15. Mary	20. Rudy

What is the correlation between the two sets of rankings? Is the relationship between behavior in the two classes significant?

5. The conductor of a small community orchestra thought he was noticing a pattern in arrival times for rehearsal: The women musicians seemed, on the average, to arrive earlier than the men. To check out this hypothesis, she asked the musicians to sign in as soon as they arrived at one of the rehearsals, and this is what the sign-in sheet looked like: Gloria, Enrico, Florence, Tomas, Sylvia, Sara, Kathryn, Henry, Amos, Charles, Curtis, Bradley, Phyllis, Elmer, and Ed. Does this list support his hypothesis?

6. A publisher is interested in the relationship between how much a textbook is used and how attractive its illustrations are. He has a group of 11th-grade students estimate how much they used their textbooks, and calculates overall rankings of textbook use. He also asks a panel of judges to rank the same textbooks in order of attractiveness of illustrations.

Here's what he found (low numbers indicate a favorable ranking):

Book	Usage Ranking	Illustration Ranking
Computing and You	1	7
History of Western Civilization	2	2
Trigonometry	3	8
World Literature	4	1
U.S. Government	5	6
Communication in Groups	6	3
Write On!	7	4
Personal Health	8	5

What can he conclude?

7. When I was a kid, the little farming community I lived in had a one-room grade school. We had no athletic teams to support, but we (apparently) needed something to argue about, so we became partisans of one or another brand of farm equipment then in use—even the "town kids" chose sides. Looking back on it now, I have a hunch that the townies differed from the farm kids (who actually used this stuff) in their choices. If I could go back and collect the data, and if it looked like the following table, would it bear out my hunch?

	Farmall	John Deere	Case	Totals
Farm Kids	4	7	1	12
Town Kids	6	2	2	10
Totals	10	9	3	22

8. As a demonstration of randomness, a math teacher put 10 black and 10 white beans in a jar, shook them up, and then had a blindfolded student draw them out one at a time. The beans were drawn in the following order: W, B, B, B, B, W, W, W, B, W, B, B, W, W, B, B, W, W, B, W. He assigned each bean a number according to the order in which it was drawn, and then divided them into a group of black and a group of white beans. Then he did a Mann-Whitney U test to determine whether the beans were drawn in an order that was other than random. What result did the test yield?

9. At O-Y-Didicum Summer Camp, cabins were rated at the beginning of each week for general neatness. One of the counselors, who happened to be interested in statistics, decided to compare a set of these ratings with the camping experience of the campers. After reranking the cabins in terms of camping experience, the data looked like this:

Cabin	Neatness Ranking	Experience Ranking
Jays	1	6
Hawks	2	5
Buzzards	3	7
Eagles	4	3
Robins	5	4
Ducks	6	1
Swans	7	2

What can the counselor conclude about the relationship between neatness and participation?

10. The research committee of the Tight Tummy Club decided to find out if dessert choices are related to marital status. At their annual banquet, they kept track of who ordered what for dessert; they then used club registration information to find out people's marital status. Their final data were as follows:

	Single	Married	Divorced	Widowed	Totals
Pie	3	5	4	2	14
Cake	1	4	2	3	10
Ice cream	4	2	2	1	9
Fresh fruit	12	1	10	4	27
Totals	20	12	18	10	60

Do these data support the hypothesis that dessert choice and marital status are related?

10

Postscript

Well, you did it! You got all the way through this book! Whether you realize it or not, this means that you have covered a great deal of material, learned (probably) quite a bit more than you think you did, and are now able to do—or at least understand—most of the statistics that you will need for a large percentage of the research that you may become involved with. No small accomplishment!

In case you are inclined to discount what you've done, let's review it: This will not only give you further ammunition for self-congratulation, but will also help to consolidate all the information you've been taking in.

Statistics, as a field of study, can be divided into two (not so equal) parts, descriptive and inferential. You've been introduced to both. First, the descriptive.

You've learned how to describe sets of data in terms of graphs (histograms, frequency polygons, cumulative frequency polygons), of middleness (mean, median, mode), and of spread (range, variance, standard deviation). You've learned that a distribution—and even that word was probably somewhat unfamiliar when you began all this—can be symmetrical or skewed, and you've learned what happens to the middleness measures when you skew a distribution.

You've also learned a lot about how two distributions—two sets of data—can be related. You learned how to compute a correlation coefficient and what a correlation coefficient means. You learned what a scatter plot is and how the

general shape of a scatter plot relates to the value of r. You learned how to use something called a regression equation to predict a score on one variable, based on an individual's performance on a related variable, and to use something called the standard error of the estimate to tell you how much "play" there is in that prediction. You learned how to compute a correlation coefficient on data comprised of ranks instead of measurements. You even learned how to calculate the relationship among more than two variables and to partial out the influence of one variable in order to get a clearer idea about the relationship between two others.

And then along came inferential statistics: using a set of observable information to make inferences about larger groups that can't be observed. You started this section by absorbing a lot of general ideas and principles. You learned about probability, and how it relates to sampling. You learned why it's important that a sample be unbiased, and how to use random-sampling techniques to get an unbiased sample. You learned what a null hypothesis is, why we need to use a null hypothesis, and what kinds of error are associated with mistakenly rejecting or failing to reject the null hypothesis. You learned that it's a great big No-No to talk about "accepting" the null hypothesis, and why! You learned what it means for a result to be statistically significant, and you got acquainted with a friendly Greek named α, as well as something called "magnitude of effect."

Then you moved into actual statistical tests, starting with the t test. Using the t test, you now know how to decide whether two groups are significantly different from each other, and you know that correlated or matched groups have to be treated differently from independent groups. You also know what a one-tailed test and a two-tailed test are and when it's appropriate to use each kind.

As if looking at two groups weren't enough, you moved right in to explore comparisons among three or more groups. You learned about the workhorse of social science statistics, the analysis of variance. Although you didn't learn to do all the calculations, you learned that the principles used in dealing with the one-way ANOVA are the basis for much more complicated ANOVA designs. And you learned how to do a post-hoc test, to look at those three or more groups in even more detail.

Finally, you rummaged around in a bag of tricks designed to allow you to work with data that don't fit the rules for the other techniques that you've learned. You learned a fine, important sounding new word: *nonparametric*. You learned nonparametric tests that let you examine frequencies and ranked data.

You really have done a lot!

And we haven't even mentioned the single most important, and impressive, thing you've done. Imagine your reaction just a few months ago if someone had handed you the first paragraphs of this chapter and said, "Read this— this is what you will know at the end of this term." The very fact of your being able to think about statistics now without feeling frightened or overwhelmed or nauseous is much more significant than the facts and techniques that you've learned. Because your changed attitude means that you're able to actually use all this stuff, rather than just being intimidated by it. If you can't remember some statistical something now, you can go look it up, instead of giving up. If you can't find out where to look it up, you can ask somebody about it and have a reasonable expectation of understanding their answer.

Moreover, you're ready to move on to the next level: You've poured yourself a good, solid foundation that you can build on, just about as high as you want to go. There is more to statistics than we've been able to cover, of course. There are all the mathematical implications and "pre-plications" (well, what else do you call something that comes before and influences the thing you're interested in?) of the techniques you've learned. There are the fascinating nooks and crannies of those techniques—the sophisticated rules about when to use them, the exceptions to the rules, the suggestions for what to do instead. There are the extensions: applying the basic principles of correlation or regression or ANOVA to larger and more complex designs. And then there are the brand new techniques, things like analysis of covariance, and factor analysis, and multiple regression, and lots and lots of clever nonparametric tricks. Why, you might even learn to *enjoy* this stuff!

But whether you learn to enjoy it or not, whether you go on to more advanced work or just stay with what you now know, whether you actively use your statistics or simply become an informed consumer—whatever you do with it—nobody can change or take away the fact that you did learn it, and you did survive. And it wasn't as bad as you thought it would be—truly, now, was it?

APPENDIX A

Answers to Problems

CHAPTER 1

1. **(a)** $M_A = 5.86$; Md = 6; Mo = 3
   (b) $M_B = 5.9$; Md = 6; Mo = 2
   (c) $M_C = 5.82$; Md = 5; Mo = 3 and 8
   (d) $M_D = 5$; Md = 4; Mo = 4
2. $M = 11.71$
   Md = 11
   Mo = there is none
3. $M = 11.71$
   $$\text{Md} = \frac{10.5 + 11}{2} = \frac{21.5}{2} = 10.75$$
   Mo = 15
   The median is closer to the mean than is the mode.
4. **(a)** $R = 8$; $s^2 = 7.50$; $s = 2.574$
   (b) $R = 80$; $s^2 = 750.00$; $s = 27.39$
   (c) $R = 8$; $s^2 = 7.50$; $s = 2.74$
   (d) $R = .8$; $s^2 = .075$; $s = .27$
   (e) $R = 5$; $s^2 = 3.70$; $s = 1.92$
   (f) Achievement: $R = 10$; $s^2 = 12.80$; $s = 3.58$
   Comprehension: $R = 18$; $s^2 = 51.3$; $s = 7.16$
   (g) $R = 39$; $s^2 = 255.3$; $s = 15.98$
   $R = 25$; $s^2 = 86.97$; $s = 9.33$
   $R = 12$; $s^2 = 16$; $s = 4$
   $R = 20$; $s^2 = 43.75$; $s = 6.61$
   (h) A: $R = 7$; $s^2 = 7.14$; $s = 2.67$
   B: $R = 9$; $s^2 = 10.77$; $s = 3.28$
   C: $R = 10$; $s^2 = 9.96$; $s = 3.16$
   D: $R = 6$; $s^2 = 4.75$; $s = 2.18$

(i) $R = 24$; $s^2 = 56.90$; $s = 7.54$
(j) $R = 19$; $s^2 = 17.96$; $s = 4.24$

CHAPTER 2

1. 50% **2.** 15.87% **3.** 2.28% **4.** .13% **5.** 68.26%
6. 95.44% **7.** 13.59% **8.** 97.72% **9.** 99.87%
10. 400 mg; 100 mg **11.** 4′8″ to 6″ **12.** 15.87%
13. 2 minutes, 32 seconds—and *nobody* can run the mile this fast. The distribution of times isn't normal; the low times bunch together at one end. The estimates we are doing only work for normal distributions.
14. 48%

CHAPTER 3

1. In a distribution with $M_X = 31.27$ and $s = 22.43$
    6 (raw score) = −1.12 (Z score) = 38 (T score)
    18 (raw score) = −.60 (Z score) = 44 (T score)
    47 (raw score) = +.70 (Z score) = 57 (T score)
    78 (raw score) = +2.08 (Z score) = 71 (T score)
Since the scores are not normally distributed, the table of values for a normal curve can't be used to convert these scores to percentiles.
2. 500 (raw score) = 0 (Z score) = 50 (T score) = 50th percentile
    510 (raw score) = .1 (Z score) = 51 (T score) = 54th percentile
    450 (raw score) = −.5 (Z score) = 45 (T score) = 31st percentile
    460 (raw score) = −.4 (Z score) = 46 (T score) = 34th percentile
    650 (raw score) = 1.5 (Z score) = 65 (T score) = 93rd percentile
    660 (raw score) = 1.6 (Z score) = 66 (T score) = 95th percentile

3.

Name	Raw Score	Z score	T Score	Percentile Rank
Jack	73	+ .2	52	58
Jill	52	−1.2	38	11.5
James	85	+1.0	60	84
John	59	− .7	42	23

4. (a)

Raw score	20
Z score	0
T score	50
percentile	50

(b)

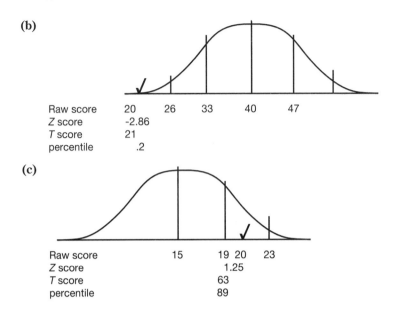

Raw score	20	26	33	40	47
Z score	-2.86				
T score	21				
percentile	.2				

(c)

Raw score		15	19 20	23
Z score			1.25	
T score			63	
percentile			89	

CHAPTER 4

1. **(a)** significant; **(b)** significant; **(c)** significant; **(d)** n.s. (not significant); **(e)** n.s.

2. With $n = 10$ and df = 8, and $r_{\text{crit}_{\alpha = .05}} = .55$,

$$r_{XY} = -.61; \text{ n.s.; coefficient of determination} = .37$$

$$r_{XZ} = .88; \text{ significant; coefficient of determination} = .77$$

$$r_{YZ} = -.66; \text{ significant; coefficient of determination} = .44$$

The correlation between I.Q. and Exam Scores (.77) is high enough to have some predictive value, since I.Q. accounts for more than 3/4 of the variability in exam scores. Whether the other two would have usefulness depends on the specific thing you want to do with them, and what other measures might be available.

3. For height and weight, $r = .80$ and the coefficient of determination = .64. Significant at the .02 level.

For height and shoe size, $r = .76$ and the coefficient of determination = .58. Significant at the .05 level.

For height and ring size, $r = .65$ and the coefficient of determination = .42. Not significant.

For weight and shoe size, $r = .94$ and the coefficient of determination = .88. Significant.

For weight and ring size, $r = .87$ and the coefficient of determination = .76. Significant.

For shoe size and ring size, $r = .79$ and the coefficient of determination = .62. Significant.

CHAPTER 5

1. **(a)** 99.51 roaches; **(b)** 5.5 packets of roach killer
2. **(a)** 10.63 months; **(b)** 15.05 months
3. **(a)** $s_{est} = .96$; **(b)** $s_{est} = 3.48$; **(c)** Jake will talk between 11.57 and 18.53 months
4. $r_{Ij.salary} = .19$
5. **(a)** $b = 12.86$; **(b)** $b = .01$; **(c)** $b = 2.25$; **(d)** $b = .26$
6. **(a)** $R = .77$; **(b)** $R = .60$; **(c)** $R = .79$
7. **(a)** $r_{f,wt.water} = .74$; **(b)** $r_{wt,water.f} = -.24$; **(c)** $r_{f,water.wt} = .65$; **(d)** that when the effects of food are partialled out, weight and water are negatively related—the more water consumed, the lower the weight.

CHAPTER 6

1. **(a)** M and s are sample values, and μ and σ are population values
   (b) The value of s, like the value of s^2, is obtained from a formula that includes a correction for bias. If this correction weren't in the formula, the obtained value would tend to be too small. M doesn't need such a correction because it is already an unbiased estimate. μ and σ don't need correction because they are themselves population values.
2. **(a)** Not random because all members of the population didn't have an equal chance of being included (kids who were ill or stayed inside during recess couldn't be chosen).
   (b) Not random because selection wasn't independent (once a given child was selected, anyone else with that last name was included, too).
   (c) Not random, because kids who had very thick files (which usually means they caused some sort of problem) would have a better chance of being selected).
   (d) (Okay, okay, so it was too easy. . . .) Random.
3. **(a)** $\mu_{left} = \mu_{right}$
   (b) $\mu_{left\text{-}handed\ people} \leq \mu_{right\text{-}handed\ people}$
   (c) $\mu_{20-25} \geq \mu_{15-20}$
   (d) $\mu_{RN} = \mu_{LPN}$;
   (e) $\mu_{kennel} = \mu_{home}$
4. **(a)** Type I; **(b)** Type II; **(c)** Type I;
   (d) Neither—but even more wrong! You can never accept the null hypothesis on the basis of collected data; you can only fail to reject it.
   (e) Type II

5. (a) If we performed this experiment over and over and if the null hypothesis were true, we could expect to get these results just by chance only 5 times out of 100.

  (b) We use the .01 level when we need to be *very* sure that we are not making a Type I error. The drawback is that as we reduce the probability of a Type I error, the likelihood of a Type II error goes up.

CHAPTER 7

1. (a) H_0: $\mu_{Men} = \mu_{Women}$
    t test for independent samples; two-tailed test
    $\sigma_p^2 = 3.85$; $\sigma_{M_{men} - M_{Women}} = 1.24$
    $t_{obt} = 1.77$; df = 8; $t_{crit} = 2.306$; do not reject H_0
  (b) H_0: $\mu_{Men} = \mu_{Women}$
    t test for nonindependent samples; two-tailed test
    $t_{obt} = 2.63$; df = 4; $t_{crit} = 2.776$; do not reject H_0

2. H_0: $\mu_{Adopted} \leq \mu_{Foster}$
    t test for nonindependent samples; one-tailed test
    $t_{obt} = .394$; df = 5; $t_{crit} = 2.571$; do not reject H_0

3. (a) H_0: $\mu_2 = \mu_3$
    t test for independent samples; two-tailed test
    $t_{obt} = 2.12$; df = 9; $t_{crit} = 2.262$; do not reject H_0
  (b) H_0: $\mu_1 = \mu_2$
    t test for independent samples; two-tailed test
    $t_{obt} = 4.30$; df = 8; $t_{crit} = 2.306$; reject H_0
  (c) H_0: $\mu_1 \leq \mu_2$
    t test for independent samples; one-tailed test
    $t_{obt} = 8.2$; df = 7; $t_{crit} = 1.895$; reject H_0

4. H_0: $\mu_{Pre} \geq \mu_{Post}$
    t test for nonindependent samples; one-tailed test
    $t_{obt} = .55$; df = 11; $t_{crit} = 1.796$; do not reject H_0

5. H_0: $\mu_{Weekdays} \geq \mu_{Weekends}$
    t test for independent samples; two-tailed test
    $t_{obt} = .43$; df = 18; $t_{crit} = 1.734$; do not reject H_0

6. H_0: $\mu_{Morning} = \mu_{Evening}$
    t test for nonindependent samples; two-tailed test
    $t_{obt} = .42$; df = 14; $t_{crit} = 2.145$; do not reject H_0

7. H_0: $\mu_{Males} \leq \mu_{Females}$
    t test for independent samples; one-tailed test
    $t_{obt} = 1.22$; df = 13; $t_{crit} = 1.771$; do not reject H_0
    (For this problem, I added the morning and evening values for each dog and used the total food per day as my data.)

8. H_0: $\mu_{Major chosen} = \mu_{Major not chosen}$
    t test for independent samples; two-tailed test
    $t_{obt} = 2.27$; df = 18; $t_{crit} = 2.101$; reject H_0

CHAPTER 8

1. (I've given you some intermediate steps here, in case you got confused.) Since F_{crit} for $\alpha = .05$, with 2 and 15 df, is 3.68, the obtained value of F does not reach the critical value and we cannot reject H_0.

	Blondes	Brunettes	Redheads	
n	6	6	6	$N_T = 18$
ΣX	31	22	17	$\Sigma X_T = 70$

$$I = \frac{(\Sigma X_T)^2}{N_T} = \frac{70^2}{18} = 272.22$$

ΣX_2	199	88	71	$II = 358$
$\dfrac{(\Sigma X)^2}{N}$	160.17	80.67	48.17	$III = 289.01$
M_X	5.17	3.67	2.83	

Source	df	Sums of Squares	Mean Square	F
Between	2	16.79	8.4	1.83
Within	15	68.99	4.6	

2. The null hypothesis can be rejected at the .01 level; the differences among the groups are significant ($p < .01$). Scheffé's test, using C_{crit} of 2.63 (for $\alpha = .05$) indicates no significant differences between bus drivers and professors ($C < 1$), but significant differences between bus drivers and U.S. presidents ($C = 3.24$) and between college professors and U.S. presidents ($C = 3.03$).

3. The ANOVA summary table looks like this:

Source of Variation	Degrees of Freedom (df)	Sum of Squares	Mean Square	F
Between groups	3	3050.31	1016.77	4.37
Within groups	26	6053.16	232.81	
Total	29	9103.47		

An F_{obs} of 4.37 exceeds the .05 level of significance ($F_{crit} = 2.98$), and the null hypothesis is rejected. The apparent differences among the group means were, in fact, greater than could have been expected just by chance. However, only the "no music" group and the "trumpet" groups are significantly different from each other ($C_{crit} = 2.99$; $C_{obs} = 2.94$).

4. The librarian has apparently done an ANOVA, since we can see part of his ANOVA summary table. With 2 df between groups and 344 df within groups, all his F values are significant at the .01 level. Graduate students check out significantly more books than undergrads, and psych majors check out more books than math majors.

   We can't tell about the math major to education major comparison or the education major to psych major comparison, without post-hoc testing (which we can't do, because we don't know the values of N for any of the groups). As for the interaction, here's a graph:

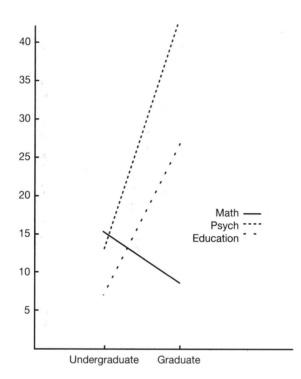

The education and psych majors read lots more books as grads than as undergrads, but the math majors read fewer.

CHAPTER 9

1. $\chi^2 = 9.2$. χ^2_{crit} with $\alpha = .05$ and 1 df is 3.84; the relationship between seating and gender is significant.

2. $\chi^2 = 24.5$. χ^2_{crit} with $\alpha = .01$ and 8 df is 20.09; the relationship between hair color and major is significant.

3. A nonparametric test, the Mann-Whitney, must be used because the data are rankings, not independent measurements. $U_1 = 35$; $N_1 = N_2 = 10$; $z = 1.13$; H_0 cannot be rejected.

4. $r_S = .17$; the relationship is not significantly different from what might be expected to occur by chance alone.

5. $U_{Females} = 40$; $U_{Males} = 14$; $z = 1.53$. The probability of a z this far (or farther) from the mean is $.06 + .06 = .12$; the conductor's hypothesis is not supported.

6. $r_S = -.17$, with $n = 8$. The data do not support the hypothesis that there is a relationship between textbook usage and textbook attractiveness.

7. $\chi^2 = 3.36$; df = 2; my hunch is not supported at a statistically significant level.

8. A U test for the two groups yields $U_1 = 41$; $U_2 = 59$; $z = .68$. A value of z this large or larger would be expected to occur almost exactly half the time. (That's an especially nice result, since I got the original data from a random-number table!)

9. $r_S = -.82$ with $n = 7$. This exceeds the critical value of .786. There is a significant negative relationship between neatness and experience.

10. $\chi^2 = 13.21$. χ^2_{crit} with $\alpha = .05$ and 9 df is 16.92; the hypothesis of no differences among the groups cannot be rejected. In this case, however, it couldn't be rejected no matter how large X^2 was, because the committee violated one of the assumptions of the chi-square test: Only 3 of the 16 cells had an expected frequency of 5 or more.

APPENDIX B

Basic Math Review

Being terrified of math didn't just happen to you overnight. Chances are that you have been having bad experiences with math for many years. Most people who have these sorts of bad experiences have not learned some of the basic rules for working with numbers. Because they don't know the rules, the problems don't make sense—sort of like trying to play baseball without knowing the difference between a ball and a strike, or what it means to steal a base.

When the problems don't make sense, but everyone else seems to understand them, we are likely to decide that there's something wrong with us. We'll just never be able to do it and, besides, we hate math anyhow. So we tune out, turn off—and the bad situation gets worse.

This book is designed to help you get past that kind of head space. The appendix you're starting now will give you a chance to review the rules that you need in order to play with numbers and come up with the same answers as everyone else. Some of the material will be very familiar to you; other parts may seem completely new. Let me make a few suggestions about how to use this appendix:

1. If, after a couple of pages or so, you're completely bored and have found nothing you don't already know, just skim through the rest and get on with Chapter 1.
2. If it seems familiar, but you're still a little shaky, go to the problems at the end of each section and work them through. That will tell you which parts you need to spend more time on.
3. If much of it feels new to you—take your time with it! Most of us "word people" absorb numerical information and ideas quite slowly and need lots of practice before it really sinks in and becomes part of our way of thinking. Give it a chance. Learning the rules now will allow you to understand the rest of the book in a way that will probably surprise you.

I've divided the basic rules into six sections: (1) positive and negative numbers, (2) fractions and percents, (3) roots and exponents, (4) order of computation, (5) summation, and (6) equations.

POSITIVE AND NEGATIVE NUMBERS

In a perfect and orderly world, all numbers would be positive (they'd be whole, too—no fractions or decimals). But the world isn't perfect, and negative numbers have to be dealt with. Actually, they're not so bad; you just have to show them who's boss.

If you're a visually oriented person, it may help to think of numbers as standing for locations on a straight line, with zero as your starting point. The number 2 is 2 steps to the right from zero; add 4 more steps and you're 6 steps out, and so on. The negative numbers are just steps in the opposite direction. If I'm 6 positive steps (6 to the right) away from zero, and I add −4 to that, I take 4 steps back toward zero; now I'm at 2.

If you're not visually oriented, the last paragraph may confuse you; if so, just ignore it and follow the rules I'm about to give you.

Rule 1.   If a number or an expression is written without a sign, it's positive.

$$+ 2 = 2 \qquad + x = x$$

Rule 2.   When adding numbers of the same sign, add them up and prefix them with the same sign as the individual numbers had.

$$+3 + (+5) = +8 \qquad 2 + 7 = 9$$

Rule 3.   When summing up a group of numbers with mixed signs, think of the process as having three steps:

1. Add the positive numbers; add the negative numbers as if they were positive.
2. Subtract the smaller sum from the larger sum.
3. Prefix your answer with the sign of the larger sum.

$$5 - 3 + 2 - 1 \rightarrow (5 + 2) \text{ and } (3 + 1) = (7) \text{ and } (4)$$
$$7(\text{larger}) - 4 \text{ (smaller)} = 3$$

The answer is +3 because the positive sum (7) was larger.

$$-2 + 6 - 14 + 3 - 4 \rightarrow (6 + 3) \text{ and } (2 + 14 + 4) = (9) \text{ and } (20)$$
$$20 \text{ (larger)} - 9 \text{ (smaller)} = 11$$

The answer is –11 because the negative sum (20) was larger.

Rule 4.   Subtracting a positive number is the same as adding a negative number; adding a negative number is the same as subtracting a positive number. Subtracting a negative is the same as adding a positive. In other words, two negative signs make a positive sign; a positive and a negative make a negative (you visuals, work it out on the number line).

$$5 - (+3) = 5 + (-3) = 5 - 3 = 2$$
$$7 + (-12) = 7 - (+12) = 7 - 12 = -5$$
$$5 - (-4) = 5 + 4 = 9$$

Rule 5.   When multiplying or dividing two numbers with the same sign, the answer is always *positive*.

$$3 \times 7 = 21 \qquad -8 \cdot -3 = 24 \qquad 12(8) = 96$$

Notice the three different ways of indicating multiplication: an × sign, a "center dot" (·) between the numbers, or no sign at all. Parentheses around an expression just means to treat what's inside as a single number; we'll talk about that more a little later.

$$15 \div 5 = 3 \qquad (-9) \div (-1) = 9 \qquad \frac{-6}{-4} = 1.5$$

Rule 6.   When multiplying or dividing two numbers with different signs, the answer is always *negative*.

$$3 \times -7 = -21 \qquad -8 \cdot 3 = -24 \qquad (12)(-8) = -96$$
$$-15 \div 5 = -3 \qquad (9) \div (-1) = -9 \qquad \frac{-6}{4} = -1.5$$

Rules 5 and 6 aren't as "sensible" as some of the other rules, and the number line won't help you much with them. Just memorize.

Rule 7.   With more than two numbers to be multiplied or divided, just take them pairwise, in order, and follow rules 5 and 6. (The rule for multiplication and division is that if there are an odd number of negative numbers, the answer will be negative; with an even number of negatives, the answer will be positive. If this helps, use it. If not, forget it.)

$$3 \times -2 \times -4 \times 3 = -6 \times -4 \times 3 = 24 \times 3 = 72$$
$$40 \div 2 \div 2 \div -2 = 20 \div 2 \div -2 = 10 \div -2 = -5$$
$$6 \div 3 \times -1 \div 5 = 2 \times -1 \div 5 = -2 \div 5 = -.4$$

Problems[1]

1. $-5 + 4 = ?$ 2. $6 - (-2) = ?$ 3. $-6 - 4 + 2 = ?$

4. $3(-4) = ?$ 5. $3 \cdot 4 = ?$ 6. $(-3)(-4) = ?$

7. $(-3)(+4) = ?$ 8. $(-4)(1)(2)(-3) = ?$ 9. $(-a)(-b)(c)(-d) = ?$

10. $-4 \div -3 = ?$ 11. $(-10)(3) \div 2 = ?$ 12. $(-1)(-1)(-1)(-1) \div (-1) = ?$

FRACTIONS

Rule 1. A fraction is another way of symbolizing division. A fraction means "divide the first (top) expression (the numerator) by the second (bottom) expression (the denominator)." Fractions answer the question, "If I cut (the top number) up into (the bottom number) of equal pieces, how much will be in each piece?"

$$1 \div 2 = .5 \qquad 4 \div 2 = 2 \qquad 4 \div -2 = -2$$

$$\frac{-9}{3} = -3 \qquad \frac{6}{4-1} = 2 \qquad \frac{(13-3)(7+3)}{-3+2} = \frac{(10)(10)}{-1} = -100$$

Rule 2. Dividing any number by 0 is impossible. Think about it. If any problem in this book seems to be asking you to divide by zero, you've made an arithmetic mistake somewhere.

Rule 3. You can turn any expression into a fraction by making the original expression the numerator, and putting a 1 into the denominator.

$$3 = \frac{3}{1} \qquad -6.2 = \frac{-6.2}{1} \qquad 3x + 4 = \frac{3x+4}{1}$$

Rule 4. To multiply fractions, multiply their numerators together and multiply their denominators together.

$$\frac{2}{3} \cdot \frac{1}{2} = \frac{2}{6} = .33 \qquad \frac{1}{5} \cdot 10 = \frac{1}{5} \cdot \frac{10}{1} = \frac{10}{5} = 2 \qquad 3xy \cdot \frac{3}{4} = \frac{3xy}{1} \cdot \frac{3}{4} = \frac{3(3xy)}{4} = \frac{9xy}{4}$$

Rule 5. Multiplying both the numerator and the denominator of a fraction by the same number doesn't change its value.

[1]The answers to all Appendix B problems are given at the end of this appendix.

$$\frac{1}{2} = \frac{2 \cdot 1}{2 \cdot 2} = \frac{2}{4} = \frac{100}{200} = \frac{\left(\dfrac{1}{200}\right) \cdot 100}{\left(\dfrac{1}{200}\right) \cdot 200} = \frac{.5}{1} = .5$$

Rule 6.   To divide by a fraction, invert and multiply. That is, take the fraction you're dividing by (the divisor), switch the denominator and numerator, and then multiply it times the thing into which you're dividing (the dividend).

$$21 \div \frac{3}{5} = \frac{21}{1} \div \frac{3}{5} = \frac{21}{1} \cdot \frac{5}{3} = \frac{105}{3} = 35$$

$$\frac{3x}{4} \div \frac{-1}{3} = \frac{3x}{4} \cdot \frac{3}{-1} = \frac{9x}{-4} = \frac{9}{-4} \cdot \frac{x}{1} = -\frac{9}{4}x$$

(I cheated a little in that last example and used some algebra. If you don't understand it yet, come back to it after you've read the "Equations" section of this appendix.)

Rule 7.   To add or subtract fractions, they must have a common denominator; that is, their denominators must be the same. For example, you can't add 2/3 and 1/5 as they are. You have to change them to equivalent fractions with a common denominator. How? By multiplying the denominators (and, of course, the numerators) by some number that will make the denominators equal. And, of course, you don't have to use the same number for each fraction. Multiply each fraction by the smallest numbers that will make the denominators equal. You may have heard of the "least common denominator": That's what you're looking for. 2/3 = 10/15 and 1/5 = 3/15. Then add or subtract the numerators, leaving the denominator unchanged.

$$\frac{2}{3} + \frac{1}{2} = \frac{2 \cdot 2}{2 \cdot 3} + \frac{3 \cdot 1}{3 \cdot 2} = \frac{4}{6} + \frac{3}{6} = \frac{7}{6} = 1\frac{1}{6}$$

$$\frac{1}{5} + \frac{1}{10} = \frac{2 \cdot 1}{2 \cdot 5} + \frac{1 \cdot 1}{1 \cdot 10} = \frac{2}{10} + \frac{1}{10} = \frac{3}{10}$$

$$\frac{5}{8} - \frac{1}{2} = \frac{1 \cdot 5}{1 \cdot 8} - \frac{4 \cdot 1}{4 \cdot 2} = \frac{5}{8} - \frac{4}{8} = \frac{1}{8}$$

$$\frac{1}{3} + \frac{1}{2} + \frac{3}{4} - \frac{1}{12} = \frac{4}{12} + \frac{6}{12} + \frac{9}{12} - \frac{1}{12} = \frac{18}{12} = 1\frac{6}{12} = 1\frac{1}{2}$$

Problems

1. $\frac{6}{3} = ?$

2. $-4 \div -3 = ?$

3. $\frac{3}{4}(-1) = ?$

4. $\frac{1}{2} \cdot \frac{2}{3} = ?$

5. $5 \cdot \frac{1}{2} \cdot 2 \cdot \frac{6}{3} = ?$

6. $\frac{7}{3} \div \frac{1}{2} = ?$

7. $\frac{1}{2} + \frac{5}{6} = ?$

8. $\frac{7}{3} - \frac{1}{2} = ?$

9. $5 - \frac{8}{2} = ?$

10. $7 + \frac{1}{2} - \frac{1}{3} + \frac{1}{4} - \frac{1}{5} = ?$

DECIMALS AND PERCENTS

Rule 1.   Decimals indicate that the part of the number following the decimal point is a fraction with 10, 100, 1000, and so on, as the denominator. Rather than trying to find words to express the rule, let me just show you:

$$3.2 = 3\frac{2}{10} \qquad 3.25 = 3\frac{25}{100} \qquad 3.257 = 3\frac{257}{1000}$$

and so on. See how it works? Not particularly complicated.

Rule 2.   Some fractions, divided out, produce decimals that go on and on and on. To get rid of unneeded decimal places, we can *round off* a number. Say you have the number 1.41421 and you want to express it with just two decimal places. Should your answer be 1.41 or 1.42? The first step in deciding is to create a new number from the digits left over after you take away the ones you want to keep, with a decimal point in front of it. In our example, we keep 1.41, and the newly created number is .421. Next steps:

(a) If the new decimal number is less than .5, just throw it away; you're done with the rounding-off process.

(b) If the new decimal is .5 or greater, throw it away but increase the last digit in your "kept" number by 1. For example, 1.41684 would round to 1.42.

Rule 3.   Percents are simply fractions of 100 (two-place decimals).

$$45\% = 45/100 = .45 \qquad 1.3\% = 1.3/100 = .013 \qquad 110\% = 110/100 = 1.1$$

Problems

1. Round off the following to two decimal places:

   (a) 3.5741;   (b) 10.1111111;   (c) 90.0054;   (d) 9.0009;   (e) 43.52500

2. Convert the following to percents:

   (a) .75;   (b) .7532;   (c) 1.5;   (d) 2/3;   (e) $1 - .77$

3. 20% of 100 = ?

4. .2 of $100 = ?$

5. $.20(100) = ?$

EXPONENTS AND ROOTS

Rule 1. An exponent is a small number placed slightly higher than and to the right of a number or expression. For example, 3^3 has an exponent of 3; $(x - y)^2$ has an exponent of 2. An exponent tells how many times a number or expression is to be multiplied by itself.

$$5^2 = 5 \cdot 5 = 25 \qquad 10^3 = 10 \cdot 10 \cdot 10 = 1,000 \qquad Y^4 = Y \cdot Y \cdot Y \cdot Y$$

Rule 2. Roots are like the opposite of exponents. You can have square roots (the opposite of an exponent of 2), cube roots (opposite of an exponent of 3), and so on. In statistics, we often use square roots, and seldom any other kind, so I'm just going to talk about square roots here.

Rule 3. The square root of a number is the value that, when multiplied by itself, equals that number. For example, the square root of 9 is 3 $(3 \cdot 3 = 9)$. The instruction to compute a square root (mathematicians call it "extracting" a square root, but I think that has unfortunate associations to wisdom teeth) is a "radical" sign: $\sqrt{}$. You take the square root of everything that's shown under the "roof" of the radical.

$$\sqrt{9} = 3 \quad \sqrt{8100} = 90 \quad \sqrt{36 + 13} = \sqrt{49} = 7 \quad \sqrt{36} + 13 = 6 + 13 = 19$$

When extracting a square root, you have three alternatives:

(a) Use a calculator with a square root button.
(b) Learn how to use a table of squares and square roots.
(c) Find a sixth grader who has just studied square roots in school.

I simply cannot recommend alternative (a) too strongly, given the inconvenience of using tables and the unreliability of sixth graders.

Problems

1. $5^2 = ?$ **2.** $32^2 = ?$ **3.** $3^2 = ?$ **4.** $\sqrt{4^2} = ?$

5. $\sqrt{22547} = ?$ **6.** $\sqrt{14727} = ?$ **7.** $\sqrt{71.234} = ?$ **8.** $\sqrt{.0039} = ?$

ORDER OF COMPUTATION

Rule 1.   When an expression is enclosed in parentheses (like this), treat what's inside like a single number. Do any operations on that expression first, before going on to what's outside the parentheses. With nested parentheses, work from the inside out.

$$4(7 - 2) = 4(5) = 20$$
$$9 \div (-4 + 1) = 9 \div -3 = -3$$
$$12 \times (5 - (6 \times 2)) = 12 \times (5 - 12) = 12 \times -7 = -84$$
$$12 \times (5 - 6) \times 2 = 12 \times (-1) \times 2 = -12 \times 2 = -24$$

With complicated fractions, treat the numerator and the denominator as if each were enclosed in parentheses. In other words, calculate the whole numerator and the whole denominator first, and then divide the numerator by the denominator:

$$\frac{3 + 2}{5 \cdot (7 - 3)} = \frac{5}{5 \cdot 4} = \frac{5}{20} = \frac{1}{4}$$

Rule 2.   If you don't have parentheses to guide you, do all multiplication and division before you add or subtract.

$$5 + 3 \cdot 2 - 4 = 5 + (3 \cdot 2) - 4 = 5 + 6 - 4 = 7$$
$$8 \div 2 + 9 - 1 - (-2) \cdot (-5) - 5 = 4 + 9 - 1 - (+10) - 5 = -3$$

An algebra teacher in North Dakota taught her students a mnemonic to help them remember the correct order of operation: **M**y **D**ear **A**unt **S**ally —> Multiply, Divide, Add, Subtract.

Rule 3.   Exponents and square roots are treated as if they were a single number. That means you square numbers or take square roots first of all—before adding, subtracting, multiplying, or dividing. Maybe we should treat My Dear Aunt Sally like a mean landlord and make the rule be "Roughly Evict My Dear Aunt Sally," in order to get the Roots and Exponents first in line!

Here are some examples of how the order of computation rules work together:

$$5 - (3 \times 4) \times (8 - 2^2)(-3 + 1) \div 3$$

$= 5 - (3 \times 4) \times (8 - 4)(-3 + 1) \div 3$	(*exponent*)
$= 5 - (12) \times (4) \times (-2) \div 3$	(*things inside parentheses*)
$= 5 - 48 \times -2 \div 3$	(*multiply*)
$= 5 - -96 \div 3$	(*multiply again*)
$= 5 - (-32)$	(*divide*)
$= 37$	(*and the addition comes last*)

Did you remember that subtracting a negative number is the same as adding a positive number?

$$2x - 3^2 \div (3 + 2) - \sqrt{25} \cdot 10 + (8 - (3 + 4))$$
$$= 2x - 9 \div (3 + 2) - 5 \cdot 10 + (8 - (3 + 4))$$
$$= 2x - 9 \div 5 - 5 \cdot 10 + (8 - 7)$$
$$= 2x - 9 \div 5 - 5 \cdot 10 + 1$$
$$= 2x - 1.8 - 50 + 1$$
$$= 2x - 50.8$$

Problems

1. $3 + 2 \cdot 4 \div 5 = ?$ **2.** $3 + 2 \cdot (4 \div 5) = ?$ **3.** $(3 \div 2) \cdot 4 \div 5 = ?$

4. $(3 + 2 \cdot 4) \div 5 = ?$ **5.** $\dfrac{\dfrac{1}{2} + \dfrac{7}{4}}{2 + \dfrac{1}{2}} = ?$ **6.** $(1 \div 2 + 7 \div 4) \div (2 + 1 \div 2) = ?$

SUMMATION

A summation sign looks like a goat's footprint: Σ. Its meaning is pretty simple—add up what comes next. Most of the time, "what comes next" is obvious from the context. If you have a variable designated as x, with individual values x_1, x_2, x_3, and so on, then Σx refers to the sum of all those individual values.

Actually, Σx is a shorthand version of $\sum_{i=1}^{N} x$, which means that there are N individual x's. Each x is called x_i, and the values of i run from 1 to N. When $i = 10$ and $N = 50$, x_i would be the tenth in a set of 50 variables; $\sum_{i=1}^{N} x$ would mean to find the sum of all 50 of them. For our purposes, a simple Σx says the same thing and we'll just use that.

There are a few rules that you should know, though, about doing summation. Let's look at an example. Five people take a pop quiz, and their scores are 10, 10, 8, 12, and 10. In other words, $x_1 = 10$, $x_2 = 10$, $x_3 = 8$, $x_4 = 12$, and $x_5 = 10$. $\Sigma x = 50$. What about Σx^2 ? Well, that would be $100 + 100 + 64 + 144 + 100$. $\Sigma x^2 = 508$.

Now, does it make sense to you that $\Sigma x^2 \neq (\Sigma x)^2$? This is a key idea, and it has to do with the order of computation. $(\Sigma x)^2$ is read "sum of x, quantity squared," and the parentheses mean that you add up all the x's first, and square the sum: $(\Sigma x)^2 = (50)^2 = 2500$.

Now, just to make things interesting, we'll throw in another variable. Let y stand for scores on another quiz. $y_1 = 4$, $y_2 = 5$, $y_3 = 6$, $y_4 = 5$, and $y_5 = 4$. $\Sigma y = 24$, $\Sigma y^2 = 118$, and $(\Sigma y)^2 = 576$. And we have some new possibilities:

$$\Sigma x + \Sigma y \quad \Sigma x^2 + \Sigma y^2 \quad \Sigma(x + y) \quad \Sigma(x^2 + y^2) \quad \Sigma(x + y)^2 \quad (\Sigma(x + y))^2$$

See if you can figure out these values on your own, and then we'll go through each one.

$\Sigma x + \Sigma y$ Add up the x values, add up the y values, add them together: 74.

$\Sigma x^2 + \Sigma y^2$ Add up the squared x values, add up the squared y values, add them together: 626.

$\Sigma(x + y)$ Add each x, y pair together, and add up the sums: $14 + 15 + 14 + 17 + 14 = 74$. Yup, $\Sigma x + \Sigma y = \Sigma(x + y)$. Every time.

$\Sigma(x^2 + y^2)$ Square an x and add it to its squared y partner; then add up the sums: $116 + 125 + 100 + 169 + 116 = 626$. $\Sigma(x^2 + y^2) = \Sigma x^2 + \Sigma y^2$.

$\Sigma(x + y)^2$ Add each x, y pair together, square the sums, and add them up: 1102.

$(\Sigma(x + y))^2$ Did those double parentheses throw you? Use them like a road map, to tell you where to go first. Starting from the inside, you add each x, y pair together. Find the sum of the pairs, and last of all square that sum: 5476.

Problems

Use these values to solve the following problems:

x	y
1	5
2	4
3	3
4	2
5	1

1. $\Sigma x + \Sigma y$ 2. $\Sigma x^2 + \Sigma y^2$ 3. $\Sigma(x + y)$ 4. $\Sigma(x^2 + y^2)$ 5. $\Sigma(x + y)^2$ 6. $(\Sigma(x + y))^2$

EQUATIONS

An equation is two expressions joined by an equal sign. Not surprisingly, the value of the part in front of the equal sign is exactly equal to the value of the part after the equal sign.

Rule 1.   Adding or subtracting the same number from each side of an equation is acceptable; the two sides will still be equivalent.

$$5 + 3 = 9 - 1 \qquad 5 + 3 + 5 = 9 - 1 + 5 \qquad 5 + 3 - 5 = 9 - 1 - 5$$
$$8 = 8 \qquad\qquad 13 = 13 \qquad\qquad\qquad 3 = 3$$

$$6 \div 4 + 1 \div 2 = 2 \qquad 6 \div 4 + 1 \div 2 + 5 = 2 + 5 \qquad 6 \div 4 + 1 \div 2 - 5 = 2 - 5$$
$$2 = 2 \qquad\qquad 7 = 7 \qquad\qquad\qquad -3 = -3$$

$$12 - 2 = (2)(5) \qquad 12 - 2 + 5 = (2)(5) + 5 \qquad 12 - 2 - 5 = (2)(5) - 5$$
$$10 = 10 \qquad\qquad 15 = 15 \qquad\qquad\qquad 5 = 5$$

Notice that I've used italics in these examples just to indicate the numbers that we are adding or subtracting. The italics have no mathematical significance; they are just there to clarify what we are doing.

Rule 2.   If you add or subtract a number from one side of an equation, you must add or subtract it from the other side as well if the equation is to *balance,* that is, if both sides are to remain equal.

$$8 - 2 = 3 + 3 \qquad 8 - 2 + 2 = 3 + 3 + 2 \qquad 8 = 8$$
$$2x + 7 = 35 \qquad 2x + 7 - 7 = 35 - 7 \qquad 2x = 28$$

Rule 3.   If you multiply or divide one side of an equation by some number, you must multiply or divide the other side by the same number. You can't multiply or divide just one part of each side; you have to multiply or divide the whole thing.

$$3 + 2 - 1 = 7 - 5 + 2$$

Multiply both sides by 6:

$$6 \cdot (3 + 2 - 1) = 6 \cdot (7 - 5 + 2)$$
$$6 \cdot (4) = 6 \cdot (4)$$
$$24 = 24$$

Look what would happen if you multiplied just one of the numbers on each side by 6:

$$6 \cdot (3) + 2 - 1 = 6 \cdot (7) - 5 + 2$$
$$18 + 2 - 1 = 42 - 5 + 2$$
$$19 = 39$$

Writing out these kinds of rules is a lot like eating hot buttered popcorn: It's hard to know when to quit. And, as with popcorn, it's a lot better to quit too soon than to quit too late; the former leaves you ready for more tomorrow, while the latter can make you swear off the stuff for months.

We could go on and on here, and end up with the outline for a freshman math course, but that's not our purpose. These rules will allow you to do all the math in this book and a great deal of the math in more advanced statistics courses. So let's get going on the fun part!

Problems

1. Use the equation $2 \cdot 3 + 4 = 10$ to answer the following:
    (a) Demonstrate that you can add the same number to each side of the equation without changing its balance.
    (b) Show the same thing using subtraction.
    (c) Multiply both sides of the equation by 2.
    (d) Divide both sides of the equation by 2.
2. Use addition and/or subtraction to solve these equations:
    (a) $5 + x = 3 - 7$
    (b) $x - 3 = 10$
    (c) $x - 3 + 2 = 8 \div 4$
3. Use multiplication and/or division to solve these equations:
    (a) $3x = 12$
    (b) $x \div 4 = 3$
    (c) $2x - 7 = 8$

ANSWERS

Positive and Negative Numbers

1. -1 2. 8 3. -8
4. -12 5. 12 6. 12
7. -12 8. 24 9. $-(abcd)$
10. $4/3$ or 1.33 11. -15 12. -1

Fractions

1. 2 2. $1\frac{1}{3}$
3. $-\frac{3}{4}$ 4. $\frac{2}{6} = \frac{1}{3}$
5. $\frac{5}{1} \cdot \frac{1}{2} \cdot \frac{2}{1} \cdot \frac{6}{3} = \frac{60}{6} = 10$ 6. $\frac{7}{3} \cdot \frac{2}{1} = \frac{14}{3} = 4\frac{2}{3}$
7. $\frac{3}{6} + \frac{5}{6} = \frac{8}{6} = 1\frac{2}{6} = 1\frac{1}{3}$ 8. $\frac{14}{6} - \frac{3}{6} = \frac{11}{6} = 1\frac{5}{6}$
9. $\frac{10}{2} - \frac{8}{2} = \frac{2}{2} = 1$ 10. $7 + \frac{30}{60} - \frac{20}{60} + \frac{15}{60} - \frac{12}{60} = 7\frac{13}{60}$

Decimals and Percents

1. **(a)** 3.57;   **(b)** 10.11;   **(c)** 90.01;   **(d)** 9.00;   **(e)** 43.53
2. **(a)** 75%;   **(b)** 75%;   **(c)** 150%;   **(d)** 67%;   **(e)** 23%
3. 20   **4.** 20   **5.** 20

Exponents and Roots

1. 25   **2.** 1024   **3.** 9   **4.** 4
5. 150.16   **6.** 121.35   **7.** 8.44   **8.** .06

Order of Computation

1. 4.6   **2.** 4.6   **3.** 1.2   **4.** 2.2
5. $\dfrac{9}{4} \div \dfrac{5}{2} = \dfrac{9}{4} \cdot \dfrac{2}{5} = \dfrac{18}{20} = \dfrac{9}{10}$ **6.** *Exactly the same as answer 5*

Summation

1. 30   **2.** 110   **3.** 30   **4.** 110   **5.** 180   **6.** 900

Equations

1. **(a)** $2 \cdot 3 + 4 = 10$ $2 \cdot 3 + 4 + 100 = 10 + 100$ $10 = 10; 110 = 110$
   (b) $2 \cdot 3 + 4 = 10$ $2 \cdot 3 + 4 - 100 = 10 - 100$ $10 = 10; -90 = -90$
   (c) $2 \cdot 3 + 4 = 10$ $2(2 \cdot 3 + 4) = 2(10)$ $10 = 10; 20 = 20$
   (d) $2 \cdot 3 + 4 = 10$ $\dfrac{2 \cdot 3 + 4}{2} = \dfrac{10}{2}$ $\dfrac{10}{2} = \dfrac{10}{2}$

2. **(a)** $5 + x = 3 - 7$ **(b)** $x - 3 = 10$
   $5 - 5 + x = 3 - 7 - 5$ $x - 3 + 3 = 10 + 3$
   $x = -9$ $x = 13$

2. **(c)** $x - 3 + 2 = 8 \div 4$
   $x - 1 = 2$
   $x - 1 + 1 = 2 + 1$
   $x = 3$

3. **(a)** $3x = 12$ **(b)** $\dfrac{x}{4} = 3$

   $\dfrac{3x}{3} = \dfrac{12}{3}$ $4 \cdot \dfrac{x}{4} = 4 \cdot 3$

   $x = 4$ $x = 12$

3. (c) $2x - 7 = 8$

$$\frac{2x - 7}{2} = \frac{8}{2}$$

$$\frac{2x}{2} - \frac{7}{2} = 4$$

$$x - 3.5 = 4$$

$$x - 3.5 + 3.5 = 4 + 3.5$$

$$x = 7.5$$

APPENDIX C

Proportions of Area under the Standard Normal Curve

z	0 z	0 z	z	0 z	0 z	z	0 z	0 z
0.00	.0000	.5000	0.17	.0675	.4325	0.34	.1331	.3669
0.01	.0040	.4960	0.18	.0714	.4286	0.35	.1368	.3632
0.02	.0080	.4920	0.19	.0753	.4247	0.36	.1406	.3594
0.03	.0120	.4880	0.20	.0793	.4207	0.37	.1443	.3557
0.04	.0160	.4840	0.21	.0832	.4168	0.38	.1480	.3520
0.05	.0199	.4801	0.22	.0871	.4129	0.39	.1517	.3483
0.06	.0239	.4761	0.23	.0910	.4090	0.40	.1554	.3446
0.07	.0279	.4721	0.24	.0948	.4052	0.41	.1591	.3409
0.08	.0319	.4681	0.25	.0987	.4013	0.42	.1628	.3372
0.09	.0359	.4641	0.26	.1026	.3974	0.43	.1664	.3336
0.10	.0398	.4602	0.27	.1064	.3936	0.44	.1700	.3300
0.11	.0438	.4562	0.28	.1103	.3897	0.45	.1736	.3264
0.12	.0478	.4522	0.29	.1141	.3859	0.46	.1772	.3228
0.13	.0517	.4483	0.30	.1179	.3821	0.47	.1808	.3192
0.14	.0557	.4443	0.31	.1217	.3783	0.48	.1844	.3156
0.15	.0596	.4404	0.32	.1255	.3745	0.49	.1879	.3121
0.16	.0636	.4364	0.33	.1293	.3707	0.50	.1915	.3085

Source: Runyon and Haber, *Fundamentals of Behavioral Statistics,* 2nd ed., 1971, Addison-Wesley, Reading, Mass.

APPENDIX C (continued)

z	0 z	0 z	z	0 z	0 z	z	0 z	0 z
0.51	.1950	.3050	0.89	.3133	.1867	1.27	.3980	.1020
0.52	.1985	.3015	0.90	.3159	.1841	1.28	.3997	.1003
0.53	.2019	.2981	0.91	.3186	.1814	1.29	.4015	.0985
0.54	.2054	.2946	0.92	.3212	.1788	1.30	.4032	.0968
0.55	.2088	.2912	0.93	.3238	.1762	1.31	.4049	.0951
0.56	.2123	.2877	0.94	.3264	.1736	1.32	.4066	.0934
0.57	.2157	.2843	0.95	.3289	.1711	1.33	.4082	.0918
0.58	.2190	.2810	0.96	.3315	.1685	1.34	.4099	.0901
0.59	.2224	.2776	0.97	.3340	.1660	1.35	.4115	.0885
0.60	.2257	.2743	0.98	.3365	.1635	1.36	.4131	.0869
0.61	.2291	.2709	0.99	.3389	.1611	1.37	.4147	.0853
0.62	.2324	.2676	1.00	.3413	.1587	1.38	.4162	.0838
0.63	.2357	.2643	1.01	.3438	.1562	1.39	.4177	.0823
0.64	.2389	.2611	1.02	.3461	.1539	1.40	.4192	.0808
0.65	.2422	.2578	1.03	.3485	.1515	1.41	.4207	.0793
0.66	.2454	.2546	1.04	.3508	.1492	1.42	.4222	.0778
0.67	.2486	.2514	1.05	.3531	.1469	1.43	.4236	.0764
0.68	.2517	.2483	1.06	.3554	.1446	1.44	.4251	.0749
0.69	.2549	.2451	1.07	.3577	.1423	1.45	.4265	.0735
0.70	.2580	.2420	1.08	.3599	.1401	1.46	.4279	.0721
0.71	.2611	.2389	1.09	.3621	.1379	1.47	.4292	.0708
0.72	.2642	.2358	1.10	.3643	.1357	1.48	.4306	.0694
0.73	.2673	.2327	1.11	.3665	.1335	1.49	.4319	.0681
0.74	.2704	.2296	1.12	.3686	.1314	1.50	.4332	.0668
0.75	.2734	.2266	1.13	.3708	.1292	1.51	.4345	.0655
0.76	.2764	.2236	1.14	.3729	.1271	1.52	.4357	.0643
0.77	.2794	.2206	1.15	.3749	.1251	1.53	.4370	.0630
0.78	.2823	.2177	1.16	.3770	.1230	1.54	.4382	.0618
0.79	.2852	.2148	1.17	.3790	.1210	1.55	.4394	.0606
0.80	.2881	.2119	1.18	.3810	.1190	1.56	.4406	.0594
0.81	.2910	.2090	1.19	.3830	.1170	1.57	.4418	.0582
0.82	.2939	.2061	1.20	.3849	.1151	1.58	.4429	.0571
0.83	.2967	.2033	1.21	.3869	.1131	1.59	.4441	.0559
0.84	.2995	.2005	1.22	.3888	.1112	1.60	.4452	.0548
0.85	.3023	.1977	1.23	.3907	.1093	1.61	.4463	.0537
0.86	.3051	.1949	1.24	.3925	.1075	1.62	.4474	.0526
0.87	.3078	.1922	1.25	.3944	.1056	1.63	.4484	.0516
0.88	.3106	.1894	1.26	.3962	.1038	1.64	.4495	.0505

APPENDIX C (continued)

z	0 z	0 z	z	0 z	0 z	z	0 z	0 z
1.65	.4505	.0495	2.03	.4788	.0212	2.41	.4920	.0080
1.66	.4515	.0485	2.04	.4793	.0207	2.42	.4922	.0078
1.67	.4525	.0475	2.05	.4798	.0202	2.43	.4925	.0075
1.68	.4535	.0465	2.06	.4803	.0197	2.44	.4927	.0073
1.69	.4545	.0455	2.07	.4808	.0192	2.45	.4929	.0071
1.70	.4554	.0446	2.08	.4812	.0188	2.46	.4931	.0069
1.71	.4564	.0436	2.09	.4817	.0183	2.47	.4932	.0068
1.72	.4573	.0427	2.10	.4821	.0179	2.48	.4934	.0066
1.73	.4582	.0418	2.11	.4826	.0174	2.49	.4936	.0064
1.74	.4591	.0409	2.12	.4830	.0170	2.50	.4938	.0062
1.75	.4599	.0401	2.13	.4834	.0166	2.51	.4940	.0060
1.76	.4608	.0392	2.14	.4838	.0162	2.52	.4941	.0059
1.77	.4616	.0384	2.15	.4842	.0158	2.53	.4943	.0057
1.78	.4625	.0375	2.16	.4846	.0154	2.54	.4945	.0055
1.79	.4633	.0367	2.17	.4850	.0150	2.55	.4946	.0054
1.80	.4641	.0359	2.18	.4854	.0146	2.56	.4948	.0052
1.81	.4649	.0351	2.19	.4857	.0143	2.57	.4949	.0051
1.82	.4656	.0344	2.20	.4861	.0139	2.58	.4951	.0049
1.83	.4664	.0336	2.21	.4864	.0136	2.59	.4952	.0048
1.84	.4671	.0329	2.22	.4868	.0132	2.60	.4953	.0047
1.85	.4678	.0322	2.23	.4871	.0129	2.61	.4955	.0045
1.86	.4686	.0314	2.24	.4875	.0125	2.62	.4956	.0044
1.87	.4693	.0307	2.25	.4878	.0122	2.63	.4957	.0043
1.88	.4699	.0301	2.26	.4881	.0119	2.64	.4959	.0041
1.89	.4706	.0294	2.27	.4884	.0116	2.65	.4960	.0040
1.90	.4713	.0287	2.28	.4887	.0113	2.66	.4961	.0039
1.91	.4719	.0281	2.29	.4890	.0110	2.67	.4962	.0038
1.92	.4726	.0274	2.30	.4893	.0107	2.68	.4963	.0037
1.93	.4732	.0268	2.31	.4896	.0104	2.69	.4964	.0036
1.94	.4738	.0262	2.32	.4898	.0102	2.70	.4965	.0035
1.95	.4744	.0256	2.33	.4901	.0099	2.71	.4966	.0034
1.96	.4750	.0250	2.34	.4904	.0096	2.72	.4967	.0033
1.97	.4756	.0244	2.35	.4906	.0094	2.73	.4968	.0032
1.98	.4761	.0239	2.36	.4909	.0091	2.74	.4969	.0031
1.99	.4767	.0233	2.37	.4911	.0089	2.75	.4970	.0030
2.00	.4772	.0228	2.38	.4913	.0087	2.76	.4971	.0029
2.01	.4778	.0222	2.39	.4916	.0084	2.77	.4972	.0028
2.02	.4783	.0217	2.40	.4918	.0082	2.78	.4973	.0027

APPENDIX C (continued)

z	0 z	0 z	z	0 z	0 z	z	0 z	0 z
2.79	.4974	.0026	2.98	.4986	.0014	3.17	.4992	.0008
2.80	.4974	.0026	2.99	.4986	.0014	3.18	.4993	.0007
2.81	.4975	.0025	3.00	.4987	.0013	3.19	.4993	.0007
2.82	.4976	.0024	3.01	.4987	.0013	3.20	.4993	.0007
2.83	.4977	.0023	3.02	.4987	.0013	3.21	.4993	.0007
2.84	.4977	.0023	3.03	.4988	.0012	3.22	.4994	.0006
2.85	.4978	.0022	3.04	.4988	.0012	3.23	.4994	.0006
2.86	.4979	.0021	3.05	.4989	.0011	3.24	.4994	.0006
2.87	.4979	.0021	3.06	.4989	.0011	3.25	.4994	.0006
2.88	.4980	.0020	3.07	.4989	.0011	3.30	.4995	.0005
2.89	.4981	.0019	3.08	.4990	.0010	3.35	.4996	.0004
2.90	.4981	.0019	3.09	.4990	.0010	3.40	.4997	.0003
2.91	.4982	.0018	3.10	.4990	.0010	3.45	.4997	.0003
2.92	.4982	.0018	3.11	.4991	.0009	3.50	.4998	.0002
2.93	.4983	.0017	3.12	.4991	.0009	3.60	.4998	.0002
2.94	.4984	.0016	3.13	.4991	.0009	3.70	.4999	.0001
2.95	.4984	.0016	3.14	.4992	.0008	3.80	.4999	.0001
2.96	.4985	.0015	3.15	.4992	.0008	3.90	.49995	.00005
2.97	.4985	.0015	3.16	.4992	.0008	4.00	.49997	.00003

APPENDIX D

Pearson Product-Moment Correlation Coefficient Values

df = N − 2	Level of Significance for a Nondirectional (Two-Tailed) Test				
	.10	.05	.02	.01	.001
1	.9877	.9969	.9995	.9999	1.0000
2	.9000	.9500	.9800	.9900	.9990
3	.8054	.8783	.9343	.9587	.9912
4	.7293	.8114	.8822	.9172	.9741
5	.6694	.7545	.8329	.8745	.9507
6	.6215	.7067	.7887	.8343	.9249
7	.5822	.6664	.7498	.7977	.8982
8	.5494	.6319	.7155	.7646	.8721
9	.5214	.6021	.6851	.7348	.8471
10	.4973	.5760	.6581	.7079	.8233
11	.4762	.5529	.6339	.6835	.8010
12	.4575	.5324	.6120	.6614	.7800
13	.4409	.5139	.5923	.6411	.7603
14	.4259	.4973	.5742	.6226	.7420
15	.4124	.4821	.5577	.6055	.7246

Source: This table is taken from Table VII of Fisher and Yates, *Statistical Tables for Biological, Agricultural, and Medical Research,* published by Longman Group Ltd., London (previously published by Oliver and Boyd, Ltd., Edinburgh), and by permission of the authors and publishers.

APPENDIX D (continued)

df = $N - 2$	Level of Significance for a Nondirectional (Two-Tailed) Test				
	.10	.05	.02	.01	.001
16	.4000	.4683	.5425	.5897	.7084
17	.3887	.4555	.5285	.5751	.6932
18	.3783	.4438	.5155	.5614	.6787
19	.3687	.4329	.5034	.5487	.6652
20	.3598	.4227	.4921	.5368	.6524
25	.3233	.3809	.4451	.4869	.5974
30	.2960	.3494	.4093	.4487	.5541
35	.2746	.3246	.3810	.4182	.5189
40	.2573	.3044	.3578	.3932	.4896
45	.2428	.2875	.3384	.3721	.4648
50	.2306	.2732	.3218	.3541	.4433
60	.2108	.2500	.2948	.3248	.4078
70	.1954	.2319	.2737	.3017	.3799
80	.1829	.2172	.2565	.2830	.3568
90	.1726	.2050	.2422	.2673	.3375
100	.1638	.1946	.2301	.2540	.3211

APPENDIX E

Table of Random Numbers

USING THE RANDOM-NUMBER TABLE TO DRAW A SAMPLE

Step 1. Define your population, for example, all the fifth-grade students in the six elementary schools in Kokomo, Indiana.

Step 2. List all the members of the population. In our example, you would have to go to the individual schools or to the Board of Education and get this information. (This is the hardest step.)

Step 3. Assign a number to each member of the population: 1, 2, 3, 4, 5, and on out through the last student on your list.

Step 4. Decide on the size of your sample. This will depend on all sorts of things: the kind of experiment you plan to do, the consequences of drawing a wrong conclusion (the likelihood of error goes down as the sample size goes up), the amount of money available. Let's say you decide to draw a sample of 50.

Step 5. The numbers in the random-number table are grouped into five-digit sets. These groupings are merely for your convenience, to help you keep your place. Select a column of as many adjacent numbers as the number of digits in your sample size. Since your sample has 50, you'll need to use two-digit columns. For a sample of 200, you would use sets of three adjacent columns. Your columns of digits can come from any grouping, from anywhere in that grouping, or can even span across groupings if you wish. Decide where you want to enter your set of columns by closing your eyes and putting your finger on the column.

Step 6. The first number you find, if it is 50 or less, is the number of the first child in your sample. Find the child with that number, and record his or her name. The next number identifies the next child. Keep on identifying sample members this way until you have 50 of them, discarding any numbers that are repeated or that are above 50.

RANDOMLY ASSIGNING SUBJECTS TO TREATMENT GROUPS

Suppose that you have 30 subjects and that you want to assign 10 subjects to each of three treatment groups:

1. In the table of random numbers, make a blind selection of a two-digit column (because your total N, 30, has two digits).
2. List the first 30 numbers from that column on a piece of paper (or on your word processor).
3. Write or type the names of your 30 subjects in a second list, pairing each name with one of the numbers from step 2.
4. Rearrange the names on the list so that they are in numerical order according to the numbers assigned to them.
5. Put the first 10 names into treatment group 1, the next 10 into treatment group 2, and the last 10 into treatment group 3.

00	54463	22662	65905	70639	79365	67382	29085	69831	47058	08186
01	15389	85205	18850	39226	42249	90669	96325	23248	60933	26927
02	85941	40756	82414	02015	13858	78030	16269	65978	01385	15345
03	61149	69440	11286	88218	58925	03638	52862	62733	33451	77455
04	05219	81619	10651	67079	92511	59888	84502	72095	83463	75577
05	41417	98326	87719	92294	46614	50948	64886	20002	97365	30976
06	28357	94070	20652	35774	16249	75019	21145	05217	47286	76305
07	17783	00015	10806	83091	91530	36466	39981	62481	49177	75779
08	40950	84820	29881	85966	62800	70326	84740	62660	77379	90279
09	82995	64157	66164	41180	10089	41757	78258	96488	88629	37231
10	96754	17676	55659	44105	47361	34833	86679	23930	53249	27083
11	34357	88040	53364	71726	45690	66334	60332	22554	90600	71113
12	06318	37403	49927	57715	50423	67372	63116	48888	21505	80182
13	62111	52820	07243	79931	89292	84767	85693	73947	22278	11551
14	47534	09243	67879	00544	23410	12740	02540	54440	32949	13491
15	98614	75993	84460	62846	59844	14922	48730	73443	48167	34770
16	24856	03648	44898	09351	98795	18644	39765	71058	90368	44104
17	96887	12479	80621	66223	86085	78285	02432	53342	42846	94771
18	90801	21472	42815	77408	37390	76766	52615	32141	30268	18106
19	55165	77312	83666	36028	28420	70219	81369	41943	47366	41067
20	75884	12952	84318	95108	72305	64620	91318	89872	45375	85436
21	16777	37116	58550	42958	21460	43910	01175	87894	81378	10620
22	46230	43877	80207	88877	89380	32992	91380	03164	98656	59337
23	42902	66892	46134	01432	94710	23474	20423	60137	60609	13119
24	81007	00333	39693	28039	10154	95425	39220	19774	31782	49037
25	68089	01122	51111	72373	06902	74373	96199	97017	41273	21546
26	20411	67081	89950	16944	93054	87687	96693	87236	77054	33848
27	58212	13160	06468	15718	82627	76999	05999	58680	96739	63700
28	70577	42866	24969	61210	76046	67699	42054	12696	93758	03283
29	94522	74358	71659	62038	79643	79169	44741	05437	39038	13163
30	42626	86819	85651	88678	17401	03252	99547	32404	17918	62880
31	16051	33763	57194	16752	54450	19031	58580	47629	54132	60631
32	08244	27647	33851	44705	94211	46716	11738	55784	95374	72655
33	59497	04392	09419	89964	51211	04894	72882	17805	21896	83864
34	97155	13428	40293	09985	58434	01412	69124	82171	59058	82859
35	98409	66162	95763	47420	20792	61527	20441	39435	11859	41567
36	45476	84882	65109	96597	25930	66790	65706	61203	53634	22557
37	89300	69700	50741	30329	11658	23166	05400	66669	48708	03887
38	50051	95137	91631	66315	91428	12275	24816	68091	71710	33258
39	31753	85178	31310	89642	98364	02306	24617	09609	83942	22716
40	79152	53829	77250	20190	56535	18760	69942	77448	33278	48805
41	44560	38750	83635	56540	64900	42912	13953	79149	18710	68618
42	68328	83378	63369	71381	39564	05615	42451	64559	97501	65747
43	46939	38689	58625	08342	30459	85863	20781	09284	26333	91777
44	83544	86141	15707	96256	23068	13782	08467	89469	93842	55349
45	91621	00881	04900	54224	46177	55309	17852	27491	89415	23466
46	91896	67126	04151	03795	59077	11848	12630	98375	52068	60142
47	55751	62515	21108	80830	02263	29303	37204	96926	30506	09808
48	85156	87689	95493	88842	00664	55017	55539	17771	69448	87530
49	07521	56898	12236	60277	39102	62315	12239	07105	11844	01117

Source: Adapted from *Statistical Methods,* 6th ed., by G. W. Snedecor and W. G. Cochran. Copyright © by Iowa State University Press, Ames, Iowa. Reprinted by permission.

00	59391	58030	52098	82718	87024	82848	04190	96574	90464	29065
01	99567	76364	77204	04615	27062	96621	43918	01896	83991	51141
02	10363	97518	51400	25670	98342	61891	27101	37855	06235	33316
03	86859	19558	64432	16706	99612	59798	32803	67708	15297	28612
04	11258	24591	36863	55368	31721	94335	34936	02566	80972	08188
05	95068	88628	35911	14530	33020	80428	39936	31855	34334	64865
06	54463	47237	73800	91017	36239	71824	83671	39892	60518	37092
07	16874	62677	57412	13215	31389	62233	80827	73917	82802	84420
08	92494	63157	76593	91316	03505	72389	96363	52887	01087	66091
09	15669	56689	35682	40844	53256	81872	35213	09840	34471	74441
10	99116	75486	84989	23476	52967	67104	39495	39100	17217	74073
11	15696	10703	65178	90637	63110	17622	53988	71087	84148	11670
12	97720	15369	51269	69620	03388	13699	33423	67453	43269	56720
13	11666	13841	71681	98000	35979	39719	81899	07449	47985	46967
14	71628	73130	78783	75691	41632	09847	61547	18707	85489	69944
15	40501	51089	99943	91843	41995	88931	73631	69361	05375	15417
16	22518	55576	98215	82068	10798	86211	36584	67466	69373	40054
17	75112	30485	62173	02132	14878	92879	22281	16783	86352	00077
18	80327	02671	98191	84342	90813	49268	95441	15496	20168	09271
19	60251	45548	02146	05597	48228	81366	34598	72856	66762	17002
20	57430	82270	10421	05540	43648	75888	66049	21511	47676	33444
21	73528	39559	34434	88596	54086	71693	43132	14414	79949	85193
22	25991	65959	70769	64721	86413	33475	42740	06175	82758	66248
23	78388	16638	09134	59880	63806	48472	39318	35434	24057	74739
24	12477	09965	96657	57994	59439	76330	24596	77515	09577	91871
25	83266	32883	42451	15579	38155	29793	40914	65990	16255	17777
26	76970	80876	10237	39515	79152	74798	39357	09054	73579	92359
27	37074	65198	44785	68624	98336	84481	97610	78735	46703	98265
28	83712	06514	30101	78295	54656	85417	43189	60048	72781	72606
29	20287	56862	69727	94443	64936	08366	27227	05158	50326	59566
30	74261	32592	86538	27041	65172	85532	07571	80609	39285	65340
31	64081	49863	08478	96001	18888	14810	70545	89755	59064	07210
32	05617	75818	47750	67814	29575	10526	66192	44464	27058	40467
33	26793	74951	95466	74307	13330	42664	85515	20632	05497	33625
34	65988	72850	48737	54719	52056	01596	03845	35067	03134	70322
35	27366	42271	44300	73399	21105	03280	73457	43093	05192	48657
36	56760	10909	98147	34736	33863	95256	12731	66598	50771	83665
37	72880	43338	93643	58904	59543	23943	11231	83268	65938	81581
38	77888	38100	03062	58103	47961	83841	25878	23746	55903	44115
39	28440	07819	21580	51459	47971	29882	13990	29226	23608	15873
40	63525	94441	77033	12147	51054	49955	58312	76923	96071	05813
41	47606	93410	16359	89033	89696	47231	64498	31776	05383	39902
42	52669	45030	96279	14709	52372	87832	02735	50803	72744	88208
43	16738	60159	07425	62369	07515	82721	37875	71153	21315	00132
44	59348	11695	45751	15865	74739	05572	32688	20271	65128	14551
45	12900	71775	29845	60774	94924	21810	38636	33717	67598	82521
46	75086	23537	49939	33595	13484	97588	28617	17979	70749	35234
47	99495	51434	29181	09993	38190	42553	68922	52125	91077	40197
48	26075	31671	45386	36583	93459	48599	52022	41330	60651	91321
49	13636	93596	23377	51133	95126	61496	42474	45141	46660	42338

50	64249	63664	39652	40646	97306	31741	07294	84149	46797	82487
51	26538	44249	04050	48174	65570	44072	40192	51153	11397	58212
52	05845	00512	78630	55328	18116	69296	91705	86224	29503	57071
53	74897	68373	67359	51014	33510	83048	17056	72506	82949	54600
54	20872	54570	35017	88132	25730	22626	86723	91691	13191	77212
55	31432	96156	89177	75541	81355	24480	77243	76690	42507	84362
56	66890	61505	01240	00660	05873	13568	76082	79172	57913	93448
57	48194	57790	79970	33106	86904	48119	52503	24130	72824	21627
58	11303	87118	81471	52936	08555	28420	49416	44448	04269	27029
59	54374	57325	16947	45356	78371	10563	97191	53798	12693	27928
60	64852	34421	61046	90849	13966	39810	42699	21753	76192	10508
61	16309	20384	09491	91588	97720	89846	30376	76970	23063	35894
62	42587	37065	24526	72602	57589	98131	37292	05967	26002	51945
63	40177	98590	97161	41682	84533	67588	62036	49967	01990	72308
64	82309	76128	93965	26743	24141	04838	40254	26065	07938	76236
65	79788	68243	59732	04257	27084	14743	17520	95401	55811	76099
66	40538	79000	89559	25026	42274	23489	34502	75508	06059	86682
67	64016	73598	18609	73150	62463	33102	45205	87440	96767	67042
68	49767	12691	17903	93871	99721	79109	09425	26904	07419	76013
69	76974	55108	29795	08404	82684	00497	51126	79935	57450	55671
70	23854	08480	85983	96025	50117	64610	99425	62291	86943	21541
71	68973	70551	25098	78033	98573	79848	31778	29555	61446	23037
72	36444	93600	65350	14971	25325	00427	52073	64280	18847	24768
73	03003	87800	07391	11594	21196	00781	32550	57158	58887	73041
74	17540	26188	36647	78386	04558	61463	57842	90382	77019	24210
75	38916	55809	47982	41968	69760	79422	80154	91486	19180	15100
76	64288	19843	69122	42502	48508	28820	59933	72998	99942	10515
77	86809	51564	38040	39418	49915	19000	58050	16899	79952	57849
78	99800	99566	14742	05028	30033	94889	53381	23656	75787	59223
79	92345	31890	95712	08279	91794	94068	49337	88674	35355	12267
80	90363	65162	32245	82279	79256	80834	06088	99462	56705	06118
81	64437	32242	48431	04835	39070	59702	31508	60935	22390	52246
82	91714	53662	28373	34333	55791	74758	51144	18827	10704	76803
83	20902	17646	31391	31459	33315	03444	55743	74701	58851	27427
84	12217	86007	70371	52281	14510	76094	96579	54853	78339	20839
85	45177	02863	42307	53571	22532	74921	17735	42201	80540	54721
86	28325	90814	08804	52746	47913	54577	47525	77705	95330	21866
87	29019	28776	56116	54791	64604	08815	46049	71186	34650	14994
88	84979	81353	56219	67062	26146	82567	33122	14124	46240	92973
89	50371	26347	48513	63915	11158	25563	91915	18431	92978	11591
90	53422	06825	69711	67950	64716	18003	49581	45378	99878	61130
91	67453	35651	89316	41620	32048	70225	47597	33137	31443	51445
92	07294	85353	74819	23445	68237	07202	99515	62282	53809	26685
93	79544	00302	45338	16015	66613	88968	14595	63836	77716	79596
94	64144	85442	82060	46471	24162	39500	87351	36637	42833	71875
95	90919	11883	58318	00042	52402	28210	34075	33272	00840	73268
96	06670	57353	86275	92276	77591	46924	60839	55437	03183	13191
97	36634	93976	52062	83678	41256	60948	18685	48992	19462	96062
98	75101	72891	85745	67106	26010	62107	60885	37503	55461	71213
99	05112	71222	72654	51583	05228	62056	57390	42746	39272	96659

50	32847	31282	03345	89593	69214	70381	78285	20054	91018	16742
51	16916	00041	30236	55023	14253	76582	12092	86533	92426	37655
52	66176	34047	21005	27137	03191	48970	64625	22394	39622	79085
53	46299	13335	12180	16861	38043	59292	62675	63631	37020	78195
54	22847	47839	45385	23289	47526	54098	45683	55849	51575	64689
55	41851	54160	92320	69936	34803	92479	33399	71160	64777	83378
56	28444	59497	91586	95917	68553	28639	06455	34174	11130	91994
57	47520	62378	98855	83174	13088	16561	68559	26679	06238	51254
58	34978	63271	13142	82681	05271	08822	06490	44984	49307	62717
59	37404	80416	69035	92980	49486	74378	75610	74976	70056	15478
60	32400	65482	52099	53676	74648	94148	65095	69597	52771	71551
61	89262	86332	51718	70663	11623	29834	79820	73002	84886	03591
62	86866	09127	98021	03871	27789	58444	44832	36505	40672	30180
63	90814	14833	08759	74645	05046	94056	99094	65091	32663	73040
64	19192	82756	20553	58446	55376	88914	75096	26119	83898	43816
65	77585	52593	56612	95766	10019	29531	73064	20953	53523	58136
66	23757	16364	05096	03192	62386	45389	85332	18877	55710	96459
67	45989	96257	23850	26216	23309	21526	07425	50254	19455	29315
68	92970	94243	07316	41467	64837	52406	25225	51553	31220	14032
69	74346	59596	40088	98176	17896	86900	20249	77753	19099	48885
70	87646	41309	27636	45153	29988	94770	07255	70908	05340	99751
71	50099	71038	45146	06146	55211	99429	43169	66259	97786	59180
72	10127	46900	64984	75348	04115	33624	68774	60013	35515	62556
73	67995	81977	18984	64091	02785	27762	42529	97144	80407	64524
74	26304	80217	84934	82657	69291	35397	98714	35104	08187	48109
75	81994	41070	56642	64091	31229	02595	13513	45148	78722	30144
76	59537	34662	79631	89403	65212	09975	06118	86197	58208	16162
77	51228	10937	62396	81460	47331	91403	95007	06047	16846	64809
78	31089	37995	29577	07828	42272	54016	21950	86192	99046	84864
79	38207	97938	93459	75174	79460	55436	57206	87644	21296	43395
80	88666	31142	09474	89712	63153	62333	42212	06140	42594	43671
81	53365	56134	67582	92557	89520	33452	05134	70628	27612	33738
82	89807	74530	38004	90102	11693	90257	05500	79920	62700	43325
83	18682	81038	85662	90915	91631	22223	91588	80774	07716	12548
84	63571	32579	63942	25371	09234	94592	98475	76884	37635	33608
85	68927	56492	67799	95398	77642	54913	91853	08424	81450	76229
86	56401	63186	39389	88798	31356	89235	97036	32341	33292	73757
87	24333	95603	02359	72942	46287	95382	08452	62862	97869	71775
88	17025	84202	95199	62272	06366	16175	97577	99304	41587	03686
89	02804	08253	52133	20224	68034	50865	57868	22343	55111	03607
90	08298	03879	20995	19850	73090	13191	18963	82244	78479	99121
91	59883	01785	82403	96062	03785	03488	12970	64896	38336	30030
92	46982	06682	62864	91837	74021	89094	39952	64158	79614	78235
93	31121	47266	07661	02051	67599	24471	69843	83696	71402	76287
94	97867	56641	63416	17577	30161	87320	37752	73276	48969	41915
95	57364	86746	08415	14621	49430	22311	15836	72492	49372	44103
96	09559	26263	69511	28064	75999	44540	13337	10918	79846	54809
97	53873	55571	00608	42661	91332	63956	74087	59008	47493	99581
98	35531	19162	86406	05299	77511	24311	57257	22826	77555	05941
99	28229	88629	25695	94932	30721	16197	78742	34974	97528	45447

APPENDIX F

Critical Values of *t*

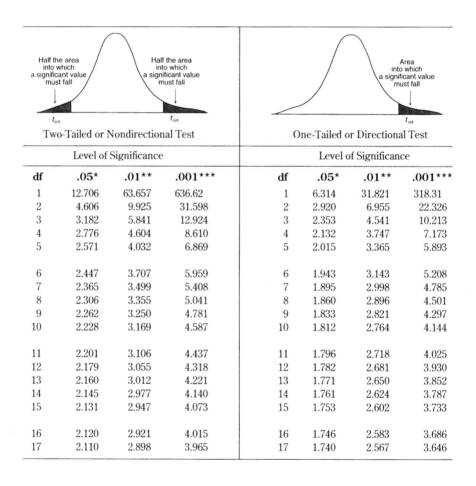

	Level of Significance				Level of Significance		
df	**.05***	**.01****	**.001*****	**df**	**.05***	**.01****	**.001*****
1	12.706	63.657	636.62	1	6.314	31.821	318.31
2	4.606	9.925	31.598	2	2.920	6.955	22.326
3	3.182	5.841	12.924	3	2.353	4.541	10.213
4	2.776	4.604	8.610	4	2.132	3.747	7.173
5	2.571	4.032	6.869	5	2.015	3.365	5.893
6	2.447	3.707	5.959	6	1.943	3.143	5.208
7	2.365	3.499	5.408	7	1.895	2.998	4.785
8	2.306	3.355	5.041	8	1.860	2.896	4.501
9	2.262	3.250	4.781	9	1.833	2.821	4.297
10	2.228	3.169	4.587	10	1.812	2.764	4.144
11	2.201	3.106	4.437	11	1.796	2.718	4.025
12	2.179	3.055	4.318	12	1.782	2.681	3.930
13	2.160	3.012	4.221	13	1.771	2.650	3.852
14	2.145	2.977	4.140	14	1.761	2.624	3.787
15	2.131	2.947	4.073	15	1.753	2.602	3.733
16	2.120	2.921	4.015	16	1.746	2.583	3.686
17	2.110	2.898	3.965	17	1.740	2.567	3.646

Two-Tailed or Nondirectional Test				One-Tailed or Directional Test			
Level of Significance				Level of Significance			
df	.05*	.01**	.001***	df	.05*	.01**	.001***
18	2.101	2.878	3.922	18	1.734	2.552	3.610
19	2.093	2.861	3.883	19	1.729	2.539	3.579
20	2.086	2.845	3.850	20	1.725	2.528	3.552
21	2.080	2.831	3.819	21	1.721	2.518	3.527
22	2.074	2.819	3.792	22	1.717	2.508	3.505
23	2.069	2.807	3.767	23	1.714	2.500	3.485
24	2.064	2.797	3.745	24	1.711	2.492	3.467
25	2.060	2.787	3.725	25	1.708	2.485	3.450
26	2.056	2.779	3.707	26	1.706	2.479	3.435
27	2.052	2.771	3.690	27	1.703	2.473	3.421
28	2.048	2.763	3.674	28	1.701	2.467	3.408
29	2.045	2.756	3.659	29	1.699	2.462	3.396
30	2.042	2.750	3.646	30	1.697	2.457	3.385
40	2.021	2.704	3.551	40	1.684	2.423	3.307
60	2.000	2.660	3.460	60	1.671	2.390	3.232
120	1.980	2.617	3.373	120	1.658	2.358	3.160
∞	1.960	2.576	3.291	∞	1.645	2.326	3.090

USING THIS TABLE

For a two-tailed test of significance (i.e., when you have not predicted ahead of time which group will have higher scores or measurements than the other), use the values on the left side of the table. For a one-tailed test (when you knew beforehand which group ought to score higher), use the values on the right side.

If the two groups are independent of each other, df = $N_1 + N_2 - 2$; if the two groups are not independent (correlated), df = $N - 1$, where N is the number of pairs of scores.

APPENDIX G

Critical Values of F

Between-group df

Within-group df	1	2	3	4	5	6	7	8	9	10	11	12	14	16	20	24	30	40	50	75	100	200	500	∞
1	161 **4,052**	200 **4,999**	216 **5,403**	225 **5,625**	230 **5,764**	234 **5,859**	237 **5,928**	239 **5,981**	241 **6,022**	242 **6,056**	243 **6,082**	244 **6,106**	245 **6,142**	246 **6,169**	248 **6,208**	249 **6,234**	250 **6,258**	251 **6,286**	252 **6,302**	253 **6,323**	253 **6,334**	254 **6,352**	254 **6,361**	254 **6,366**
2	18.51 **98.49**	19.00 **99.00**	19.16 **99.17**	19.25 **99.25**	19.30 **99.30**	19.33 **99.33**	19.36 **99.34**	19.37 **99.36**	19.38 **99.38**	19.39 **99.40**	19.40 **99.41**	19.41 **99.42**	19.42 **99.43**	19.43 **99.44**	19.44 **99.45**	19.45 **99.46**	19.46 **99.47**	19.47 **99.48**	19.47 **99.48**	19.48 **99.49**	19.49 **99.49**	19.49 **99.49**	19.50 **99.50**	19.50 **99.50**
3	10.13 **34.12**	9.55 **30.82**	9.28 **29.46**	9.12 **28.71**	9.01 **28.24**	8.94 **27.91**	8.88 **27.67**	8.84 **27.49**	8.81 **27.34**	8.78 **27.23**	8.76 **27.13**	8.74 **27.05**	8.71 **26.92**	8.69 **26.83**	8.66 **26.69**	8.64 **26.60**	8.62 **26.50**	8.60 **26.41**	8.58 **26.35**	8.57 **26.27**	8.56 **26.23**	8.54 **26.18**	8.54 **26.14**	8.53 **26.12**
4	7.71 **21.20**	6.94 **18.00**	6.59 **16.69**	6.39 **15.98**	6.26 **15.52**	6.16 **15.21**	6.09 **14.98**	6.04 **14.80**	6.00 **14.66**	5.96 **14.54**	5.93 **14.45**	5.91 **14.37**	5.87 **14.24**	5.84 **14.15**	5.80 **14.02**	5.77 **13.93**	5.74 **13.83**	5.71 **13.74**	5.70 **13.69**	5.68 **13.61**	5.66 **13.57**	5.65 **13.52**	5.64 **13.48**	5.63 **13.46**
5	6.61 **16.26**	5.79 **13.27**	5.41 **12.06**	5.19 **11.39**	5.05 **10.97**	4.95 **10.67**	4.88 **10.45**	4.82 **10.27**	4.78 **10.15**	4.74 **10.05**	4.70 **9.96**	4.68 **9.89**	4.64 **9.77**	4.60 **9.68**	4.56 **9.55**	4.53 **9.47**	4.50 **9.38**	4.46 **9.29**	4.44 **9.24**	4.42 **9.17**	4.40 **9.13**	4.38 **9.07**	4.37 **9.04**	4.36 **9.02**
6	5.99 **13.74**	5.14 **10.92**	4.76 **9.78**	4.53 **9.15**	4.39 **8.75**	4.28 **8.47**	4.21 **8.26**	4.15 **8.10**	4.10 **7.98**	4.06 **7.87**	4.03 **7.79**	4.00 **7.72**	3.96 **7.60**	3.92 **7.52**	3.87 **7.39**	3.84 **7.31**	3.81 **7.23**	3.77 **7.14**	3.75 **7.09**	3.72 **7.02**	3.71 **6.99**	3.69 **6.94**	3.68 **6.90**	3.67 **6.88**
7	5.59 **12.25**	4.74 **9.55**	4.35 **8.45**	4.12 **7.85**	3.97 **7.46**	3.87 **7.19**	3.79 **7.00**	3.73 **6.84**	3.68 **6.71**	3.63 **6.62**	3.60 **6.54**	3.57 **6.47**	3.52 **6.35**	3.49 **6.27**	3.44 **6.15**	3.41 **6.07**	3.38 **5.98**	3.34 **5.90**	3.32 **5.85**	3.29 **5.78**	3.28 **5.75**	3.25 **5.70**	3.24 **5.67**	3.23 **5.65**
8	5.32 **11.26**	4.46 **8.65**	4.07 **7.59**	3.84 **7.01**	3.69 **6.63**	3.58 **6.37**	3.50 **6.19**	3.44 **6.03**	3.39 **5.91**	3.34 **5.82**	3.31 **5.74**	3.28 **5.67**	3.23 **5.56**	3.20 **5.48**	3.15 **5.36**	3.12 **5.28**	3.08 **5.20**	3.05 **5.11**	3.03 **5.06**	3.00 **5.00**	2.98 **4.96**	2.96 **4.91**	2.94 **4.88**	2.93 **4.86**
9	5.12 **10.56**	4.26 **8.02**	3.86 **6.99**	3.63 **6.42**	3.48 **6.06**	3.37 **5.80**	3.29 **5.62**	3.23 **5.47**	3.18 **5.35**	3.13 **5.26**	3.10 **5.18**	3.07 **5.11**	3.02 **5.00**	2.98 **4.92**	2.93 **4.80**	2.90 **4.73**	2.86 **4.64**	2.82 **4.56**	2.80 **4.51**	2.77 **4.45**	2.76 **4.41**	2.73 **4.36**	2.72 **4.33**	2.71 **4.31**
10	4.96 **10.04**	4.10 **7.56**	3.71 **6.55**	3.48 **5.99**	3.33 **5.64**	3.22 **5.39**	3.14 **5.21**	3.07 **5.06**	3.02 **4.95**	2.97 **4.85**	2.94 **4.78**	2.91 **4.71**	2.86 **4.60**	2.82 **4.52**	2.77 **4.41**	2.74 **4.33**	2.70 **4.25**	2.67 **4.17**	2.64 **4.12**	2.61 **4.05**	2.59 **4.01**	2.56 **3.96**	2.55 **3.93**	2.54 **3.91**
11	4.84 **9.65**	3.98 **7.20**	3.59 **6.22**	3.36 **5.67**	3.20 **5.32**	3.09 **5.07**	3.01 **4.88**	2.95 **4.74**	2.90 **4.63**	2.86 **4.54**	2.82 **4.46**	2.79 **4.40**	2.74 **4.29**	2.70 **4.21**	2.65 **4.10**	2.61 **4.02**	2.57 **3.94**	2.53 **3.86**	2.50 **3.80**	2.47 **3.74**	2.45 **3.70**	2.42 **3.66**	2.41 **3.62**	2.40 **3.60**
12	4.75 **9.33**	3.88 **6.93**	3.49 **5.95**	3.26 **5.41**	3.11 **5.06**	3.00 **4.82**	2.92 **4.65**	2.85 **4.50**	2.80 **4.39**	2.76 **4.30**	2.72 **4.22**	2.69 **4.16**	2.64 **4.05**	2.60 **3.98**	2.54 **3.86**	2.50 **3.78**	2.46 **3.70**	2.42 **3.61**	2.40 **3.56**	2.36 **3.49**	2.35 **3.46**	2.32 **3.41**	2.31 **3.38**	2.30 **3.36**
13	4.67 **9.07**	3.80 **6.70**	3.41 **5.74**	3.18 **5.20**	3.02 **4.86**	2.92 **4.62**	2.84 **4.44**	2.77 **4.30**	2.72 **4.19**	2.67 **4.10**	2.63 **4.02**	2.60 **3.96**	2.55 **3.85**	2.51 **3.78**	2.46 **3.67**	2.42 **3.59**	2.38 **3.51**	2.34 **3.42**	2.32 **3.37**	2.28 **3.30**	2.26 **3.27**	2.24 **3.21**	2.22 **3.18**	2.21 **3.16**
14	4.60 **8.86**	3.74 **6.51**	3.34 **5.56**	3.11 **5.03**	2.96 **4.69**	2.85 **4.46**	2.77 **4.28**	2.70 **4.14**	2.65 **4.03**	2.60 **3.94**	2.56 **3.86**	2.53 **3.80**	2.48 **3.70**	2.44 **3.62**	2.39 **3.51**	2.35 **3.43**	2.31 **3.34**	2.27 **3.26**	2.24 **3.21**	2.21 **3.14**	2.19 **3.11**	2.16 **3.06**	2.14 **3.02**	2.13 **3.00**
15	4.54 **8.68**	3.68 **6.36**	3.29 **5.42**	3.06 **4.89**	2.90 **4.56**	2.79 **4.32**	2.70 **4.14**	2.64 **4.00**	2.59 **3.89**	2.55 **3.80**	2.51 **3.73**	2.48 **3.67**	2.43 **3.56**	2.39 **3.48**	2.33 **3.36**	2.29 **3.29**	2.25 **3.20**	2.21 **3.12**	2.18 **3.07**	2.15 **3.00**	2.12 **2.97**	2.10 **2.92**	2.08 **2.89**	2.07 **2.87**
16	4.49 **8.53**	3.63 **6.23**	3.24 **5.29**	3.01 **4.77**	2.85 **4.44**	2.74 **4.20**	2.66 **4.03**	2.59 **3.89**	2.54 **3.78**	2.49 **3.69**	2.45 **3.61**	2.42 **3.55**	2.37 **3.45**	2.33 **3.37**	2.28 **3.25**	2.24 **3.18**	2.20 **3.10**	2.16 **3.01**	2.13 **2.96**	2.09 **2.89**	2.07 **2.86**	2.04 **2.80**	2.02 **2.77**	2.01 **2.75**

Source: Adapted from *Statistical Methods*, 6th ed., by G. W. Snedecor and W. G. Cochran. Copyright © 1967 by Iowa State University Press, Ames, Iowa. Reprinted by permission .05 level (lightface type) and .01 level (**boldface type**).

Between-group df (Continued)

Within-group df	1	2	3	4	5	6	7	8	9	10	11	12	14	16	20	24	30	40	50	75	100	200	500	∞
17	4.45 / 8.40	3.59 / 6.11	3.20 / 5.18	2.96 / 4.67	2.81 / 4.34	2.70 / 4.10	2.62 / 3.93	2.55 / 3.79	2.50 / 3.68	2.45 / 3.59	2.41 / 3.52	2.38 / 3.45	2.33 / 3.35	2.29 / 3.27	2.23 / 3.16	2.19 / 3.08	2.15 / 3.00	2.11 / 2.92	2.08 / 2.86	2.04 / 2.79	2.02 / 2.76	1.99 / 2.70	1.97 / 2.67	1.96 / 2.65
18	4.41 / 8.28	3.55 / 6.01	3.16 / 5.09	2.93 / 4.58	2.77 / 4.25	2.66 / 4.01	2.58 / 3.85	2.51 / 3.71	2.46 / 3.60	2.41 / 3.51	2.37 / 3.44	2.34 / 3.37	2.29 / 3.27	2.25 / 3.19	2.19 / 3.07	2.15 / 3.00	2.11 / 2.91	2.07 / 2.83	2.04 / 2.78	2.00 / 2.71	1.98 / 2.68	1.95 / 2.62	1.93 / 2.59	1.92 / 2.57
19	4.38 / 8.18	3.52 / 5.93	3.13 / 5.01	2.90 / 4.50	2.74 / 4.17	2.63 / 3.94	2.55 / 3.77	2.48 / 3.63	2.43 / 3.52	2.38 / 3.43	2.34 / 3.36	2.31 / 3.30	2.26 / 3.19	2.21 / 3.12	2.15 / 3.00	2.11 / 2.92	2.07 / 2.84	2.02 / 2.76	2.00 / 2.70	1.96 / 2.63	1.94 / 2.60	1.91 / 2.54	1.90 / 2.51	1.88 / 2.49
20	4.35 / 8.10	3.49 / 5.85	3.10 / 4.94	2.87 / 4.43	2.71 / 4.10	2.60 / 3.87	2.52 / 3.71	2.45 / 3.56	2.40 / 3.45	2.35 / 3.37	2.31 / 3.30	2.28 / 3.23	2.23 / 3.13	2.18 / 3.05	2.12 / 2.94	2.08 / 2.86	2.04 / 2.77	1.99 / 2.69	1.96 / 2.63	1.92 / 2.56	1.90 / 2.53	1.87 / 2.47	1.85 / 2.44	1.84 / 2.42
21	4.32 / 8.02	3.47 / 5.78	3.07 / 4.87	2.84 / 4.37	2.68 / 4.04	2.57 / 3.81	2.49 / 3.65	2.42 / 3.51	2.37 / 3.40	2.32 / 3.31	2.28 / 3.24	2.25 / 3.17	2.20 / 3.07	2.15 / 2.99	2.09 / 2.88	2.05 / 2.80	2.00 / 2.72	1.96 / 2.63	1.93 / 2.58	1.89 / 2.51	1.87 / 2.47	1.84 / 2.42	1.82 / 2.38	1.81 / 2.36
22	4.30 / 7.94	3.44 / 5.72	3.05 / 4.82	2.82 / 4.31	2.66 / 3.99	2.55 / 3.76	2.47 / 3.59	2.40 / 3.45	2.35 / 3.35	2.30 / 3.26	2.26 / 3.18	2.23 / 3.12	2.18 / 3.02	2.13 / 2.94	2.07 / 2.83	2.03 / 2.75	1.98 / 2.67	1.93 / 2.58	1.91 / 2.53	1.87 / 2.46	1.84 / 2.42	1.81 / 2.37	1.80 / 2.33	1.78 / 2.31
23	4.28 / 7.88	3.42 / 5.66	3.03 / 4.76	2.80 / 4.26	2.64 / 3.94	2.53 / 3.71	2.45 / 3.54	2.38 / 3.41	2.32 / 3.30	2.28 / 3.21	2.24 / 3.14	2.20 / 3.07	2.14 / 2.97	2.10 / 2.89	2.04 / 2.78	2.00 / 2.70	1.96 / 2.62	1.91 / 2.53	1.88 / 2.48	1.84 / 2.41	1.82 / 2.37	1.79 / 2.32	1.77 / 2.28	1.76 / 2.26
24	4.26 / 7.82	3.40 / 5.61	3.01 / 4.72	2.78 / 4.22	2.62 / 3.90	2.51 / 3.67	2.43 / 3.50	2.36 / 3.36	2.30 / 3.25	2.26 / 3.17	2.22 / 3.09	2.18 / 3.03	2.13 / 2.93	2.09 / 2.85	2.02 / 2.74	1.98 / 2.66	1.94 / 2.58	1.89 / 2.49	1.86 / 2.44	1.82 / 2.36	1.80 / 2.33	1.76 / 2.27	1.74 / 2.23	1.73 / 2.21
25	4.24 / 7.77	3.38 / 5.57	2.99 / 4.68	2.76 / 4.18	2.60 / 3.86	2.49 / 3.63	2.41 / 3.46	2.34 / 3.32	2.28 / 3.21	2.24 / 3.13	2.20 / 3.05	2.16 / 2.99	2.11 / 2.89	2.06 / 2.81	2.00 / 2.70	1.96 / 2.62	1.92 / 2.54	1.87 / 2.45	1.84 / 2.40	1.80 / 2.32	1.77 / 2.29	1.74 / 2.23	1.72 / 2.19	1.71 / 2.17
26	4.22 / 7.72	3.37 / 5.53	2.98 / 4.64	2.74 / 4.14	2.59 / 3.82	2.47 / 3.59	2.39 / 3.42	2.32 / 3.29	2.27 / 3.17	2.22 / 3.09	2.18 / 3.02	2.15 / 2.96	2.10 / 2.86	2.05 / 2.77	1.99 / 2.66	1.95 / 2.58	1.90 / 2.50	1.85 / 2.41	1.82 / 2.36	1.78 / 2.28	1.76 / 2.25	1.72 / 2.19	1.70 / 2.15	1.69 / 2.13
27	4.21 / 7.68	3.35 / 5.49	2.96 / 4.60	2.73 / 4.11	2.57 / 3.79	2.46 / 3.56	2.37 / 3.39	2.30 / 3.26	2.25 / 3.14	2.20 / 3.06	2.16 / 2.98	2.13 / 2.93	2.08 / 2.83	2.03 / 2.74	1.97 / 2.63	1.93 / 2.55	1.88 / 2.47	1.84 / 2.38	1.80 / 2.33	1.76 / 2.25	1.74 / 2.21	1.71 / 2.16	1.68 / 2.12	1.67 / 2.10
28	4.20 / 7.64	3.34 / 5.45	2.95 / 4.57	2.71 / 4.07	2.56 / 3.76	2.44 / 3.53	2.36 / 3.36	2.29 / 3.23	2.24 / 3.11	2.19 / 3.03	2.15 / 2.95	2.12 / 2.90	2.06 / 2.80	2.02 / 2.71	1.96 / 2.60	1.91 / 2.52	1.87 / 2.44	1.81 / 2.35	1.78 / 2.30	1.75 / 2.22	1.72 / 2.18	1.69 / 2.13	1.67 / 2.09	1.65 / 2.06
29	4.18 / 7.60	3.33 / 5.42	2.93 / 4.54	2.70 / 4.04	2.54 / 3.73	2.43 / 3.50	2.35 / 3.33	2.28 / 3.20	2.22 / 3.08	2.18 / 3.00	2.14 / 2.92	2.10 / 2.87	2.05 / 2.77	2.00 / 2.68	1.94 / 2.57	1.90 / 2.49	1.85 / 2.41	1.80 / 2.32	1.77 / 2.27	1.73 / 2.19	1.71 / 2.15	1.68 / 2.10	1.65 / 2.06	1.64 / 2.03
30	4.17 / 7.56	3.32 / 5.39	2.92 / 4.51	2.69 / 4.02	2.53 / 3.70	2.42 / 3.47	2.34 / 3.30	2.27 / 3.17	2.21 / 3.06	2.16 / 2.98	2.12 / 2.90	2.09 / 2.84	2.04 / 2.74	1.99 / 2.66	1.93 / 2.55	1.89 / 2.47	1.84 / 2.38	1.79 / 2.29	1.76 / 2.24	1.72 / 2.16	1.69 / 2.13	1.66 / 2.07	1.64 / 2.03	1.62 / 2.01
32	4.15 / 7.50	3.30 / 5.34	2.90 / 4.46	2.67 / 3.97	2.51 / 3.66	2.40 / 3.42	2.32 / 3.25	2.25 / 3.12	2.19 / 3.01	2.14 / 2.94	2.10 / 2.86	2.07 / 2.80	2.02 / 2.70	1.97 / 2.62	1.91 / 2.51	1.86 / 2.42	1.82 / 2.34	1.76 / 2.25	1.74 / 2.20	1.69 / 2.12	1.67 / 2.08	1.64 / 2.02	1.61 / 1.98	1.59 / 1.96
34	4.13 / 7.44	3.28 / 5.29	2.88 / 4.42	2.65 / 3.93	2.49 / 3.61	2.38 / 3.38	2.30 / 3.21	2.23 / 3.08	2.17 / 2.97	2.12 / 2.89	2.08 / 2.82	2.05 / 2.76	2.00 / 2.66	1.95 / 2.58	1.89 / 2.47	1.84 / 2.38	1.80 / 2.30	1.74 / 2.21	1.71 / 2.15	1.67 / 2.08	1.64 / 2.04	1.61 / 1.98	1.59 / 1.94	1.57 / 1.91
36	4.11 / 7.39	3.26 / 5.25	2.86 / 4.38	2.63 / 3.89	2.48 / 3.58	2.36 / 3.35	2.28 / 3.18	2.21 / 3.04	2.15 / 2.94	2.10 / 2.86	2.06 / 2.78	2.03 / 2.72	1.98 / 2.62	1.93 / 2.54	1.87 / 2.43	1.82 / 2.35	1.78 / 2.26	1.72 / 2.17	1.69 / 2.12	1.65 / 2.04	1.62 / 2.00	1.59 / 1.94	1.56 / 1.90	1.55 / 1.87
38	4.10 / 7.35	3.25 / 5.21	2.85 / 4.34	2.62 / 3.86	2.46 / 3.54	2.35 / 3.32	2.26 / 3.15	2.19 / 3.02	2.14 / 2.91	2.09 / 2.82	2.05 / 2.75	2.02 / 2.69	1.96 / 2.59	1.92 / 2.51	1.85 / 2.40	1.80 / 2.32	1.76 / 2.22	1.71 / 2.14	1.67 / 2.08	1.63 / 2.00	1.60 / 1.97	1.57 / 1.90	1.54 / 1.86	1.53 / 1.84
40	4.08 / 7.31	3.23 / 5.18	2.84 / 4.31	2.61 / 3.83	2.45 / 3.51	2.34 / 3.29	2.25 / 3.12	2.18 / 2.99	2.12 / 2.88	2.07 / 2.80	2.04 / 2.73	2.00 / 2.66	1.95 / 2.56	1.90 / 2.49	1.84 / 2.37	1.79 / 2.29	1.74 / 2.20	1.69 / 2.11	1.66 / 2.05	1.61 / 1.97	1.59 / 1.94	1.55 / 1.88	1.53 / 1.84	1.51 / 1.81

Within-group df	1	2	3	4	5	6	7	8	9	10	11	12	14	16	20	24	30	40	50	75	100	200	500	∞	
42	4.07 / 7.27	3.22 / 5.15	2.83 / 4.29	2.59 / 3.80	2.44 / 3.49	2.32 / 3.26	2.24 / 3.10	2.17 / 2.96	2.11 / 2.86	2.06 / 2.77	2.02 / 2.70	1.99 / 2.64	1.94 / 2.54	1.89 / 2.46	1.82 / 2.35	1.78 / 2.26	1.73 / 2.17	1.68 / 2.08	1.64 / 2.02	1.60 / 1.94	1.57 / 1.91	1.54 / 1.85	1.51 / 1.80	1.49 / 1.78	42
44	4.06 / 7.24	3.21 / 5.12	2.82 / 4.26	2.58 / 3.78	2.43 / 3.46	2.31 / 3.24	2.23 / 3.07	2.16 / 2.94	2.10 / 2.84	2.05 / 2.75	2.01 / 2.68	1.98 / 2.62	1.92 / 2.52	1.88 / 2.44	1.81 / 2.32	1.76 / 2.24	1.72 / 2.15	1.66 / 2.06	1.63 / 2.00	1.58 / 1.92	1.56 / 1.88	1.52 / 1.82	1.50 / 1.78	1.48 / 1.75	44
46	4.05 / 7.21	3.20 / 5.10	2.81 / 4.24	2.57 / 3.76	2.42 / 3.44	2.30 / 3.22	2.22 / 3.05	2.14 / 2.92	2.09 / 2.82	2.04 / 2.73	2.00 / 2.66	1.97 / 2.60	1.91 / 2.50	1.87 / 2.42	1.80 / 2.30	1.75 / 2.22	1.71 / 2.13	1.65 / 2.04	1.62 / 1.98	1.57 / 1.90	1.54 / 1.86	1.51 / 1.80	1.48 / 1.76	1.46 / 1.72	46
48	4.04 / 7.19	3.19 / 5.08	2.80 / 4.22	2.56 / 3.74	2.41 / 3.42	2.30 / 3.20	2.21 / 3.04	2.14 / 2.90	2.08 / 2.80	2.03 / 2.71	1.99 / 2.64	1.96 / 2.58	1.90 / 2.48	1.86 / 2.40	1.79 / 2.28	1.74 / 2.20	1.70 / 2.11	1.64 / 2.02	1.61 / 1.96	1.56 / 1.88	1.53 / 1.84	1.50 / 1.78	1.47 / 1.73	1.45 / 1.70	48
50	4.03 / 7.17	3.18 / 5.06	2.79 / 4.20	2.56 / 3.72	2.40 / 3.41	2.29 / 3.18	2.20 / 3.02	2.13 / 2.88	2.07 / 2.78	2.02 / 2.70	1.98 / 2.62	1.95 / 2.56	1.90 / 2.46	1.85 / 2.39	1.78 / 2.26	1.74 / 2.18	1.69 / 2.10	1.63 / 2.00	1.60 / 1.94	1.55 / 1.86	1.52 / 1.82	1.48 / 1.76	1.46 / 1.71	1.44 / 1.68	50
55	4.02 / 7.12	3.17 / 5.01	2.78 / 4.16	2.54 / 3.68	2.38 / 3.37	2.27 / 3.15	2.18 / 2.98	2.11 / 2.85	2.05 / 2.75	2.00 / 2.66	1.97 / 2.59	1.93 / 2.53	1.88 / 2.43	1.83 / 2.35	1.76 / 2.23	1.72 / 2.15	1.67 / 2.06	1.61 / 1.96	1.58 / 1.90	1.52 / 1.82	1.50 / 1.78	1.46 / 1.71	1.43 / 1.66	1.41 / 1.64	55
60	4.00 / 7.08	3.15 / 4.98	2.76 / 4.13	2.52 / 3.65	2.37 / 3.34	2.25 / 3.12	2.17 / 2.95	2.10 / 2.82	2.04 / 2.72	1.99 / 2.63	1.95 / 2.56	1.92 / 2.50	1.86 / 2.40	1.81 / 2.32	1.75 / 2.20	1.70 / 2.12	1.65 / 2.03	1.59 / 1.93	1.56 / 1.87	1.50 / 1.79	1.48 / 1.74	1.44 / 1.68	1.41 / 1.63	1.39 / 1.60	60
65	3.99 / 7.04	3.14 / 4.95	2.75 / 4.10	2.51 / 3.62	2.36 / 3.31	2.24 / 3.09	2.15 / 2.93	2.08 / 2.79	2.02 / 2.70	1.98 / 2.61	1.94 / 2.54	1.90 / 2.47	1.85 / 2.37	1.80 / 2.30	1.73 / 2.18	1.68 / 2.09	1.63 / 2.00	1.57 / 1.90	1.54 / 1.84	1.49 / 1.76	1.46 / 1.71	1.42 / 1.64	1.39 / 1.60	1.37 / 1.56	65
70	3.98 / 7.01	3.13 / 4.92	2.74 / 4.08	2.50 / 3.60	2.35 / 3.29	2.23 / 3.07	2.14 / 2.91	2.07 / 2.77	2.01 / 2.67	1.97 / 2.59	1.93 / 2.51	1.89 / 2.45	1.84 / 2.35	1.79 / 2.28	1.72 / 2.15	1.67 / 2.07	1.62 / 1.98	1.56 / 1.88	1.53 / 1.82	1.47 / 1.74	1.45 / 1.69	1.40 / 1.62	1.37 / 1.56	1.35 / 1.53	70
80	3.96 / 6.96	3.11 / 4.88	2.72 / 4.04	2.48 / 3.56	2.33 / 3.25	2.21 / 3.04	2.12 / 2.87	2.05 / 2.74	1.99 / 2.64	1.95 / 2.55	1.91 / 2.48	1.88 / 2.41	1.82 / 2.32	1.77 / 2.24	1.70 / 2.11	1.65 / 2.03	1.60 / 1.94	1.54 / 1.84	1.51 / 1.78	1.45 / 1.70	1.42 / 1.65	1.38 / 1.57	1.35 / 1.52	1.32 / 1.49	80
100	3.94 / 6.90	3.09 / 4.82	2.70 / 3.98	2.46 / 3.51	2.30 / 3.20	2.19 / 2.99	2.10 / 2.82	2.03 / 2.69	1.97 / 2.59	1.92 / 2.51	1.88 / 2.43	1.85 / 2.36	1.79 / 2.26	1.75 / 2.19	1.68 / 2.06	1.63 / 1.98	1.57 / 1.89	1.51 / 1.79	1.48 / 1.73	1.42 / 1.64	1.39 / 1.59	1.34 / 1.51	1.30 / 1.46	1.28 / 1.43	100
125	3.92 / 6.84	3.07 / 4.78	2.68 / 3.94	2.44 / 3.47	2.29 / 3.17	2.17 / 2.95	2.08 / 2.79	2.01 / 2.65	1.95 / 2.56	1.90 / 2.47	1.86 / 2.40	1.83 / 2.33	1.77 / 2.23	1.72 / 2.15	1.65 / 2.03	1.60 / 1.94	1.55 / 1.85	1.49 / 1.75	1.45 / 1.68	1.39 / 1.59	1.36 / 1.54	1.31 / 1.46	1.27 / 1.40	1.25 / 1.37	125
150	3.91 / 6.81	3.06 / 4.75	2.67 / 3.91	2.43 / 3.44	2.27 / 3.14	2.16 / 2.92	2.07 / 2.76	2.00 / 2.62	1.94 / 2.53	1.89 / 2.44	1.85 / 2.37	1.82 / 2.30	1.76 / 2.20	1.71 / 2.12	1.64 / 2.00	1.59 / 1.91	1.54 / 1.83	1.47 / 1.72	1.44 / 1.66	1.37 / 1.56	1.34 / 1.51	1.29 / 1.43	1.25 / 1.37	1.22 / 1.33	150
200	3.89 / 6.76	3.04 / 4.71	2.65 / 3.88	2.41 / 3.41	2.26 / 3.11	2.14 / 2.90	2.05 / 2.73	1.98 / 2.60	1.92 / 2.50	1.87 / 2.41	1.83 / 2.34	1.80 / 2.28	1.74 / 2.17	1.69 / 2.09	1.62 / 1.97	1.57 / 1.88	1.52 / 1.79	1.45 / 1.69	1.42 / 1.62	1.35 / 1.53	1.32 / 1.48	1.26 / 1.39	1.22 / 1.33	1.19 / 1.28	200
400	3.86 / 6.70	3.02 / 4.66	2.62 / 3.83	2.39 / 3.36	2.23 / 3.06	2.12 / 2.85	2.03 / 2.69	1.96 / 2.55	1.90 / 2.46	1.85 / 2.37	1.81 / 2.29	1.78 / 2.23	1.72 / 2.12	1.67 / 2.04	1.60 / 1.92	1.54 / 1.84	1.49 / 1.74	1.42 / 1.64	1.38 / 1.57	1.32 / 1.47	1.28 / 1.42	1.22 / 1.32	1.16 / 1.24	1.13 / 1.19	400
1000	3.85 / 6.66	3.00 / 4.62	2.61 / 3.80	2.38 / 3.34	2.22 / 3.04	2.10 / 2.82	2.02 / 2.66	1.95 / 2.53	1.89 / 2.43	1.84 / 2.34	1.80 / 2.26	1.76 / 2.20	1.70 / 2.09	1.65 / 2.01	1.58 / 1.89	1.53 / 1.81	1.47 / 1.71	1.41 / 1.61	1.36 / 1.54	1.30 / 1.44	1.26 / 1.38	1.19 / 1.28	1.13 / 1.19	1.08 / 1.11	1000
∞	3.84 / 6.64	2.99 / 4.60	2.60 / 3.78	2.37 / 3.32	2.21 / 3.02	2.09 / 2.80	2.01 / 2.64	1.94 / 2.51	1.88 / 2.41	1.83 / 2.32	1.79 / 2.24	1.75 / 2.18	1.69 / 2.07	1.64 / 1.99	1.57 / 1.87	1.52 / 1.79	1.46 / 1.69	1.40 / 1.59	1.35 / 1.52	1.28 / 1.41	1.24 / 1.36	1.17 / 1.25	1.11 / 1.15	1.00 / 1.00	∞

APPENDIX H

Critical Values of Chi Square (χ^2)

df	.01	.05	.10
1	6.64	3.84	2.71
2	9.21	5.99	4.60
3	11.34	7.82	6.25
4	13.28	9.49	7.78
5	15.09	11.07	9.24
6	16.81	12.59	10.64
7	18.48	14.07	12.02
8	20.09	15.51	13.36
9	21.67	16.92	14.68
10	23.21	18.31	15.99
11	24.72	19.68	17.28
12	26.22	21.03	18.55
13	27.69	22.36	19.81
14	29.14	23.68	21.06
15	30.58	25.00	22.31
16	32.00	26.97	23.54
17	33.41	27.59	24.77

Source: Abridged from Table IV of Fisher and Yates, *Statistical Tables for Biological, Agricultural, and Medical Research,* published by Oliver and Boyd Ltd., Edinburgh, and by permission of the authors and publishers.

(The significance level for each value is given at the top of the column.)

APPENDIX H (continued)

df	.01	.05	.10
18	34.80	28.87	25.99
19	36.19	30.14	27.20
20	37.57	31.41	28.41
21	38.93	32.67	29.62
22	40.29	33.92	30.81
23	41.64	35.17	32.01
24	42.98	36.42	33.20
25	44.31	37.65	34.38
26	45.64	38.88	35.56
27	46.96	40.11	36.74
28	48.28	41.34	37.92
29	49.59	42.56	39.09
30	50.89	43.77	40.26

Probabilities Associated with the Mann-Whitney U Test
(One-Tailed Test)

	$N_2 = 3$		
U \ N_1	1	2	3
0	.250	.100	.050
1	.500	.200	.100
2	.750	.400	.200
3		.600	.350
4			.500
5			.650

	$N_2 = 4$			
U \ N_1	1	2	3	4
0	.200	.067	.028	.014
1	.400	.133	.057	.029
2	.600	.267	.114	.057
3		.400	.200	.100
4		.600	.314	.171
5			.429	.243
6			.571	.343
7				.443
8				.557

Source: From "On a Test of Whether One of Two Random Variables Is Stochastically Larger than the Other," by H. B. Mann and D. R. Whitney, *Annals of Mathematical Statistics,* 1947, 18, 52, 54. Reprinted with permission.

APPENDIX I (continued)

$N_2 = 5$

U \ N_1	1	2	3	4	5
0	.167	.047	.018	.008	.004
1	.333	.095	.036	.016	.008
2	.500	.190	.071	.032	.016
3	.667	.286	.125	.056	.028
4		.429	.196	.095	.048
5		.571	.286	.143	.075
6			.393	.206	.111
7			.500	.278	.155
8			.607	.365	.210
9				.452	.274
10				.548	.345
11					.421
12					.500
13					.579

$N_2 = 6$

U \ N_1	1	2	3	4	5	6
0	.143	.036	.012	.005	.002	.001
1	.286	.071	.024	.010	.004	.002
2	.428	.143	.048	.019	.009	.004
3	.571	.214	.083	.033	.015	.008
4		.321	.131	.057	.026	.013
5		.429	.190	.086	.041	.021
6		.571	.274	.129	.063	.032
7			.357	.176	.089	.047
8			.452	.238	.123	.066
9			.548	.305	.165	.090
10				.381	.214	.120
11				.457	.268	.155
12				.545	.331	.197
13					.396	.242
14					.465	.294
15					.535	.350
16						.409
17						.469
18						.531

APPENDIX I (continued)

$$N_2 = 7$$

U \ N_1	1	2	3	4	5	6	7
0	.125	.028	.008	.003	.001	.001	.000
1	.250	.056	.017	.006	.003	.001	.001
2	.375	.111	.033	.012	.005	.002	.001
3	.500	.167	.058	.021	.009	.004	.002
4	.625	.250	.092	.036	.015	.007	.003
5		.333	.133	.055	.024	.011	.006
6		.444	.192	.082	.037	.017	.009
7		.556	.258	.115	.053	.026	.013
8			.333	.158	.074	.037	.019
9			.417	.206	.101	.051	.027
10			.500	.264	.134	.069	.036
11			.583	.324	.172	.090	.049
12				.394	.216	.117	.064
13				.464	.265	.147	.082
14				.538	.319	.183	.104
15					.378	.223	.130
16					.438	.267	.159
17					.500	.314	.191
18					.562	.365	.228
19						.418	.267
20						.473	.310
21						.527	.355
22							.402
23							.451
24							.500
25							.549

APPENDIX I (continued)

$$N_2 = 8$$

U	1	2	3	4	5	6	7	8	t	Normal
0	.111	.022	.006	.002	.001	.000	.000	.000	3.308	.001
1	.222	.044	.012	.004	.002	.001	.000	.000	3.203	.001
2	.333	.089	.024	.008	.003	.001	.001	.000	3.098	.001
3	.444	.133	.042	.014	.005	.002	.001	.001	2.993	.001
4	.556	.200	.067	.024	.009	.004	.002	.001	2.888	.002
5		.267	.097	.036	.015	.006	.003	.001	2.783	.003
6		.356	.139	.055	.023	.010	.005	.002	2.678	.004
7		.444	.188	.077	.033	.015	.007	.003	2.573	.005
8		.556	.248	.107	.047	.021	.010	.005	2.468	.007
9			.315	.141	.064	.030	.014	.007	2.363	.009
10			.387	.184	.085	.041	.020	.010	2.258	.012
11			.461	.230	.111	.054	.027	.014	2.153	.016
12			.539	.285	.142	.071	.036	.019	2.048	.020
13				.341	.177	.091	.047	.025	1.943	.026
14				.404	.217	.114	.060	.032	1.838	.033
15				.467	.262	.141	.076	.041	1.733	.041
16				.533	.311	.172	.095	.052	1.628	.052
17					.362	.207	.116	.065	1.523	.064
18					.416	.245	.140	.080	1.418	.078
19					.472	.286	.168	.097	1.313	.094
20					.528	.331	.198	.117	1.208	.113
21						.377	.232	.139	1.102	.135
22						.426	.268	.164	.998	.159
23						.475	.306	.191	.893	.185
24						.525	.347	.221	.788	.215
25							.389	.253	.683	.247
26							.433	.287	.578	.282
27							.478	.323	.473	.318
28							.522	.360	.368	.356
29								.399	.263	.396
30								.439	.158	.437
31								.480	.052	.481
32								.520		

APPENDIX J

Critical Values of Spearman's Ranked Correlation Coefficient (r_S)

n	$\alpha = .05$	$\alpha = .025$	$\alpha = .01$	$\alpha = .005$
5	0.900	—	—	—
6	0.829	0.886	0.943	—
7	0.714	0.786	0.893	—
8	0.643	0.738	0.833	0.881
9	0.600	0.683	0.783	0.833
10	0.564	0.648	0.745	0.794
11	0.523	0.623	0.736	0.818
12	0.497	0.591	0.703	0.780
13	0.475	0.566	0.673	0.745
14	0.457	0.545	0.646	0.716
15	0.441	0.525	0.623	0.689
16	0.425	0.507	0.601	0.666
17	0.412	0.490	0.582	0.645
18	0.399	0.476	0.564	0.625
19	0.388	0.462	0.549	0.608
20	0.377	0.450	0.534	0.591
21	0.368	0.438	0.521	0.576
22	0.359	0.428	0.508	0.562
23	0.351	0.418	0.496	0.549
24	0.343	0.409	0.485	0.537
25	0.336	0.400	0.475	0.526
26	0.329	0.392	0.465	0.515
27	0.323	0.385	0.456	0.505
28	0.317	0.377	0.448	0.496
29	0.311	0.370	0.440	0.487
30	0.305	0.364	0.432	0.478

Source: From "Distribution of Sums of Squares of Rank Differences for Small Numbers of Individuals," E. G. Olds, *Annals of Mathetmatical Statistics,* Volume 9 (1938). Reproduced with permission.

APPENDIX K

Overcoming Math Anxiety

If you are what might be termed a "math-anxious" or "math-avoidant" person, this appendix may be helpful to you. Most of the material in this appendix is drawn from the theory and practice of rational-emotive therapy (RET), originally developed by the psychologist Albert Ellis. RET has been shown through research to be quite effective in helping people overcome problems like yours. Unfortunately, in a book devoted to statistics, I can only introduce you to some of the basic ideas and techniques. If you are interested, you can enrich your understanding by reading books like Ellis and Harper's *A Guide to Rational Living* or Kranzler's *You Can Change How You Feel* (notice the sneaky way of getting in a plug?).

Fear of math, or math anxiety, is what is called a *debilitative* emotion. Debilitative emotions such as math anxiety are problem emotions because (1) they are extremely unpleasant, and (2) they tend to lead to self-defeating behavior, such as "freezing" on a test or avoiding courses or occupations you otherwise would enjoy.

What you do about your math anxiety (or any other problem) will depend on your theory of what is causing the problem. For example, some people believe that the cause is hereditary: "I get my fear of math from mother, who always had the same problem." Others believe that the cause lies in the environment: "Women are taught from a very young age that they are not supposed to be good in math, to avoid it, and to be afraid of it." The implication of these theories is that if the cause is hereditary, you can't do much about the problem (you can't change your genetic structure), or if the cause is the culture in which you live, by the time you can change what society does to its young, it will still be too late to help you. Although there may be some truth in both the heredity and environmental theories, I believe that they can, at most, set only general limits to your performance. Within these limits, your performance can fluctuate considerably. Though you have very little power to change society and no ability to change your heredity, you still have enormous power to change yourself if you choose to do so, if you know how to bring about that change, and if you work hard at it.

Let's begin with the *ABC*'s. *A* stands for *A*ctivating event or experience, such as taking a difficult math test; *C* stands for the emotional *C*onsequence, such as extreme nervousness. Most people seem to believe that *A* causes *C*. In fact, this theory seems to be built right into our language. Consider:

Activating Event	Cause	Emotional Consequence
(Something happens . . .	that causes me . . .	to feel . . .)
"When you talk about math . . .	you make me . . .	so upset."
"This test . . .	makes me . . .	nervous."

The implications of this *A*-causes-*C* theory are (1) you can't help how you feel, and (2) the way to deal with the problem is to avoid or escape from activating events such as math tests.

But is the *A*-causes-*C* theory true? Respond to the following items by indicating how you would feel if you were to experience the event. Use a scale that ranges from –5, indicating very unpleasant emotions (such as rage, depression, or extreme anxiety), to +5, to indicate an emotion that is extremely positive (such as elation or ecstasy); or use a 0 if you would experience neutral, neither positive nor negative, feelings:

1. Handling snakes.
2. Giving a speech in front of one of your classes.
3. Seeing your eight-year-old son playing with dolls.
4. The death of a loved one in an automobile accident.

I have administered items like this to hundreds of people and have found that for items 1 through 3 the responses have ranged all the way from –5 to +5. On the item concerning the death of a loved one, most people respond with a –5, but when questioned, they have heard of cultures where even death is considered to be a positive event (in the United States everyone wants to go to Heaven but nobody wants to die). Why is it that, given the same *A*ctivating event, people's emotional *C*onsequences vary so much?

Differing responses like this suggest that maybe *A* —> *C* isn't the whole story. There must be something else, something that accounts for the different ways people respond to the same stimulus. I believe that it is not *A*, the activating event, that causes *C*, the emotional consequence. Rather, it is *B*, your Belief about *A*, that causes you to feel as you do at point *C*. Take the example of observing your eight-year-old son playing with dolls. What does the person who experiences feelings of joy believe about what he or she sees? Perhaps something like, "Isn't that wonderful! He's learning nurturing attitudes and tenderness. I really like that!" But the person who experiences very negative feelings probably is thinking, "Isn't that awful! If he keeps that up, he'll surely turn into an effeminate man, or even be gay, and that really would be terrible!"

Ellis has identified some specific beliefs that most of us have learned and that cause us a great deal of difficulty. He calls these beliefs "irrational beliefs." A number of these beliefs have particular relevance to the phenomenon of math anxiety:

> I must be competent and adequate in all possible respects if I am to consider myself to be a worthwhile person. (If I'm not good at math, I'm not a very smart person.)
>
> It's catastrophic when things are not the way I'd like them to be. (It's terrible and awful to have trouble with statistics.)
>
> When something seems dangerous or about to go wrong, I must constantly worry about it. (I can't control my worrying and fretting about statistics.)
>
> My unhappiness is externally caused. I can't help feeling and acting as I do and I can't change my feelings or actions. (Having to do math simply makes me feel awful; that's just what it does to me.)
>
> Given my childhood experiences and the past I have had, I can't help being as I am today and I'll remain this way indefinitely. (I'll never change; that's just how I am.)
>
> I can't settle for less than the right or perfect solution to my problems. (Since I can't be a math whiz, there's no sense in trying to do math at all.)
>
> It is better for me to avoid life's frustrations and difficulties than to deal with them. (Since math always makes me feel bad, the only sensible thing to do is to avoid math.)

Do any of these sound familiar? If they do, chances are good that you not only learned to believe them a long time ago, but also that you keep the belief going by means of self-talk. The first step in changing is to increase your awareness of the kind of self-talk that you do. When you think, you think with words, sentences, and images. If you pay attention to these cognitive events, you may notice one or more of the following types of self-talk, which may indicate your underlying irrational beliefs.

Catastrophizing

This type of self-talk is characterized by the use of terms or phrases such as "It's awful!" "It's terrible!" or "I can't stand it!" Now, there are some events that most of us would agree are extremely bad, such as bombing innocent people and earthquakes that kill thousands. Chances are good that you will never be the victim of such an event. But your mind is powerful: If you *believe* that your misfortunes are catastrophes, then you will *feel* accordingly. Telling yourself how catastrophic it is to do badly on a stats test will almost guarantee that you will feel awful about it. And that emotional response, in turn, can affect how you deal with the situation. It is appropriate to be *concerned* about doing well on a test, because concern motivates you to prepare and to do your best. But when you are *overconcerned,* you can make yourself so nervous that your performance goes down instead of up.

Do you see how all this relates to the first irrational belief on our list? Performing poorly on a stats test would be *awful* because you believe that you *must* be competent in all possible respects. If you were to fail at something important to you, that would make you a *failure:* someone who couldn't respect himself or herself. One of the oddest things about irrational beliefs like this is the uneven way we apply them. Your friend could bomb a test, and you'd still think him or her a worthwhile person. But do badly yourself, and the sky falls in!

When you indoctrinate yourself with catastrophic ideas, when you tell yourself over and over again how *horrible* it would be if you were to perform poorly, then you defeat yourself, because you become so anxious that you help bring about the very thing you're afraid of, or you avoid the experience that could benefit you.

Overgeneralizing Self-Talk

When you overgeneralize, you take a bit of evidence and draw conclusions that go beyond the data. If you experienced difficulty with math as a child, you may have concluded, "I'll *never* be good at math" or "I'm stupid in math." If you failed a math course, then you tended to think of yourself as a failure who will never be able to succeed, and trying harder would be completely useless.

Rationally, though, failing once doesn't make you a "failure." Because you had difficulty in the past doesn't prove that you will never succeed. If it did, nobody would ever learn to walk!

The most pernicious form of overgeneralizing is self-evaluation. We have a tendency to tie up our feelings of self-worth with our performance. When we do well at something, we say, "Hey! I'm a pretty good [or competent or worthwhile] person!" But when we perform poorly, we tend to believe that we are now worthless as a person. This process begins in childhood. When Johnny does something we consider bad, we tend to encourage overgeneralization by saying, "Johnny, you are a *bad boy*" (i.e., you are worth less as a person).

If you were a worthless or stupid person, you wouldn't have gotten far enough in your education to be reading this book. True, in the past, you may have had difficulty in math, and math may be difficult for you now. But how does that prove that you can't learn it? There is absolutely no evidence that your situation is hopeless or that it is useless to try. The only way to make it hopeless is to tell yourself, over and over, how hopeless it is.

Demanding Self-talk

This type of self-talk includes the use of words such as "should," "must," and "need." If you are math-anxious, chances are that you use these words to beat up on yourself. You make a mistake and say, "I shouldn't have made that mistake! How could I have been so stupid?" I have a tennis partner who informed me that she finds it difficult to concentrate on her work for the rest of the day after she has played poorly. She believes that she *should* have done better. Instead of being calmly regretful for having made some errors and thinking about how to do better next time, she bashes herself over the head psychologically for not doing perfectly well, every time.

"But," you may say, "I *need* to be successful" or "I *have* to pass this course." Have to? The first time? Or you can't survive? It would be nice to be successful because of the advantages it would bring you, but lots of people do manage to function in life even after doing badly in a statistics course. To the degree that you believe you *need* a certain level of performance, to that degree you will experience anxiety about possible failure and thereby increase the chance of failure.

HOW TO DEAL WITH MATH ANXIETY

What can you do about a way of thinking that seems so automatic, so ingrained? Here is a series of steps that will probably help. I'd suggest that you try them out, in order, even though you may not expect them to work for you. You might just be surprised!

Step 1.   Record your feelings. When you notice that you are feeling anxious, guilty, angry, or depressed about some aspect of your statistics course, record your emotional experience. Describe your feelings as accurately as you can. You might write things such as, "I feel guilty about not having taken more math as an underclassman," or "I feel really nervous about the test we're having next week," or "I'm too shy to ask questions in class," or "I just get furious that they make us take statistics when I'll never have to use it." Write down all the unpleasant feelings you have at the time. When you have done this, you will have described *C*, the emotional *C*onsequence part of the *ABC* paradigm.

Step 2.   Describe the Activating event or experience (*A*). Briefly write down what it was that seemed to trigger your feelings. Here are some common activating events for math anxiety. When you write your own, record the thing that is most likely to have happened. Find the *immediate* trigger, the thing that happened just before your experiencing of the negative emotion.

I was assigned some difficult statistics problems, and I don't know how to do them.

I thought about a test coming up, one that I will almost surely fail.

I discovered that I need more information about some of the material, but I'm afraid to ask about it in class because I'll look stupid.

Step 3.   Identify your irrational beliefs. As accurately as you can, record what you were saying to yourself before and during the time when you experienced the emotions you recorded in step 1. The first few times you do this, you may have difficulty, because you don't usually pay much attention to the thoughts that seem to race through your head. Although it is difficult to become aware of your thoughts, it is not impossible. One technique you can use is to ask yourself, "What must I have been saying to myself about A (the activating event) at point B in order to experience C (the emotional consequence)?"

Suppose your first three steps looked like this:

Step 1. (Describing *C*, the emotional Consequence) I feel really nervous and miserable.

Step 2. (The Activating event, *A*) My advisor told me I need to take a statistics class.

Step 3. Identify *B*, the Belief that leads from *A* to *C*. Obviously, you're not saying, "Wow, I'm really going to enjoy that class!" You must have been saying something like:

"If I fail, that'll be *awful!*"

"I'll be a real failure!"

"I'll *never* be any good at statistics!"

"I'm going to have a terrible term and hate every minute of it."

"What will the other students and the professor think of me when I do badly?"

Step 4.   Challenge each of the beliefs you have identified. After you have written down your self-talk in step 3, look at each statement and dispute it. One question you can ask to test the rationality of any belief is, "Where's the evidence for this belief?" Let's look at each of the examples listed in step 3:

1. Where's the evidence that it will be awful if I fail? True, failure would be unfortunate, but would it be catastrophic? I'd do better to remember that if I'm overconcerned with doing well, I will be even more likely to fail.
2. Where's the evidence that if I fail the test, I, as a person, will be a failure? The worst I can possibly be is an FHB (a fallible human being) along with the rest of the human race.
3. Where's the evidence that I'll never be good in statistics? I may have some evidence that similar material was difficult for me in the past, but how can that prove anything about the future?
4. Where's the evidence that I will hate every single minute of the term? This statement has several irrational beliefs to be challenged: that I'll

hate the course (I might have a great teacher, with a wonderful sense of humor, and actually enjoy it), that the discomfort will generalize to the entire term (I might dislike my statistics class but very much enjoy my other courses), and that I will spend every single minute of the term feeling hateful (no help needed to challenge this one, right?).

5. This statement appears to be a rhetorical question. Chances are that I'm not really wondering what others will think of me if I fail, but rather telling myself all the bad things they'll think—and how awful that will be. Both parts of this can be challenged: Where's the evidence that they'll think bad things about me and, even if they do, would that be catastrophic?

Step 5. Once you have identified and challenged an irrational belief, the next step is to replace it with a rational one. Ask yourself what you would rather believe—what your best friend might believe—what John Wayne or Jack Kennedy or Mother Teresa probably would believe. Then, every time you find yourself moving into that old irrational self-talk, answer it with the new alternative belief.

Step 6. Do rational-emotive imagery. After you have practiced replacing your irrational beliefs a few times, you may feel better. Some people, however, report that they now understand that their beliefs cause their unpleasant emotions, and they realize that those beliefs are irrational, but they still feel much the same way as before. If this is true of you, you may benefit from doing some imagery. I will discuss both mastery and coping imagery techniques because some of my students have reported that one approach is more effective for them than the other. Before attempting either kind of imagery, however, do spend several days practicing steps 1 through 5.

Mastery Imagery. In the mastery imagery approach, you are to imagine yourself mastering the situation, that is, feeling and acting in an appropriate way in the presence of the activating event. If you are anxious about a statistics test, imagine feeling calm or at most slightly concerned while taking the test, answering the questions as well as you can, calmly leaving the exam, and being able to look back on the experience with some satisfaction. Imagine speaking rationally to yourself during the whole experience (taken from your material in step 5). Make the image (the daydream, if you want to call it that) as vivid and real as possible. If you feel very upset during the experience, terminate the imagery; go back and reread step 4 and attempt the imagery again the next day. For any kind of positive imagery to be effective, you will need to work at it for at least a half-hour per day for a week; don't expect immediate results.

Coping Imagery. Again, imagine yourself in the experience that you're having problems with, for example, taking a statistics test. This time include having difficulty and starting to experience anxiety. Then imagine dealing with the anxiety by saying to yourself, "Stop! Relax!" Try to force yourself to feel more calm. Breathe deeply a few times, remind yourself of rational self-talk, and try to change the extremely anxious feelings to ones that are more calm. Imagine coping with the problem. Again, you won't experience immediate success; it usually takes at least a week of imagery work before you begin to get results.

***Step* 7**. Activity homework. You can only live in your imagination so long if you want to attain objectives in the real world. Sooner or later you need to take a deep breath and DO SOMETHING. If you experience math anxiety, one such "something" might be to work your way through this book. As you begin to make this sort of conscious, real-world changes, be aware of your self-talk. When you notice yourself feeling emotionally upset, dispute your irrational beliefs as actively as you can. If things don't get better immediately, don't give up—keep using these techniques for at least a couple of weeks. Remember, the odds are in your favor!

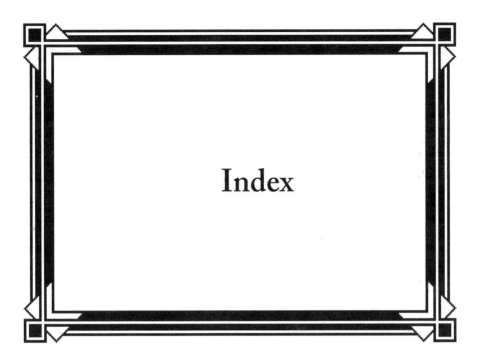

Index